WALKING WITH BEARS

On Bridges to Earth's New Era

Dr. Will Taegel

2nd Tier Publishing

Published by:
    2nd Tier Publishing
    13501 Ranch Road 12, STE 103
    Wimberley, TX 78676

ISBN 978-0-692-96686-0

Table of Contents

THIS BOOK BELONGS TO

PROLOGUE

The sun rises on my seventy-seventh year, and I look back on a long shamanic walk with Bear Heart Williams, revered Muskogee/Creek shaman. Together, we covered much ground until we came to a bridge that led to a mysterious landscape on the other side, a new era still taking shape.

As we walked toward the bridge, Bear Heart assisted me and others in letting go of the story of our dominant culture, indeed a deep relinquishing of our personality patterns. Step-by-step I came to question my core understanding of myself and, eventually, the foundations of current civilization.

Gradually, I realized I was rethinking thinking, even refeeling feeling.

Then, before we made it fully onto the bridge, Bear Heart stepped across another span we call death. How, I asked myself, could I become a *Bridge Walker* to a new era without his guidance? Over the next decades, archetypal bears showed up in my dreams and visions, and eventually Bear Heart returned as an ancestral visitor to walk with me and others.

Additionally, on hikes in mountain forests, I sometimes encountered black bears and grizzlies. These bears in real time taught me what it is like to be in a domain where human control is tested and shown its limits.

Trekking with these bears taught me what it feels like not to be at the top of the food chain; indeed, what it feels like to be viewed as food. Inside the food chain as food, I could wholeheartedly become part of the landscape.

Both the spirit and real-time bears gave me the same message, "You humans aren't the top of everything. Much of what you have been taught about how our creation works is an illusion. You must cross over from where you are to meet the truth."

This book is about a full-on sprint or, maybe, a jog out of our current illusions toward ecological steps to another world.

Regina WaterSpirit was Bear Heart's spouse, a medicine partner, and trusted sojourner. When she asked me to consider writing the preface to a book Bear Heart had been working on when he died, I perked up because I had long been interested in writing about my journey with this grizzled sage, an ambling that spanned the 1980s to the 21st Century.

In the unfinished draft that Reginah sent me, I read fascinating narratives that revealed more about Bear Heart's character and teachings. Included were reams of material that built on his first book, *The Wind Is My Mother*, and then transcended to include a new batch of teachings. The proposed title of his new book was *The Bear Is My Father* and, if finished, would have balanced the two influences of Wind and Bear, Grandmother and Grandfather, that lived in his big heart.

At that point, I agreed to write the preface. But, as I dug into the document, I realized that the notes, though well-written, needed much work. Coherence seemed a distant and tall mountain. So, I sat in council with my spirit guides for several months puzzling over the course to take.

Reginah's invitation sent me scurrying into my own notes and memories long stored and valued but not recently reviewed. I discovered markings, pictures, and scribblings in odd places. From a pile in my closet, I uncovered a small juniper box in which I stored feathers for safe keeping. Hiding in the box underneath three decades of feather collecting, I found personal notes to me from Bear Heart in his own hand, a neat but tiny printing that required me to get my glasses.

As part of our relationship, he had taught me basic features of the Muskogee/Creek language, though I was not persistent enough to become fluent. These lost notes included his personal reflections on key words in his native tongue, a language very close to the Mother Tongue, the primary language of the Universe. The abundance of his teaching came through in an intimacy made possible through the fascia of shamanic visions revealed as I pieced together memories and encounters.

As I perused through these important notes taken when Bear Heart wanted to make a certain point, fresh insights flooded my awareness. I found myself in a profound conversation between my scientific side and the part steeped in Bear Heart's ancient teaching. My research had taken me into the intersecting circles of psychology, ecology, and eco-field physics, a confluence that pulsated and swirled with rich interaction, conflict, and, sometimes, collaboration.

When I put the ancient visions together with the paradigm shattering breakthroughs of eco-psychology and field physics, I had quite a brew, one that might make a book.

During the reviewing of my notes, Bear Heart appeared to me in various shamanic journeys from the invisible domain. We walked together in dreams and visions. He amplified in those appearances what he had taught me in a decades long and mutual training process. Mysteriously, people who did not know Bear Heart and who had little familiarity with my work were having similar experiences of his teaching them in spirit-form through dreams.

These appearances, especially the ones with people not connected to him or me in a historical manner, grabbed me and shook me with a passion until my teeth rattled. What was the meaning of his appearances? Was he amplifying his work through linking the two worlds?

Gradually, a plan formed. I would write a book integrating the Bear Heart who once walked the Earth with the ancestral Bear Heart who, by all accounts, was continuing his service of love, healing, and teaching through trans-ordinary consciousness.

Then, I realized that Bear Heart's and my stories were intermingled in a way that had been implicate but needed to be explicate. Ours was not a usual apprentice or mentoring relationship; rather, it was and continues to be a rich dialogue of co-creativity. Sometimes, I thought of myself as an apprentice while at other moments I found myself offering my more scientific and psychological perspective to my elder.

A desire arose to tell the larger narrative of the intertwining of our lives, the calling we experienced, our work, and, ultimately, the service to Grandmother Earth.

At first I thought of a book about walking with bears as a personal growth journey, but, then, I realized there was something much bigger going on. Without realizing it, I found myself in a passageway between realms. Eventually, people were attracted to a similar walk, and it became apparent that we were on our way from one cycle of civilization to another.

With this intention well grounded inside myself, Reginah and I talked of a plan to honor Bear Heart with a book based on his notes, my markings and memoirs, other resources, and his new appearances from the imaginal realm. In no way do I claim to be the only, or even the principal, inheritor of Bear Heart's wisdom.

It is not unusual for people who know us both to remark that what I attribute to Bear Heart often is actually my own. Our teachings overlap, dance, pull apart, and come back together until woven into an unbroken wholeness.

Given Bear Heart's ancestral appearances, I consulted him about the proposed writing in a dream. He answered me very directly.

He said, "Listen to Reginah."

"What did you say?" I stammered, recoiling a bit from his directness, an approach needed because I don't always listen to him.

I said, as his voice became steely, "Listen to Reginah."

Properly directed, I spoke to Reginah, and she suggested a title that would embrace both the sacred feminine and masculine since she knew that was a major dynamic in my adventure in this integral consciousness. Through the months of our conversations, I settled on *Walking With Bears*. In a moment, I will tell you about how the bridge emerged as a key in the subtitle.

A synergy unfolded with this title as a carrier of the inherent truths of the two Bear Hearts: the one who lived locally in Oklahoma and New Mexico, and the one who now dwells in what quantum physicists call nonlocality.

Of related importance is my own unfolding into an integration of my scientific and shamanic work. Indeed, the friendship of the bear of scientific inquiry and the bear of shamanic experience constitutes the élan vital of my life. Writing this book is an effort for these two bears of my interior to get along, though their sibling rivalry is sometimes fierce.

At its most basic layer, according to the newer science of quantum physics, reality doesn't principally show itself to us in a linear or logical fashion. The Universe Story does not unfold—at least most of the time—in neat movement from points A to B to C. Rather, reality swirls in circles, cycles, waves, troughs, and spirals.

Einstein showed us that space-time is a continuum, a smooth fabric that has wrinkles in it, wrinkles we call material objects. In my reading of Einstein, the separation of past, present, and future is merely a "stubbornly persistent illusion."[1] Particles constitute the basis of our Universe and do not travel in a linear fashion but rather go up, down, and around in space.

They bump into and dodge other particles seeking a path, maybe even choosing a direction from myriad possibilities. And, astoundingly, the particles under certain conditions enter a domain beyond space and time called nonlocality wherein they talk to each other, exchanging information instantaneously in a surprising intimacy. Not traveling faster than the speed of light but beyond speed and light in a mysterious, quantum dimension.

My experience of Bear Heart's Universe, in both his historical and ancestral forms, rarely moves in linear and logical sequences, and—now that I think about it—neither does my life or yours.

To get in the spirit of our walk, I am asking you to suspend a need for usual sequencing.

I will tell our interwoven stories in the fashion of the movement of subatomic particles: circling, spiraling, moving through troughs, bumping into past, present, and future.

As I tell you about his appearances to me as an ancestor, I begin with the ending that leads to the beginning of his life and mine, and then bumps into the middle. Along the way, the bears and I hope to mingle with your narrative through the power of eco-field intimacy, an intimacy that widens the angle of our lens into life itself.

We may even see ourselves as expressions of a larger consciousness.

Soon after our conversation about this book, Reginah sent me a narrative that speaks to different layers in the writing. She had been reading one of my other books and ran across a phrase that indicated she was a bridge between Bear Heart and the modern world, including many of his students. As she was contemplating the notion of bridge, a memory came to her.

She wrote:

In 1990, my dear mother had crossed over. I found myself in deep grief. Although I had been teaching and facilitating using the tool of Voice Dialogue, a large part of me felt lost.

On an impulse, I signed up with the Department of Labor in Albuquerque, NM, to take an aptitude test. I had expectations of finding work that did not include having to be on such intimate terms, heartfelt connections, with folks as was the case in being a co-worker with such a powerful medicine man.

Both my own work and being a "medicine helper" to Bear Heart called for a willingness to empathize with others. I was tired. Out of gas. Maybe I could do something, at least for a while, that would give me some relief from having to feel the pain of others since I was so engrossed in my own pain.

The two hour test in Albuquerque led to a conversation with a vocational counselor about my future. She told me that I had an aptitude in the area of "bridge inspecting."

Say What?

I had a good chuckle over it and quickly returned to my deeper soul and my life dedicated to deepening awareness of ourselves as the best way I knew to contribute to our world.

Exactly two years later, Bear Heart and I were on a trip to where he grew up. Nearing the place where he was born, we came to cross a bridge on a country road in Oklahoma. I was driving.

He calmly said, "Pull over here." I had learned to not question his motives and dutifully parked the car on the side of the road before the bridge.

"I want you to inspect this bridge before we cross over it for our safety."

I laughed so loud I thought I might have dislodged that bridge.

Later, I began to see how my own sincere interest in both the consciousness movement and the Native American ways I was experiencing, was like an energetic bridge. I was deeply involved in looking for ways to speak about these bridge-like connections. I cared about honoring the ideas that had been brought forward by all my teachers. I was being a "bridge inspector" of sorts.

Reginah's story sends us in the direction of viewing this book as a bridge.

A bridge between our ordinary habit patterns and the deep dimension we call soul.

A bridge between the mechanistic view and an engaged eco-field.

A bridge between an Oklahoma Indian (as Bear Heart liked to call himself) and a Llano Estacado mongrel (as I experience myself).

Come along with me to an organic experience with this remarkable medicine teacher as we become bridge builders, inspectors, and walkers to the other side.

We may learn that the biggest bear is the wild one inside who refuses to be tamed by a crumbling culture.

Keep moving.

Can you see the shadows of the other side, a new era Mother Earth is birthing?

1   ANCESTRAL BEAR WALKS

A large black stetson adorned with a silver hat band of a white egret droops over his eyes as if he is asleep, and maybe he is.

Or am I?

He certainly is relaxed as he leans into a large juniper tree as if part of its root system. As I approach, he seems to know I enter his circle and stands slowly, a bear of a man if ever I saw one, what with a barrel chest and straight spine. An ironic smile crosses his face in recognition of my being surprised by his presence.

Bear Heart ended his Earth walk on 8/8/08; the 8s, lined up as they were, spoke to an important opening between worlds through which he could move.

The Earthtribe that was created out of our work adopted 8 directions for ceremonies: East, South, West, North, Earth, Sky, Relations, and Ancestors. The 8th direction is the ancestral door through which Bear Heart moved in his appearances.

So who or what is this ancestral form? Is this a dream? A vision? Am I psychotic? Is the visage real or just a symbolic dream stimulated by the enchilada I had for dinner? I take a chance on his being a vision and invite ancestral Bear Heart to sit with me around a ceremonial fire so we can talk about his Earth walk.

What was it like in his passage from historical life to an adventure beyond? What insights does he bring from living outside time and space?

As we amble along a path near my house, I blink my eyes and question my perception, even my hold on consensual reality. Like Carl Jung in *The Red Book*, I wonder about my sanity during such vivid moments beyond the material and historical world. At the very least, I question the reality of energy forms outside current civilization's version of reality, an edition that doesn't countenance ancestral spirits.

The invisible realm challenged Jung's scientific view of reality in a series of nocturnal visits. Biblical Elijah and Salome, visitors from the ancestral domain, appeared to Jung and eventually informed him that they were not just figments of his dream life or imagination.

No, the dream spirits insisted, they were independent energy forms, completely aside from his cultural perception.[1] Visits of ancestors from another domain constitutes a large pill for our dominant civilization to swallow. In such moments, the question of sanity is put on the mainstream table.

Like most of us, I was educated to reduce everything in life to the channels of our five senses. When a form enters my awareness through my sixth sense, I do a double take.

I have explored a bridging of the two worlds for a lifetime; nevertheless, I still have to translate a lost language that converses on the boundary of waking and sleeping, of chronological and eternal time, of locality and nonlocality, and of this universe and another.

I am not fluent in a version of the Mother Tongue that bridges easily between dimensions; though, perhaps, as a gift of the aging process, I am gaining ground on a bandwidth that can include such moments.

Still, a little voice insinuates itself into my awareness, "Maybe, Will, you are exercising a vivid imagination fueled by wishful thinking. You have just been eating too much spicy salsa. Get real. Maybe, you are experiencing waves of grief and Bear Heart's appearances are merely wish fulfillments to help you in your loss of this key person in your everyday life."

That's what my psychologically trained voice offers in a diagnostic dismissal of such transcendence.

I listen to that voice, but it doesn't ring true, or at least not entirely true. To be sure, I have an active imagination that assists me, but Bear Heart's ancestral presence at the fire transcends my personal consciousness and embraces Jung's notion of the collective unconscious as a vehicle for modern people to grasp these ancient realities.

Quantum physics' discovery of nonlocality describes a contextual domain for communication and transfer of information outside time and space. This 21st century science describes a dimension that forms a fascinating bridge over which my mentor travels to be with me by the fire.

Many newer scientific discoveries make room for energy forms from a parallel reality or even another universe to visit us. Equipped with these recent discoveries, I quiet my inner skeptic, promise to listen to said skeptic at various times in this book, and proceed, hopefully with you as a companion.

Where does ancestral Bear Heart come from at 2:00 a.m. on a winter night? What is his point of origin? I just mentioned the *collective unconscious*, which is Jung's language for that terrain beyond our current personal time/space, and Jung would lovingly refer to this visage as an archetype.

Such a description is a fitting way for us to discuss an ancestral domain, but let's draw the bow of perception back farther by listening to Bear Heart in his musings about life beyond.

"Do you recall what I told you many times about going to the stars?"

He fixes a gaze on me not so much in criticizing as in poking a little fun.

"My first stop after I left New Mexico on the day I bridge walked over the mystery was at the Great Bear constellation. It's a long distance away unless you travel beyond the speed limits of light, which I did.

"I caught a ride on a moon beam. We all do when we die. Off I went to the stars shaped like a bear. That night time arrangement in the sky includes the Big Dipper and points the way to the north.

"The good red road runs north and south, so the Great Bear is very important to planet Earth right now. You can easily see humans have lost their way and need direction. The Great Bear Constellation wants to walk with you a bit. That is the main reason for my visit with you around this ceremonial fire, and we have much to discover about the teachings of bear walking."

2   LOVE AND THE CLASH OF CULTURES

Our ancestral mentor sits down next to the fire and waits in silence. He was good at the indigenous practice of *waiting* when he taught me for a decade in the 1980s. He is even better now that he is free of the space/time continuum. Let me catch you up on Bear Heart's background as a way to provide a context for his current visits.

Several chapters of Bear Heart's story were chronicled beautifully in *The Wind Is My Mother*, a narrative he and Molly Larkin authored in a stirring book by that name. In an elegant mother and son passage, Bear Heart recalls a touching moment when his biological mother dedicated him to the Great Mother.

> *When I was three days old, my mother took me to a hill-top near our home and introduced me to the elements. First she introduced me to the Four Directions—East, South, West, and North. "I'm asking special blessings for this child. May You sur-round our lives and keep us going. Please protect him and bring balance into his life."*[1]

That comely blessing by his mother speaks to the beginning education of a *medicine person*. Lately, our culture refers to this mode of work as shamanism, a term borrowed by modernity from tribes in Siberia. The early recognition by the biological mother of the gifts of her child constitutes one mark of a person called to shamanic work. From this initial ceremony, the child, Marcellus Williams, was designated as a conduit of trans-ordinary reality.

When Bear Heart took me to a place in Oklahoma near where the above ceremony occurred with his mother, Katie Williams, we looked out over the surrounding hills where Katie touched his feet to Grandmother Earth. I could almost see mother and brand new son framed against bluestem grass and black jack oak.

Katie's child, Marcellus, was a frail and vulnerable newborn. She had already lost one son at a young age, so she especially cherished Marcellus. His family sometimes called her new son, Chaboni, or *Sonny* in Creek. So this baptism was a syncretistic recognition of his calling as a caretaker of the medicine ways, a healing of his body, and a baptismal ceremony. All on the third day of his Earth walk.

Such a beginning frame for Bear Heart's life and teachings is important because everything in his body of work rotates around a human return to the web of life, as humble and conscious participants, not arrogant dominants. Later, my grandson, Will Turner, would call this return *Earth Renaisance.*

His mother, Katie, embodies the waiting arms of the Great Mother who calls her wayward human children in from a 5,000-year shopping spree that has broken the bank and covered over our souls with civilization's concrete.

Against the backdrop of this landscape where his mother dedicated him, Bear Heart told me something about his tribal history as the wind blew his Stetson so that he kept pulling it down over his forehead. The implication was clear to me as the two of us shifted from one foot to another on the dark brown soil of the Oklahoma prairie. Before we transcend into the sky to converse with the Great Bear, we needed to descend into the loins of Earth.

His voice rumbled low and deep like thunder in a distant Oklahoma storm as he spoke his name *Bear Heart* in his native language—*Nogus Fege Ematha Tustanaki*, a visionary name he would receive later in life.

Though it was nearing last light in the Oklahoma evening, he still wore sunglasses as if to look through a lens to the beyond, including some of his personal story. I wondered if his eyes were impaired because there was something odd about his left eye.

Marcellus, Bear Heart's given name at birth, was born in 1918 to the Muskogean-speaking nation, the largest of federally recognized Muskogee tribes. He was the youngest child in a large family, born to a mother who would live to 104 years—some said, 107.

In its apex, the Muskogee Nation/Creek Tribe stretched from East Texas, to Canada, to the Atlantic, and down to Florida. His older half-brother by 20 years, John Davis, became Chief of the Muskogee Nation/Creek Tribe, but it was Bear Heart whom the family and tribal friends would always call *Chief.* To his nieces and nephews, he would be *Uncle Chief,* a term of respect and endearment.

When exploring his roots with me, the pride in Bear Heart's voice shone through as he spoke of his tribe as being one of the Five Civilized Tribes—the Muskogee/Creeks, the Cherokees, the Chickasaws, the Choctaws, and the Seminoles. This term was assigned to these tribes by mainstream, European/American historians who meant by the description that the tribes adjusted easily to European life styles.

Bear Heart laughed at such egotistical and culturally ignorant pronouncements and was quick to point out that these indigenous tribes were far more civilized in their own right than the invading immigrants from

Europe. He considered such a patronizing designation by Ivy League and European trained academics to be grossly conceited, and insulting.

He summarized his feelings: "The mystery writer, Tony Hillerman, understands us better than the hide-bound academics who spend most of their time projecting their view on a world they little understand. Western academic types study us as if we were laboratory rats.

"They think they can learn about our ways by fitting us into their silly systems. But we tell them only enough to confuse them. Sometimes, we make up stories to tell them for our own entertainment. Our elders laugh at what passes for understanding indigenous ways.

"We have given up on American academia. They have no heart. They think. They don't feel."

As always Bear Heart had a laughing lilt to his stinging words that had a way of slipping underneath my usual rationality as he gently aimed at shaking me loose from the hold my various graduate degrees had on me.

That his tribe was civilized when the Europeans arrived is without question; but, in Bear Heart's mind, the encounter with Western Civilization degraded the civilization of the five tribes, which he saw as superior in many ways.

In fact, what the European Americans delineated as civilized, Bear Heart considered a serious setback to Creek sensibilities.

Most of what they learned from the French, British, and new Americans was anything but civilized, said he. The immigrant Americans diluted an indigenous civilization that had its roots in several thousand years of Mound Builders whose engineering monuments dotted tens of thousands of mounds, mostly east of the Mississippi.

These so-called mound builders may have had roots in the Pyramids of Teotihuacán since some mounds were shaped like pyramids and their descriptions of rivers carried names like *Mississippi*, a Nahuatl word, the language spoken by the people of Teotihuacán.

"Take scalping as an example of what we learned from the European-Americans," he laughed as he ruffled my shoulder length hair, in a mock appraisal of how the locks would look as a prize of battle.

"The French introduced that practice to the Creek in the French and Indian war in 1763. My elders told me that the Europeans brought scalping with them into war. They had learned it from Old World Scythians who were so good at it that they used their tanned, human scalps as napkins to wipe their mouths when they ate.

"The English, especially the Anglo Saxons, were proficient at scalping, having brought it with them to the New World as a central tactic of war."

He continued with a wry smile, "Those guys from the seat of Western Civilization taught us many bad things, and we bought into the whole package. Maybe we gave them a few of our bad habits, as well. The only thing we really have left is our deep roots in Grandmother Earth.

"Current industrial nations are going to need what we bring. Wait and see. Our day is coming. We welcome all you mixed-bloods, mongrels, and wannabes. We need everybody for the new day!"

I pushed Bear Heart a bit to see if modern culture had given his tribe anything of worth. "Coffee and old Dodge pickup trucks, especially red ones," he said, smacking his lips, knowing I mainly drank tea.

I hit the pause button here to let you know more about my learning process as it relates to Bear Heart when I was in the mentoring mode, both giving and receiving. Since childhood I have questioned everything, especially authority. My many therapists have pointed out that I, at least in my youth into mid-life, had an authority problem. Namely, I had trouble accepting outside authority. Such a diagnosis was probably accurate since I tended to question their diagnosis.

As I reflect on my time with Bear Heart from the vantage point of several decades, I see that walking with him accelerated my questioning. My mentor awakened in me a profound inquiry into the validity of accepted accounts of American history and even the roots of Western Civilization.

When Bear Heart gifted me with a sacred pipe, he laughed and called me a pipe carrier who is more of a *question carrier*. Such a perspective has served me well in scientific and spirit questing.

I also questioned most of what Bear Heart taught me, and he encouraged the questioning.

Sometimes, people ask me if Bear Heart and I started a cult. In a cult, I tell them, you don't question the leader or the group norm. In a healthy community, questioning is embraced.

Early on, we had no internet or Google, so I spent considerable time in the local library and mall bookstores checking out Bear Heart's perception of history as revealed in his tribal wisdom.

In the case of scalping, I found his oral tradition to be *mostly*, though not entirely, true. I say mostly because there was some scalping going on in the Americas before the European invasion, though it is true that the Muskogee/Creek did learn scalping from the French and British.

But the Creeks never reached the dark pleasure of using scalps as napkins as did the Europeans or even the perverse practice of some American soldiers in making necklaces of the enemies ears, a practice sometimes used in modern American warfare.[2]

Keep in mind that in 1491, there were prodigious differences between the Mound or Pyramid Builders who were grandparents to Bear Heart's tribe and the hunter-gathers of the Northern and Southern Plains, who embraced European violence more readily.

A major error in mainstream's academic understanding the new world is a failure to see the immense diversification of tribes. There are as many differences between 1491 tribes as there are, say, between a county seat town in Texas and Apple's corporate campus in Silicon Valley.

It was convenient for the infant United States to think of *Indians* as retro savages, hunter/gatherers, rather than quite sophisticated as were some of the Southeastern tribes like the Creek and Southwestern tribes like the Hopi. Hollywood has vaccinated the American mainstream with the view of natives as a monoculture, a simplistic horse culture.

It was, and is, convenient for us in the USA to live in denial of a genocide of indigenous peoples if we think of them as savages.

In addition, the cities along the Mississippi were far more evolved than London or Paris at the time of the invasion, said Bear Heart. As I indicated, I didn't really believe what he was telling me, at least at first glance. So I continued a vigorous research about his tribe and its roots.

Fueled by a fierce curiosity, I reached back into the mists of the early American narrative. What I discovered not only confirmed many of Bear Heart's indigenous stories but slowly, and painfully, reshaped my view of American history.

That liberation from civilization's dream constituted a basic intent of our walk became more and more apparent as the years passed by. Such a liberation was supported by Carl G. Jung, a major influence in my psychological research.

What we are experiencing in current global chaos, according to Jung, is "…a rude awakening from the dream of civilization."[3]

As you read this book, join me in questioning most everything you have been taught about the accepted American narratives well as the themes of this book.

We can respect, for example, George Washington, but we also know he didn't chop down a cherry tree. We know that he had 300 slaves. When a certain slave escaped, he spent decades and extensive funds trying to hunt her down. He failed. We also know that Thomas Jefferson fathered children with his slave, Sally Hemings. We know that the founding fathers gave us a heritage of trashing the environment.

We know that Abraham Lincoln oversaw a removal march of the Navajos that decimated, ironically, a similar number of Indians as people died in the 9/11 attack on the World Trade Center. To the Navajo and Apache, Lincoln—often cited by historians as our best President— might well be considered a terrorist.

Once free of the calcified views of our education about our own culture, we can make room for larger truths. Such enlargement of perspective is the purpose of reframing American history.

In his book, *1491*, Charles C. Mann shines a light on the pre-Columbian Americas with information made possible through GPS archeology and anthropology. As information has poured in with fresh images, important, even revolutionary, discoveries have been made. Using GPS directives, scientists have been guided to excavate sites by images from outer space to areas not previously known, and, ever so slowly, the view of the Western Hemisphere prior to 1492 is being revamped.

"It was, in this newer view, a thriving, stunningly diverse place, a tumult of languages, trade and culture."[4]

It also was a web of eco-fields that yielded a sustainable wisdom through some of the more advanced tribes. If we can shed the shackles of our current world views, we may discover a lost language, an affiliation with the environment, and, indeed, a profound love which can open the way for our children's children, seven generations ahead to live in harmony within our beautiful blue planet.

Diets in key tribes within indigenous Americans averaged 2,500 calories a day, far better than the foodstuffs of famine-dominated Europe. According to new research, the pre-invasion Americas were apparently free of cystic fibrosis, newborn anemia, schizophrenia, asthma, and juvenile diabetes. Although researchers have competing hypotheses, it has long been argued that there was no instance of cancer in pre-Columbian Americas.[5]

Embedded in my world view at the beginning of my sojourn with Bear Heart was a picture of a disease-riddled native population incapable of responding to the European threat. That was, indeed, true of post-1492 Americas.

But what happened after the Europeans landed to make these native civilizations so vulnerable; especially since, in many ways, they were superior to the invaders? The narrative is complex, layered, and, at times, mystifying, but let's explore briefly to get a sense of Bear Heart's background.

Although academics have been almost uniformly defensive of the notion of governmental germ warfare, I found it likely to be true. To wit Jeffery Amherst, a British commander in the French and Indian War of 1763, recorded in his diary and letters that the Europeans used the spread of disease as a tactic against Indians, a weapon the immigrant Americans used as well.[6, 7]

The population of the Americas was estimated by some scholars as 100 million in 1491. By the end of the 19th Century, the population had been drastically reduced by 90% or nearly 90 million natives. Some researchers describe the impact of invasion on the native peoples as genocide and, even more controversial, an *Amerindian Holocaust*. Andrew Jackson's presidential strategy had as its goal complete extermination.

Jackson's genocidal policy continues to this very day.

The mainstream culture no longer infects with the virus of small pox but now infects with the virus of consumerism. Wherever you go with indigenous people, you can see that this lethal virus exacts an enormous toll. The devastating disease of consuming spreads like wild fire and is on a road to destroying the environment unless we soon arrive at the bridge to a new era.

In exterminating the indigenous, it turns out we are obliterating ourselves.

In the early days of my bear walk, I—like mainline historians—had difficulty washing out of my system the view of the Americas largely shaped by European dominated academics in the educational system of the USA.

Here is an example of my Western Civilization bias. Since my psychotherapy practice in those days consisted of many clients who carried the label of schizophrenia, I was especially skeptical of Bear Heart's claim that there was little or no schizophrenia in the Americas when Columbus arrived.

How could that possibly be true?

As I labored day-after-day with clients barely holding on to the day of the week or the address of my office, his claim seemed outlandishly romantic and naive. Still, I was aware no researcher in widely accepted scientific circles really knew what schizophrenia was or what caused it.

Neither did I, but, to my great surprise, my clients improved when I provided them experiences outdoors that energized their natural selves.

A number of therapists from different states heard of my work at integrating ancient wisdom with newer therapies through professional workshops and my writing. Soon, they began visiting our ceremonial healing events to probe the possibility of help for themselves personally and also for their patients.

Around a campfire, one psychiatrist commented to Bear Heart, "This is great, but my patients are too sick for this kind of help. These people here in this Earthtribe encampment are much healthier than my case load."

Bear Heart allowed the psychiatrist to finish, and then replied:

"From what I hear many of these folk here in Will's group got themselves labeled with mental disorders before they closed the gap between themselves and these trees and that crow over there. What you see here is a group of people who are getting more and more healthy by digging their toes in dirt. Everybody is getting better, except, of course, my friend here," Bear Heart laughed and dug an elbow into my proverbial ribs.

Could it be that this ancient pathway held a key for a new paradigm for healing mental disorders, including the epidemic of addictive urges that constitute a plague in the Western World?

Though questions like this one lurked in the background, I was very slow to connect the dots. The process jolted my identity as I came along kicking and screaming; I only reluctantly admitted that indigenous mental health might indeed be better when the people still lived in harmony with the wilder forms of the eco-fields.

The more I studied the emerging picture of a 1492 hemispherical invasion of east to west, the more my inner skeptic quieted regarding Bear Heart's tribal version of American history.

But the skepticism was replaced by an inner sub-self whose blood was boiling not only about the genocide but also about the lies we tell ourselves in mainstream America. We currently are beset with an avalanche of *fake news* stories on the internet. Such fake news may be the offspring of fabricated stories taught as history in most of our schools on a daily basis.

The more I delved into the so-called historical accounts of the formation of our nation, the more I sensed a basic betrayal of truth. No wonder we are having difficulty in deciphering the difference between the fake news of Twitter from a grounded statement of facts.

And, most important to our exploration here, I wondered why Bear Heart wasn't more angry and why he was both realistic in his view of atrocities committed against his people and, at the same time, loving and forgiving in his heart.

In my late 30s and early 40s, I was just discovering my own tribal roots, which my family-of-origin had repressed. Nevertheless, the diminutive portion of native blood flowing in my veins raged.

But, on the other hand, I was confused because I also had a slave trader in my personal history, an ancestor who kidnapped my generational grandmother and dragged her as a Shawnee slave to Texas and then married her, likely against her will, or so one version of family genealogy stated.

As pieces of my family story bobbed to the surface over time I—like many mongrels—was stretched between these cultural opposites. Night after night, I tossed and turned in the tension between the anger of the victim and the guilt of the perpetrator all flowing in my veins.

I had inner sub-selves warring with each other: one, a Shawnee slave, and the other a slave trader. I was being torn apart by the split in the matrix of mainline culture. No wonder this culture produced schizophrenics.

Bear Heart told me time and again, "Go to the sweat lodge and let go of your anger and confusion; Mother Earth can recycle them. You can do no lasting good by being angry. We all have heroes and skeletons in our closets."

Our friendship was shifting my identity. I now was in search of my untamed heart, or, as Jung put it, "the natural man."[8]

To my surprise my mentor was leading me to a wild and natural essence that tapped into a more basic wellspring of love, one that showed me the potential of embracing anger and guilt within the arms of beloved community. At least on occasions, there was a conscious embrace of these opposites, and, in that recovery of the natural person, lay the possibility of healing of the terrible split of a schizophrenogenic civilization.

Such stories about the absence of schizophrenia implied that the 1491 Muskogee/Creek and likely some other tribes knew how to interact with people who might be predisposed to schizophrenia and other mental illnesses through faulty DNA or brain chemistry gone awry. Many observers note that depression and anxiety are essentially conditions that arise primarily in Western Civilization. Such thoughts led to two fundamental questions:

Who are we humans?

Where are we going?

These questions cascaded like hot water out of a deep, volcanic river and the steam loosened the super glue of my professional identity. Questions from the elders I was meeting through Bear Heart seemed to come out of left field as if from another star system, certainly another culture. On one occasion, one of the elders asked me what my day job was.

"I am a psychotherapist," I replied, wondering what he meant by "day job."

"Well, how do you get to be a psychotherapist? Is that something like a train conductor. You know Rolling Thunder is a train conductor. We all have to do something because healing doesn't pay much these days," he elbowed me and laughed, a habit of these tribal wise persons.

"You study and get a doctor's degree and a state licensure," I replied again, starting to feel defensive because I could tell the medicine council wasn't exactly buying the validity of my education.

I recalled that Carl Jung was 50 years old before he talked to a person of color or much less an indigenous person. Jung was shocked by the indigenous perspective, and I was having a similar experience with this council of elders. I also was making a good living and felt a defense of my fees coming to the surface. I didn't consider being a psychotherapist as being a day job. It was my main job—actually, my only job.

"How do people find you if they want healing?" They persisted.

Again these were the days before Google, so I said, "By searching in the Yellow Pages or word of mouth."

"Not a good way."

After a long while and a pregnant silence, I asked, "Well, how do you suggest people find a competent resource if they want *healing*." I stumbled a bit over the word, *healing*.

As a product of reductive and industrialized education, I wasn't comfortable with the term healing at the time, much less providing my clients with a deeply healing process. Like most in my field, the best I could do was to put band-aids on their depression, anxiety, disturbances, and addictions.

I had no idea what a *soul healing* was and even less a notion as to how to go about it.

Finally from my elders came a response, "If you are sick or out-of-sorts, walk in the forest with the person you think might connect you with the forest. You watch how their spine connects with Earth. You watch how their bare feet contact the path. You watch their gait. You watch to see if they notice what is around them and if a smile comes to their face when a raven flies by and a butterfly lights on their finger.

"Everything depends on the link between the healer and the land. If you are sick, then you need a better relationship with the forest, a better balance, a better harmony. It is not your degrees that matter but rather your ability to lead people in a right relationship with themselves, with you, and with the Sacred Web.

"And walking with awareness is a very good and ancient medicine."

Such conversations as this one pushed me to examine my life and profession and to consider if there were treatment methods beyond the grasp of modern psychology. Such conversations kept niggling at the edge of my awareness until I moved my work basically outdoors and translated my psychotherapeutic skills into walking, ceremony, sweating, breathing, leaning against trees, chanting, singing, and listening.

I didn't dismiss my clinical skills and education but rather placed them in the larger milieu of the natural order. In my research into quantum fields, I was discovering that everything is motion.

The Universe is not a noun but rather more like a verb. If motion is at the base of all life, then the way through our emotional tangles lies in movement, or so I was now hypothesizing. Emotions tend to find healthy expression through motion itself.

Was Spirit somehow constructing a hybrid path for our walk?

Before long, a mode of being began to poke its head through the soil in a unified thinking/feeling. Industrialized rationalism faded in my rear view mirror. As I discovered that I was linked to every aspect of the Universe, notions of extreme individualism appeared as illusory.

A possibility of pervading compassion emerged naturally when I practiced being a participant in Nature rather than a dominant. An impersonal set of anthropocentric habits were melting in a first thaw.

But another challenge disturbed me.

What was the origin of the profound love I sensed in this unusual man?

The hurt in Bear Heart's voice bled through as he told me of the Amerindian strategy of Old Hickory, President Andrew Jackson's plan to move the five sophisticated tribes from Southeastern United States to *Oklahoma*.

Few in mainstream culture know what an affront it is to many native families to use the $20 bill, adorned as it is by Jackson. It would be something like Jewish people using as a principal currency a bill with Hitler's image staring them in the face each day.

The forced march called the Trail of Tears has become known in some academic circles as President Jackson's genocidal policy. And Bear Heart's great grandmother, Yec-pe (pronounced Ye Be in English), walked the entire distance in the snow without shoes until her feet froze.

"Do you know what gangrene looks like," Bear Heart asked me, and I didn't. "My family told me the story of how Yec-pe died," he continued, "Her feet turned a greenish-black, smelled bad, and ran open sores with pus until her feet dropped off." His words could have been venomous but instead were soft and tender. A far off look came over Bear Heart as he gazed beyond the hills where we sat.

"My great grandmother is buried over yonder just east of here in a place called Ft. Gibson. She almost made it to the end of the Trail of Tears at Tahlequah, Oklahoma. Almost.

"She died moving as best she could. I can't go pay proper respects to her grave because she died without recognition by the government. The cemetery consists of a mass of white crosses with no names. I guess they felt no shame in the mass graves.

"Every once in awhile you can utter her name out of respect for her humility and courage to walk the path even when it was terrible and even when she was the target of President Jackson's abuse."

We sat for a long while.

Then, I asked Bear Heart how he could stand the pain and not give into revenge. "I learned a long time ago that love is the greatest power, that forgiveness is the fuel of the pathway, and that the greatest revenge is to sow seeds of love where there is hate and ignorance. Forgiveness is a two-way street. It is easy enough to ask for forgiveness, but the law of the spirit world is that you have to learn how to forgive. To forgive is to relinquish all the stored up toxic waste you carry in the cells of your body."

Thus, I began to understand the reason Bear Heart and I had connected, and the direction to the great bridge. Truth be known, I didn't really grasp or experience that form of love until similar suffering entered my life.

In my 70s and facing a cancer diagnosis in my beloved partner, Judith, I softened and softened until I was prepared for a larger love.

And ancestral Bear Heart's visits called me to the ceremonial fire to fill in the gaps I missed during my first walk with him. In the face of a devastating disease with my loved one, I began to grasp the meaning of the practice of relinquishing, a deep letting go that originates in the well-spring of our souls.

Little did I know when I began the walk across the bridge with this bear that letting go would entail a relinquishing of reality as I knew it.

3

STORIES AS SOIL

Next steps in our walk require a rich compost of stories. With stories, we shovel natural fertilizer around the tender plants of our yearning for guidance, shamanic and otherwise. All of us have our own sagas wherein shamanic guides—called by many names in different traditions—are seeking us out.

And for what purpose?

To lead us into intimate connections and transactions within the web of eco-fields. Often, we don't remember or notice the guides reaching out to us because of the cultural overlay that gives us amnesia. The ancient intimacy of storytelling yields watershed moments and refreshes our memories.

Early on, Bear Heart asked me to tell him a few yarns about my growing-up days to balance out many questions I had about him. We realized right away that our stories intertwined.

My boyhood town, Plainview, Texas, was about half way between the Pueblos in Taos, New Mexico, and the large Comanche reservation in Lawton, Oklahoma. Ancient pathways and tribal cross-fertilization led indigenous folk to journey from the enchantment of the Sangre de Cristo mountains through the Texas Panhandle directly through our town and eastward toward Lawton, a hot bed of shamanism that birthed the Native American Church through Quanah Parker.

All night tipi ceremonies with peyote as a sacrament attracted shaman from a variety of tribal traditions, even though at that time these deeply spiritual ceremonies were against the law in the United States, certainly in my hometown. Underground as they were, the white establishment had little or no knowledge of these practices.

Plus, these were times when Toltec and Huichol shaman from Mexico rode in beds of canvass-covered trucks to work in the fields of local ranchers and farmers, including the land owned by my mother.

Adults in our little town called these people, *braceros*, loosely translated as *one who works with his arms*. Most white adults in the township knew little or nothing about these elder teachers; they saw them as cheap labor.

Typical of the conceit of modernity, the patriarchs of my world didn't give these *braceros* the time of day or, for that matter, a living wage. Meanwhile, my boyish curiosity was piqued by a man with a sombrero who pushed a cart of tamales down our dusty streets selling door-to-door, transmitting both his wares and his worldview.

Every Saturday in the Fall of the year, Juanita, my mother, bundled me up and took me to a spot near the Running Water Draw, an eco-field of massive sycamore trees, Siberian elms, hackberry groves, and periodic spring water from the Ogallala aquifer.

The flowing water of this massive aquifer system attracted her father to the area in the late 1800s. On these adventurous Saturdays, we spent eight hour days selling her clothes to migrant workers, and, in that endeavor, I was exposed not only to hispanic but also indigenous cultures.

Left mostly to my own devices, I played with children whose native tongue was Nahuatl, an Uto-Aztecan language spoken by many migrant workers at the time. Later, when I began studying Spanish, I found that words we use commonly in English are not Spanish in origin but actually Nahuatl—*tomato, chocolate, avocado, guacamole, mesquite, coyote, tequila, tamale, Mexico, and Tabasco*, to name a few.

Some of these braceros were from the Mexica (pronounced Mee-shee-ca) tribe, and they sometimes conducted ceremonial dances punctuated with conch shells.

From the back of trucks that doubled as mobile homes, I smelled the burning of *copal* and sage and listened to talk of *temezcal sweat lodges* and *peyote*. Such exposure would, in later life, send me scurrying to Teotihuacán and its sacred pyramids.

In annual pilgrimages for the Día de Muertos—Day of the Dead—I experienced a coming home when shaman spoke a language that brought forth from my childhood smells of copal—something like hot water on freeze dried coffee crystals.

That some of these elders practiced curanderismo in a form of shamanic healing and teaching is certain. Later in life, I would discover that there were several young people tutored informally by indigenous elders, curanderos and curanderas, in our village. Such archetypal wisdom seeped into my unconscious and fueled my connections with the indigenous. Eventually, I was formally adopted into the Mexica tribe and invited to assist in ceremonies.

In some instances, I was reunited in adulthood with other young people graced by this early shamanic influence. Such was the case with Mitchell Gaynor, M.D., who became a pioneer oncologist in New York and who was the son of my mother's dentist.

In Mitch's notes about his development as a cancer doctor, he chronicles being mentored by a Mexica shaman.[1] As adult clinicians, Mitch and I exchanged information about our formative years and shamanic roots and noted that we were brothers, in a real sense, offspring of the Mexica. We marveled at how our paths had twisted through many different venues of science and spirituality to lead us to a point of integrating scientific inquiry with ancient wisdom.

It now appears that Grandmother Earth sent forth an underground of shamanic teachers in both historical and archetypal spirit-form to backwater children during a time when the mainstream was lost in new fangled television, the Cleaver family, and fascination with and dread of the atomic bomb.

My personal experience suggests a larger strategy of the spirit world in providing modern humans with shamanic guides; but, as you likely surmise in your own experience, there are major obstacles to our listening to these guides.

Search your own background, and you might find that imaginary friends might not be so much imaginary as imaginative and, thus, links us to trans-ordinary reality. As we proceed, we will explore this possibility.

Time met itself.

Three years into elementary school, I hiked in a red rock canyon a few miles from our family land. It was late July, and an afternoon thunder boomer passed by leaving its calling card of fresh air. The sun disappeared behind the rim rock of the canyon as I followed older hikers in front of me. They turned a corner and left me alone in a forest of Forsyth juniper native to the area.

A sharp and enlivening fragrance wafted across my tanned face carried by the last vestige of the storm. An olfactory presence moved through the limbs of the trees. I shuddered, and tears of boyhood joy flowed. I didn't need to know what happened, only that it happened. I didn't need a name for the presence, only that its fragrance would follow me.

Four or five years later, I was in the same canyon, summer again. This time I hiked alone wearing blue suede shoes not practical for hiking but part of an adolescent strategy of attracting female attention at a nearby church camp.

Walking along, I hummed from a favorite song, "You can do anything that you want to do, but stay off of my blue suede shoes." Following the spring-fed Ceta Canyon Creek that emerged from the Ogallala acquifer, I came to a small waterfall, cascading over slick red rocks.

Before I knew it, my beloved shoes sank into red mud up to my ankles. Greatly disturbed, I sat down to inspect them and, in doing so, I took time to listen to the music of the water as the current washed away the mud.

Then, I heard a sound, maybe a voice. Out of the late afternoon mists of the waterfall, emerged a shadowy figure who uttered something that sounded like *O-nee-ha*.

A whispering voice blended with the rushing water. The visionary figure had a slender face with eyelids that hung at half mast. His eyes were milky and sharp at the same time. A silver feather hung from each ear, and a deep crease ran vertically through his third eye.

His forehead had a few wrinkles but struck me with how smooth the skin was. His mouth was neither smiling or frowning. A golden eagle was in full flight over his head with one wing stretched out to constitute his hair. Blinking, I saw shining light coming through his body as if he could appear and reappear on demand.

Time warped.

He cleansed my windows of perception which were clouded with adolescent testosterone, and, for a moment, I saw clearly through the clutter and chaos of culture. I saw my future beyond basketball aspirations. I saw rampant and profligate consumption. I saw rambling and empty suburban sprawls. I saw the degradation of our beloved planet.

I saw water polluted, used up, and then flooding. I also saw immense possibility in the flowing whole of life through the waters falling over slick, red rock cliffs. This was the summer of 1952, and my visions—strange to me at the time—prepared me to listen closely to what would come.

Little did I know that this shamanic ancestor—like the juniper fragrance—would shadow me all my life. Though he has never given me his name—as if naming detracts from his unique power—I call him *O-nee-ha* after the sound of the waterfall I heard when I first met him.

Later in the day, after I used a safety pin to repair the elastic stretch on my blue suede loafers and after I returned from my hike, I attempted to talk about my vision with counselors at the church camp and was greeted by blank stares. Not looks of ridicule or hostility or even anxiety, but a you-might-be-from-another-planet stares.

Several such encounters with spirit-forms followed me through high school. After each of these transordinary experiences with spirits, I sought flesh and blood guidance from the visible world, a mentor to help me walk a path that was inviting but obscure. No mentors from my ordinary life appeared: at least, none who seemed conversant with visitors from the imaginal realm.

The drought of the 1950s severely limited crops and thus the presence of migrant workers who had helped shape my life. No crops; no workers; no guides, shamanic or otherwise. There was no one to talk to about mysterious occurrences happening in an otherwise typical adolescence.

I was adrift on a vast sea without a North Star.

After high school graduation in 1958, five of my friends and I hatched a plan for an expedition of two and half hours to Lake Conchas near Tucumcari, New Mexico. Our aspiration in late night bull sessions was vision questing, a term we borrowed from the Comanche in our area.

The name of Tucumcari, a town of about 5,000, is derived from the Comanche word tukamukaru, which can be translated as "waiting within a circle." Perhaps, intuitively, we knew we needed to sit in a circle in a remote area and wait before we jumped into our lives beyond.

Wait for what? Or Whom?

We didn't know; we only yearned.

Ordinarily, the climate at Lake Conchas is dry and pleasant at over 4,000' in elevation, but, when we arrived, on a June afternoon, it was hot and uncharacteristically humid. Forty miles of rocky, unpaved roads had already covered us in dust and questions.

We had no elders to guide us, so we decided on a whim to boat over to Rattlesnake Island, a destination whose name might give people other than late adolescents pause to think.

Intrepid as young men washed in high school graduation fever generally are, we launched small boats we had borrowed on the lake's south boat ramp without regard to the dangers. The ramp had been closed during the drought but had been recently opened with the spring rains of 1957–58.

Typically, Lake Conchas had a dry 17" annual rainfall, but not this abnormally wet year. Tropical storms churned up over Baja California, drifted north and east, and drenched this high desert. In so doing, the atmosphere was highly charged and ripe for late spring storms.

The lake, which is fed by the Conchas and Canadian Rivers, stretches about 25 miles from north to south. With 15-horse outboard motors we headed out to the island, which is located at a mid-point near the deepest part of the lake. The shores of the island are rocky, so we had a challenging time landing and securing our boats. We cooked a light supper and built an inviting campfire. We knew about fasting but not its benefits. Without guidance, we chose to fill our bellies with hot dogs and Oreo cookies.

Soon, we adjourned to our circles with blankets and no tents. A couple of the fellows had sleeping bags, but most of us reclined on the ground covered in horse blankets to watch the sunset. We aspired to meditate but hardly knew what the word meant. This was the 1950s, and we had not even heard of the term "yoga." We had no spiritual practice other than following our natural inclinations.

Off to the southwest, I saw a billowing cloud, yellowish black with an anvil top. Fascinated and terrified, I watched as an ominous wedge dropped out of the sky, moving north and east.

At first its fingers dangled and then formed a massive hand. Too late, it dawned that it was a tornado, bearing down on us with a characteristic train-like roar with winds exceeding 200 mph. I hugged the ground. Hail bounced off a wet blanket I stretched over my head for protection. The ground shook. The funnel danced across the lake, sucking up the water and mercifully passed by.

Had the funnel been over our island, it would have drawn trees and rocks into its core and flung them at us as deadly missiles. Instead, the hail pummeled us, and the water and wind drenched us, but no major harm.

It seemed a Grandfather Sky, with an unlimited force in reserve, had compassion for clueless seekers.

A phrase came to me in my first year of philosophy class later that fall to describe how I felt in the hands of the storm—*mysterium tremendum.* I had been knocked off my feet by a mysterious power beyond my comprehension, and I trembled. Visited by Grandfather's hand, the storm moved beyond a tap on the shoulder, passionately to shake my foundations.

If a central purpose of a vision quest is to upset usual personality and cultural patterns and push to an archetypal story, this quest was a success. My default defenses were scattered with the storm. Yet, I had no guidance to assist in processing the primal material seeking entrance into my awareness.

I had no tribe, no community to hold these potentially fecund experiences.

Years later, as an aspiring minister, I expressed some of these visions in a church sermon in my hometown of Plainview, and, after polite rebuke by the officials, was never invited back. These were good people in the congregation, but visages emerging out of waterfalls and tornadoes with hands were a bit much.

Failure on my part to communicate with those around me whetted my appetite to find a community where trans-ordinary experiences could be held and valued. I longed for fellow seekers who could say, "We not only hear your story, but we have pieces of that story in our lives."

These visions also pointed me to something ominous beneath the surface of my fledgling personality, perhaps a wound seeking to find its way to the surface. I sensed an iron box next to my soul that held pain, suffering, and, most of all, anger.

But I wasn't prepared to open the box—not yet.

Born in me was a thirst to translate the language of the storm. I wasn't fully aware of it at the time, but what I hankered for and needed was a journey guide who understood the messages of tornadoes, one who had been through the fires of his own injuries in order to prepare the way for a retrieval of his soul and mine.

O-nee-ha appeared from time-to-time as a spirit guide and helped, but I had no grounding that comes from a flesh and blood relationship. I couldn't open my inner, iron box by myself or with the assistance of my peers. I needed wisdom born of someone who could hold me and wipe away my tears. I craved an elder steeped in the flow of Nature, one who had survived his own terrors, to take me by the hand and, at times, boot my hind side.

One crisp fall day, early 1980s in the Montrose section of Houston, Bear Heart and I sat visiting in Judith's and my backyard under a native pecan tree. He often visited and stayed in our home so that we could explore in a variety of directions and dimensions.

As we batted Houston's famous subtropical mosquitoes in a fanning motion, I asked Bear Heart what he thought of modern psychology, a point of some interest but also controversy in our conversations. Psychology was my field of scientific inquiry at the time, and the reductive version of that science looked down its nose at shamanism. I largely had escaped from the silly reductionism so prevalent in that discipline, but not entirely.

"I don't know that much," he intoned, "but I really like Carl Jung." He pronounced *Jung, Young*.

I thought to myself, "If you can't pronounce his name, how could you know anything about him?"

These were thoughts typical of my mainstream arrogance during that phase of my life. Then, jolting me out of my judgements, Bear Heart waxed eloquent with regard to Jung's encounter with Och-wi-ay Beano, a Pueblo shaman in Taos, New Mexico, and emphasized the importance of the indigenous mind in the development of Jung's psychology.

Cryptically, Bear Heart asked me, "What do you know about the ancestors who guided the good doctor Jung? You might find Jung was a medicine man. Try looking beneath his research to his underlying story."

In 1925, Carl Jung journeyed to the USA with two places on his mind to visit. One was obvious: New York City. The other, not so obvious: Taos, New Mexico. When asked about his choice of places to visit, Jung commented that the two urban experiments shared a common theme of humans living in proximity, both with a canyon-like effect when he walked their streets.

Keep in mind that Jung was now fifty years old, and—typical of his day but shocking to us—he had never talked to a person of color, much less an indigenous person. He had been reared in a white, privileged ghetto dominated by European civilization's preoccupation with pessimism, linear reasoning, and homogeneity.

No wonder he was astounded when he encountered Och-wi-ay Beano, a holy person of the Pueblo tribe, whose name translates as Mountain Lake. His conversations with this little brown man astounded Jung because it was of a quality he had never experienced before.

Jung marveled at the indigenous culture, and wrote of the Taos Pueblo: "What a world this is!"[2] At a very deep level this white boy from Switzerland felt like he had come home, or was on the way home, at the very least.

Jung, then let us in on this insight into himself and our modern culture, "In talk with a European, one is constantly running up on the sand bar of things long known but never understood; with this Indian, the vessel floated freely on deep, alien seas."[3]

Och-wi-ay Biano considered Jung, drinking him in and spoke as he gazed into Jung's eyes, "See how cruel the whites look. Their lips are thin, their noses sharp, their faces furrowed and distorted by folds. Their eyes have a staring expression; they are always seeking something. They are always uneasy and restless. We do not know what they want. We do not understand them. We think they are mad."[4]

Jung was understandably shocked, especially at the notion that whites are mad. Jung had a deep split in himself between his daytime scientist and his nighttime shaman. His daytime psychiatrist diagnosed his nighttime shaman as "psychotic." That being the case, he was especially vulnerable to Och-wia-y's observation of the madness of civilized whites; the comment cut him to the quick.

Jung asked Och-wi-ay why he thought all whites were mad.

"...they think with their heads," Och-wi-ay replied.

"Why of course. What do you think with?" Jung asked him in surprise.

"We think here," the shaman said, placing his palm on his heart.

This was a Rubicon moment for one of the great scientists of the 20th Century, one he would return to time and again throughout his life. Historians have puzzled over the power of such a brief moment.

Jung's students have—with a few notable exceptions—been somewhat embarrassed by the exchange and tended to denigrate its importance. Many have asked how such a brief encounter could be axial for Jung and criticized Jung for exaggerating and misunderstanding the Pueblo culture.

Maybe, but I was learning that many scientists miss the roar of the wild bear and that Jung was beginning a wild walk on a bridge between human eras to show us the way.

Later that week, Bear Heart and I sat in a hot tub in my backyard looking at Houston's night sky. We discussed the above story, and, for the first time in my life, I saw that the shaman and the scientist could hang out together.

4   WANDERING
WITH TWO YOUTHS

One fine day early in our time together, Bear Heart drove me in his faded Dodge pick-up truck to a remote place on the west side of the Rio Grande near Albuquerque. As Bear Heart braked his old truck and parked near an overlook of the river, I could hear metal to metal as he pumped us to a stop. His brakes needed a shoe job.

The landscape along the river bank called us out of the truck to sit on a large log placed by spring floods. The river wandered through sage and sand and carried us to scenes of his childhood. Along the way, he told me a story of his wounding as a boy during his father's illness.

Nathan Williams was beloved by all, especially by his son, Mark, as Bear Heart was known at that time. In the later stages of pernicious anemia, Nathan was nearing death. It was the custom of the Creek tribe to build juniper arbors outside the house in order for the walk across the bridge of death to be infused by the sounds of the night and the breezes of the day.

Mark followed the instructions closely in how to build the arbor, noting how important it was for his father to be close to his animal friends.

Once the arbor was completed, Mark had the task of sitting all night with this man he loved so much—no small task for a twelve-year-old. At the edge of the arbor was a Coleman lantern that gradually lost its strength in the course of the night.

As the night progressed, Mark drifted off into sleep. During the day, Mark rubbed his father's back with a healing touch, following directions given by tribal healers. These same elders assisted Mark in concocting a medicine aimed at pain relief for his failing father.

Bear Heart picked up the story at this point, allowing pain to seep through, "Sitting with my father, I felt alone and abandoned, yet strangely I experienced the presence of our Creator inviting me to keep the faith, but, sometimes, I couldn't.

"My father noticed I went to sleep about 2:00 am, and he was dismayed. Somewhat sternly, he instructed me to remain alert all night. I had to obey because our tribal tradition taught that when someone was to go across the great river we call death, there were dark witches who aspired to come around and steal the heart of the loved one.

"When you die, it is important to be surrounded by the safety of your loved ones. Even so, you can imagine that I nodded off from time-to-time."

Bear Heart noticed my wrinkled brow and knew I was questioning such "superstitions" since he knew I didn't believe in witches. He waited for my wrinkles to relax and then proceeded, though I am sure he knew my questioning did not cease.

"These witches are kind of like vampires who desire to capture other people's hearts and souls to extend their powers.

"Our tribal elders teach, even today, these ancient truths that tell us about the dark side of the Universe. I was taught to look for tiny iron pots that the vampire-like witches use to cook people's hearts and souls.

"You have to stay alert and aware in order to protect a loved one who's about to go across. That is a challenge because witches know about long distance hypnosis that can put an entire household, even a tribe, or even a nation, to sleep.

"Long distance hypnosis was given to my tribe before we ever came to Oklahoma. It had been passed down to us from an advanced civilization that grew up along the Mississippi River and extended out through the creeks and streams of Alabama and Georgia.

"It was especially useful when there was very little game, and my people were hungry. The hunters put themselves into a trance-like state so they could talk with potential game. Using ancient language, they told the game they were hungry and respectfully requested their co-operation. Using this communication my people made agreements with the game that included offerings on the part of humans to their kind and to their environmental homes.

"The hunter/game agreement included our never taking more than we needed and sharing with those in our tribe who couldn't hunt for themselves. In fact, the best hunters always shared the game with the less fortunate before they ate themselves.

"Respect in the tribe centered not so much on the amount of game you could horde for yourself but on an ability to share with others. In that way, we hunted to eat but also kept balance and respect at the center of our lives. This form of communication with animals and even plants is very powerful but has been lost to most people, especially white folks, often called *wascina*."

The storyteller paused. I was stunned by the deceptive profundity of his narrative.

I recalled a phrase by Nietzsche, the *transvaluation of values*, a description that the philosopher employed to challenge the mainstream values of his day to return to the "natural values" that affirm life.

In a similar vein, Bear Heart challenged the widespread practice of our culture in recognizing the accumulation of wealth as the *gold standard* of life. Accumulating wealth is not a life-giving value; rather, vitality emerges in sharing nature's bounty.

Certainly, the hunter of excellence provided for himself and his family, but he made sure the first share went to the needy, even before his own children ate. Such a basically altruistic practice turned the values of competitive capitalism upside down.

More specifically, Bear Heart's story was challenging the foundation of ownership and accumulation dominant in my daily world.

Were the materialistic value memes of American life the vampire witches he mentioned?

I wondered.

Bear Heart continued, "These witch vampire types took this gift of long distance hypnosis and practiced it on the dark side. They would come to a sleeping person and scratch him with a thorn, just a little bit, so the person didn't know they had been wounded. The witches then traveled a ways and hollered so that the sleeping person stirred. That way they could plant whatever negative thoughts they wanted while the person was half-asleep, hypnogogic state you called it the other day.

"One of the main ways witches bewitch you is to plant negative thoughts in your head so that they go round and round inside of you.

"There is so much negative thinking planted in people through the dark side of your culture. Releasing the consequences of this negative thinking is a large part of shamanic work.

"So, I was being taught through my father how to doctor a house and, in this case, the arbor where he lay to protect him and us from these long-distance influences. One protective device he taught me was to take a particular kind of feather and put it over the doorway. If someone tried to send a dark message to the house, the feather fluttered and woke up the people because the dark influences tend to come when you are asleep.

"If you had a really lively drum, it actually would make a sharp sound on its own to wake you up. Someday, you will receive a drum that will talk to you in a number of different ways even when no one is striking it.

"You may be talking to someone in your office, and *boom* the drum will make a sound. Or you may be lying in bed at night half asleep, and the drum will make a sound to let you know that the dream or vision is important. Drums help you with dark powers.

"Some witches shoot a foreign object into a person's body where it festers and causes pain. Even if we had x-rays in those days, professionals could not have detected the object because it would move around the body.

"So, it was my job to keep watch over my father to make sure these dark influences were not sneaking into him while he was in a vulnerable state.

"It may sound strange to your ears, but my father gave me a loaded .45 pistol that I kept with me at all times that summer, or at least at night. This loaded pistol had powers beyond the usual because of some special bullets. A relative of my mother was a noted medicine man, and he stopped by the arbor to teach me how to protect myself.

"My medicine uncle sat down beside me and spoke in a low voice, 'I hear that you been sitting up all night taking care of your dad. That's a good thing. Do you get sleepy?'"

I nodded, "Yes."

My uncle continued, "I'll fix you up some medicine to use to stay awake. Nobody in this world or the invisible world will be able to put you to sleep.

"Give me your bullets, and I will fix them with a concoction. If a witch tries to invade this here arbor to get your dad's heart, you will know them because their eyes glow like fire. When you shoot, you don't even have to aim. The bullet is guided to that shadowy person."

Bear Heart paused for me to take in this information, but he seemed to give up on my digesting such a strong morsel.

"That night I put the special bullets in the pistol and sat waiting when I saw a light coming toward us in the graveyard not too far away. Was it a witch wanting to get at my father's heart? I got up and walked toward the light, pointed the gun, and pulled the trigger.

"The gun clicked but didn't fire. I pulled the trigger again, and then again for the third time. Still, no firing. I was sweating another kind of bullets. Off in the distance, I could hear the witch laughing at me, 'Heh, heh, heh.'

"The fourth time I pulled the trigger the gun fired, bang! I heard a death sound, 'Ooohh!!'

"I moved quickly over to my dad. He said nothing, but I could tell he knew I was protecting him. Even near death his hand was firm, and his eyes clear when he grasped my arm.

"In the morning, some of my female cousins came over to help my mother clean the house. That was the custom. Our tribe helped each other. We were the only Indians in that part of the country who had a telephone, and it was a party line. Our ring was two long and two short— bzzz, bzzz, bz, bz. My mother answered. The person calling was an Indian woman who was using the phone at a neighboring white man's house.

"The distressed woman cried out, 'My mother fell off the wagon last night and hurt herself. I need medication. Do you have any? I know you go to town often and keep a lot of healing stuff around.'

"So, my cousin took some of our medicine to assist the poor woman. When my cousin came back, she found us at the arbor around my father's bed. She was full of news and told us that the woman didn't actually fall off the wagon. Rather, she was shot last night near the cemetery not far from the arbor.

"I looked at my father with a catch in my chest. The woman later died of the gunshot, and her wound became mine. I kept wondering if I had accidentally killed her, or was she a witch?

"My cousin tried to comfort me by saying I was just defending my father from dark forces trying to steal his heart. Yes, that was true, but this was a wound, along with my father's early death that I carried into my twenties. I still feel it when I tell you. The great path, William, is often beset with painful memories that come back time and again."

His story distressed me because in some way it cracked the iron box that held my own injuries. So I peeked in the cold darkness and saw the absence of my own father and the death of my grandfathers and grandmothers.

I saw the rampant addictions in my extended family. With just a small look, I knew I had been infected by a cultural virus, the sickness of addiction. I knew I would have to face this potential destruction lest it be passed from one generation to the next.

Bear Heart continued: "The Creator selects us to practice the healing ways of our medicine. The Sacred Mystery taps us on the shoulder. We seek guidance, and we don't know how it turns out. We don't know if what we do is helpful.

"Maybe it hurts and we do more harm than good. We don't know if we see witches when they are not there or if they are there and we are heroes. Sometimes our very calling brings us low. We are wounded as we try to heal. We just keep going toward being whole.

"In the end, we answer to the Creator Who will say to us, 'I allowed you to have certain gifts. Tell me how you used them.'

"That is my teaching on that subject."

Bear Heart beckoned me back to his truck, but I knew there was more to the story. The next day he continued over a cup of coffee at a Denny's restaurant in Albuquerque while I dipped a tea bag.

"When my father's time neared, my mother told me to go tell my aunt, my father's older sister. She lived in a neighboring county. Even though I was still young, I drove by myself that very night.

"When I arrived late in the evening, the family members were sitting around the supper table. I sat down and looked into the eyes of my aunt, her husband, and their daughter and told them my father was about ready to cross over. They invited me to pray with them and, after an extended time, we made plans to travel back the next day. As I slept that night in a strange bed, I longed for some signal that all would be OK.

"The next day I drove ahead of them in my family's car. Just west of my house as I traveled over a bridge, the dome light in the car came on. Immediately, I knew it wasn't an accident because the switch was way up out of reach in that particular model car.

"Then, after a short distance, the light went out by itself, and that's when I knew that my beloved dad was gone. That I was on a bridge when this happened told me much about crossing over. When I drove up to the house, a black man who worked for us came out to tell me that I had just lost my father.

"But I already knew. The light had told me. I had been on the bridge. It was a traumatic moment, yet I was encouraged by the presence of spirits in the light coming on. A power was with me.

"Some of our relatives had come over as was our tribal custom to sit in a circle of prayer in the arbor under the stars. They told me that at the last moment my father raised his hand with a great smile on his face and said, 'Thy will be done.'

"I was twelve years old when my father died.

"Soon, we went to the cemetery and put him in the ground. Before we shoveled dirt in the grave, I picked up a clod and threw it in. It made a clunking sound. Others followed. An elder took the shovel and passed it around so that everyone in the circle threw in a shovelful.

"After he was gone, I felt a great sense of emptiness. The cemetery was next to our house as I mentioned yesterday, so I got up at night and went out to the grave.

"I lay down to sleep, cry, and talk to him. I couldn't let go. For days family members would get up in the night and carry me back to my bed. This was a very deep hurting. Maybe it was my shooting witches. Maybe it was just the loss of this man I loved so much. But I was heartsick.

"The same medicine man who gave me the bullets to quell the witches came over after a few weeks to offer healing for me. Other wise elders, grandfathers and grandmothers of spirit, came and built a small shelter over the grave because that was the custom.

"In later years, I traveled in Europe and went through a museum which contained Viking ships and other artifacts of their culture. There I saw a little structure that looked exactly like our *grave houses*. The museum guide told me that, yes, these ancient Viking tribes built grave houses. He also told me that the Vikings prepared a dish that a dead person liked and put it in the grave house."

Bear Heart paused and touched a leather pouch hanging around his neck. I had been introduced to the Toltecs of Teotihuacán even before I began studying with Bear Heart. I thought about them and their practice of the Day of the Dead.

Much later, I would study and experience Toltec wisdom at the pyramids there. I would recall Bear Heart's story and wonder if there was any connection between the Vikings, the Toltec, and the Muskogee Creek. Or was this an archetypal practice, or both?

Bear Heart continued.

"*Wascina* often make fun of me when I tell them of my tribal practice of putting food and drink out in the grave hut for our loved ones as they travel over the great white mountain to the other side of the stars.

"They don't understand that when folks die, they transition from the material world into the invisible. They need food and other stimulations of the senses for a short period for their travel. One white man chided my medicine guide, 'When is that dead person going to come and eat the food you put out in the grave hut?'

"Our Indian elders answered with a wry smile, 'The same time your dead come up to smell the flowers that you put on your graves.'"

A persistent grief passed through me when I heard Bear Heart's story of his boyhood because I lost connection along the way with my father and my two grandfathers.

My grandfather on my father's side was killed in a gun battle on a dusty road in a pioneer Texas town when W.R., my father, was ten. That was an era of raw violence when men settled their differences with guns they carried on their hips—a troubling tendency toward which we drift presently.

Until I was age ten, W.R. was a good, if emotionally distant, father. We hunted and fished together in my early boyhood in the rugged canyons near our land.

On Saturdays, he would come in from working our acreage and change into freshly laundered khaki pants and shirts ironed and starched at Luster's laundry. When he picked me up to hug, he smelled both clean and of Llano dirt. His hands and forearms were brown and strong, with fresh soil under his fingernails. The land nourished me through him. But, as I approached manhood, he lost his way in alcoholism and puzzled over my yearning for gifts of larger consciousness.

In the mainstream, we long for grandfathers steeped in Mother Earth, rather than emotionally remote men, themselves dislocated from their souls. They suffer as captives of the collateral damage of an absent and silent god who rears divided men and personalities.

The human split from Nature leads to a split of the soul from the personality, and then to a loss of intimacy with landscape. Bear Heart lost his father in death, and I lost mine through addiction. Like Barack Obama, we could only dream of our fathers.

Physicist, David Bohm, speaks of how the universe works: the implicate and primal order seeks to come through into our lives as explicate coherence.

All of us search to connect with an implicit love which seeks to hold us explicitly. Such a searching love is as primal as the attractor force of gravity, like the hound of heaven.

Yet, where in Western Civilization does a young woman or man find a guide to help with such an emergent love? The only person in my little town able to hear my visions when I felt that consciousness reaching out to touch me was the local minister.

We hiked in the canyons where I had encountered the spirit at the waterfall, discussing such matters as we walked. He made a Herculean effort to understand, but, he admitted, it all sounded a bit strange to his Methodist ears.

A few days later and back from the canyons, he told me he thought I was being called to the clergy. I smiled. The notion of calling was apparent to us both.

Calling? Yes, but to what?

The "what" that followed was a ten year stint in a Masters program in theology and training in pastoral counseling and spiritual guidance with Mahatma Gandhi's protégé, E. Stanley Jones.

Many benefits came my way through this sojourn in Christian mysticism, but something was missing. A bewildering intimation worked its way slowly to the surface of my inner waters as I gasped for air. These forms of spiritual mentoring, while helpful, did not address the iron box of tangled emotions that lay next to my heart.

Maybe, I thought, education as a therapist might be the solution, and, with that motivation, I veered in the direction of becoming a therapist.

In training for counseling at Grady General Hospital in Atlanta, Ga., my supervising therapist looked at me with a cigarette between his teeth, and said, "What are you so angry about?"

"I am not angry," I blurted, just below the decibel shout of denial.

But I knew he was right.

His intervention prompted me to continue my development as a therapist and to enter a variety of therapeutic processes, including extended psychoanalysis. All of these approaches were helpful but, again, I yearned for more. Two continental divide moments smacked me in the face.

One day in church I realized that I was suffocating. No elbow room. No fresh air. I looked out the window from the sanctuary and saw the wind moving through the trees, and I knew my high school pastor had been correct. I was called, but not to the tame indoors of his institution.

Sometime later, a second axial moment came when I realized as a therapist I spent my life locked in an office where left-over emotions gathered like a dark mist; once again, making it hard to breathe. I was captured by a prison of personality dynamics, air conditioning, and couches.

Added to the stifling climate of an indoor office was the very real yearning of my clients who told me they were feeling better but wanted more. They weren't so depressed. They weren't so anxious. Their suffering lessened.

"What do we do now?" They asked me.

And I didn't have a clue.

What these two turning moments shared was the insight that the pathway for me had to move into domains beyond culture with the guidance of someone who moved easily in the natural world.

I had found many father figures in psychotherapists. Emotionally, I was better, but it wasn't enough. I intuited that I needed connection beyond human-centered space. There was little or no room for a spirited, wild heart behind pulpits or seated in the therapist's office.

Off I went on the most important trek of my life, one that took me back to spirit forms I met on Rattlesnake Island as a high school graduate.

The farther I trod on my return to the natural, the more I discovered that the shift from office to forest was more than a camping trip for adult boy scouts. My psychotherapist colleagues laughed about my *Kubayah* hand holding and soul-thirst, but I knew *something* had come-by-me in the form of a tornado. I just didn't know what, or who could show me how to know more.

Painstakingly, it dawned on me that I was participating in a massive epistemological shift from one form of knowing to another. The profound urge to spread my wings with the birds of the sky was part of an evolutionary impulse for humans to rediscover their role as humble connectors within a moving and organic matrix.

I would discover that Mark Williams, not yet fully a man and not yet named through his visions, with elder guidance moved through his own turmoil as part of his initiation. One day, I would know that Mark's and Billy's wounds were one story, a story that pointed to larger awareness and compassion for the split underlying the human condition.

Questions persisted: could Bear Heart move through his boyhood wounds enough to become a consciousness guide?

Could I?

Can any of us?

5   DANCING AWAY OUR TEARS

Lying on his father's grave night after night, all seemed lost to twelve-year-old Mark. Family members were naturally concerned and contacted a local medicine man (*Owala, Hilis-ha-yah* in Creek), a shaman who also happened to be part of the young man's extended family.

Elders conferred and offered young Mark a pathway through his grief in the form of tribal rites-of-passage that included dancing, drumming, sweat lodging, and vision questing.

The *Muskokalgi*—as Creek people sometimes referred to themselves—engaged youth in what they called the *obango hadjo*, or ecstatic dances that led them through the tangle of adolescent emotions and prepared the way for questing in the wild in search of a life-directing vision.

Mark was becoming Bear Heart, but it was gradual.

Early on, Bear Heart told me stories about his working through the loss of his father through ecstatic dancing:

49

"Long ago, my people were looking for Tookebudche, a leader who was prophesied to bring them through a particularly difficult time. They searched far and wide among holy people and warriors alike to no avail. Eventually, though, they found a tall, ordinary looking man, unassuming and unremarkable in appearance. Yet, something drew them to him as a possible fulfillment of their tribal prophesy.

"The tribal seekers inquired as to who he was, and he calmly replied, 'I am *Tookebudche.*'

"'We heard you are very powerful. If so, show us your power,' the council of elders tested him. It was the custom in these nature-based communities to recognize leaders by their harmony and collaboration with nature spirits, and such collaboration had to be visible to the tribal eye.

"'All right,' Tookebudche replied cryptically, 'But I have to holler four times.'"

Bear Heart continued in his rendition of the story after taking a drink of coffee from a blue cup with chipped edges, the kind you often see on camping trips.

"On Tookebudche's first holler, the grass shook. When he hollered a second time, the leaves on the trees shook. On his third holler, the trees themselves commenced to shake. On his fourth holler even the ground itself was shaking.

"Naturally, the council of my people themselves shook with such a demonstration of power. Everybody was all shook up. Maybe, that's where Elvis got his moves. Seeing them in such a vulnerable state, Tookebudche pointed to the sky and said, 'Such power comes from on high.'"

When he told me this story, Bear Heart stood up and stomped his feet on the ground, laughing and dancing as he acted out the story. It seemed to me the ground moved beneath my feet as he kicked up the dust, but who knows what happens in such situations?

Looking at me shudder, Bear Heart saw a teaching moment and interrupted his account of Tookebudche to immerse me in a related Shawnee story since he knew of my ties with a Shawnee relative.

As he talked, I reminded myself that this form of wisdom and story telling moved in cycles, not within the confines of linear logic. It was an approach of seemingly chasing rabbits that I had to adjust to since I was accustomed to maintaining a subject theme from beginning to end.

"It seems," Bear Heart began his teaching moment, "the great Shawnee shaman, Tecumseh, visited my home tribe in July of 1811 to convince us to join in a unified effort of many tribes to stop the European invasion of our beloved, a term we use to describe North America. We Creek were slow to respond to his invitation, and so Tecumseh told the reluctant tribe that he would return to his homeland along the Ohio River and offer a sign that would convince us to unify.

"There he would take his walking stick to the banks of the Ohio River and strike it on the ground a number of times. The result would be an earthquake they would feel all the way in Georgia and Alabama where my people gathered in council.

"Tecumseh prophesied the very day of the earthquake that would shake us up. Our chiefs looked at each other in a mixture of disbelief and wonder. Could he do such a thing?

"Tecumseh's name—given at birth—translates as 'Shooting Star' or 'He who walks across the sky,' and Tecumseh promised us Creeks that he would connect with a star as well as the earthquake to prove to us the validity of his unifying efforts.

"Stars, you know William, are connected with earthquakes and other happenings here on Earth. Sure enough he arrived back at his homeland on the Ohio River on December 16, 1811. He gathered his people around, took out his medicine stick, and tapped the ground. Just as he stomped on the ground in a power dance, a rumbling shook the Earth.

"And do you know what, my good man? The earthquake was so big it shook up my ancestors back in Georgia and Alabama. It was that big a thing.

"And that's not all. The earthquakes were preceded by the appearance of a great comet, visible around our Mother Earth. It had been going on for a while but during the earthquake it shone especially bright. In fact, that particular comet became known as 'Tecumseh's Comet' since that was his name, and it was linked to the largest earthquakes in American history, at least up until that time."

Bear Heart paused and took a long drink out of his blue cup to let the Shawnee story sink in. I mentioned earlier that I fact-checked Bear Heart, mostly behind his back in hopes of catching him in an exaggeration. This habit was a funny little protection of my world view that I didn't seem to break easily. Bear Heart's story seemed so preposterous that I couldn't wait to prove him wrong. I knew little or nothing about such an earthquake.

Well, it turns out there were a series of earthquakes, known as the New Madrid Earthquakes, the biggest earthquakes in American history. The epicenter was in the Mississippi valleys, but were felt as far away as New York City, Boston, Montreal, and Washington D.C.

President James Madison and his wife, Dolly, felt the floor rumble in the White House. Church bells rang in Boston. In the weeks that followed the December 16th date, there were over 2,000 earthquakes in the central Midwest and over 6,000 earthquakes in Missouri where New Madrid is located.

Get this: the earthquakes had an epicenter near the junction of the Ohio and Mississippi Rivers just as Bear Heart had indicated. To confirm my research notes from thirty-five years ago, I visited the New Madrid Earthquake website and found this description:

"In the known history of the world, no other earthquakes have lasted so long. Three of the earthquakes are on the list of America's top earthquakes: the first one on December 16, 1811, a magnitude of 8.1 on the Richter scale; the second on January 23, 1812, at 7.8; and the third on February 7, 1812, at 8.8 magnitude.

"After the February 7 earthquake, boatmen reported that the Mississippi actually ran backwards for several hours. The force of the land upheaval 15 miles south of New Madrid created Reelfoot Lake, drowned the inhabitants of an Indian village; turned the river against itself to flow backwards; devastated thousands of acres of virgin forest, and created two temporary waterfalls in the Mississippi."[1]

If anything, Bear Heart had understated his story about Tecumseh's stomping dance; his earthquake narrative challenged my questioning mind and, at the same time, opened my heart. After the Tecumseh digression—which he loved to do—Bear Heart returned to Tookebudche and the power of dance to heal.

"We stomp on the ground throughout the dance, *o-pan-ka-ha-co*, to honor Tookebudche, and, when I was a boy who lost his father, I danced until all of the anger, sadness, and fear drained out of my feet into Mother Earth.

"At the beginning of the dance, men and women line up facing each other to chant the *iyabi*, an entreaty to *Ibofunga*, Great Spirit. Then, we form a circle holding hands to link all our joys and woes within the tribal circle. By then, we are dancing counter sun wise, the circular movement that brings forth the feminine as we form an unbroken leather band that holds us altogether.[2]

"The four elements of earth, air, fire and water move with us throughout the dance. If you dance with us, Will, we will sprinkle water on you, and not because you grew up a Methodist. It keeps the dust down but also brings together earth and water.

"Through the night, we dance so hard that we gasp for air and oxygen to acknowledge the sacred presence of our Creator, *Hesagedamesse*, as a Unifying Energy, *Ibofanga*.

"The place where the dance is performed is sometimes called *the stomp ground* because it is a sacred spot where the land and all creatures have called us forth. Just after the elders found the holy person, *Tookebudche*, he showed them forty-four different sacred areas in Northeast Oklahoma where we could dance and feel the energy of the place calling us back into what you might call resonance.

"There are about twelve of these grounds that remain holy while the others have lost their power because of plowed fields, cities, and the like. You know such places can lose their wild hearts, just like us humans."

Bear Heart paused and sat in silence for a long time, finally speaking, "Someday the ancestors may appear to you, Will, and show you a new dance that is the offspring of *o-pan-ka-ha-co*. But remember, my good man, these visions come only to those who keep the faith and who refuse to be captured by the dark forces.

"You go through an initiation into a particular dancing ground. Initiations are central to our way. A medicine man scratches you with a thorn on the calf of your leg or on your bicep four times, and, interestingly, the scratches never in my experience became infected. The scratches indicate the four hills of your life. The first hill represents your childhood. The second, your early married life. The third, when you have children. The fourth is most important, when you have grandchildren.

"At each dance or stomp ground there are four dances a year. The first occurs when Mother Earth puts on her green grass and new leaves. For our people, that is the New Year, and this first dance allows us to give thanks for the birth of another year. We take the ashes from the fires of the last dance of the old year and scatter them around the dance circle to link the past with the present and leading us to the future.

"The second dance we have is for people who have been in war and return. It is a dance of a Great Return. These soldiers have been places where blood has been shed—World War I, World War II, and Viet Nam. The blood that has been spilled through their fellow warriors, and enemies as well, shows up in both their dreams, their health, and their families. You call this trauma. We know that the way through such terrible experiences is in our ceremonial dances.

"We fix medicine for the returning warriors who avail themselves. Many of our returning Indians have been captured by your ideas and ways and find themselves in VA hospitals. It doesn't seem to help much. You have to use big medicine. By medicine I mean various plants that lift them out of the clutches of these experiences.

"You see, you can't just get over these kinds of things by talking or doing your therapy, though that helps. No, you need elders who can lead you through the dances of war to cleanse and let go of all enemies.

"Then, a wise elder says something like this, 'You didn't die in that war because you have something to do for the people to help them in some way. There was a reason behind the fact that you weren't killed. You were meant to live for a certain purpose. We come here to dance in order for you to let go and allow the Spirits to show your new purpose. Mother Earth needs you for making peace.'

"'These are the words, but they are merged into the dance. Together, the words and the movement do the healing by allowing tight parts of the humans to shake loose. Then Spirit can flow through.'"

Questions arose in the midst of the dance story about combat vets. Do we create wars because we have no nature-based initiatory rites for our youth? At some unconscious level do our political leaders keep creating wars because we have so few instances of brotherhood and sisterhood?

Are we addicted to professional athletics because we enter into the strenuous fray vicariously in a desperate attempt at connecting with our wilder selves? Are our youth attracted to terrorist organizations because we offer them few, if any, pathways to meaning that challenges them into a larger identity? These swirling questions send me back to Bear Heart's dance narrative.

"The third dance renews the arbors on the dance ground. The arbors in our area are made of willow branches, one facing east, one facing west, one facing south and one facing north. Our greatest dance is the fourth one, called *the Corn Dance, Vce-O-pan-ka-ha-co.*

"We separate the men from the women during this part of the dance, so they can minister to themselves. They fill their buckets from what we have sprinkled around. I know you told me the other day that you work with folks that upchuck, bulimia you called it. They do it to relieve fear.

"We have ceremonies to help with that, and it is very different when you go through upchucking in a ceremony with a wise person assisting you. Your young people are throwing up because they know at a deep level that they are being poisoned. Just as the European immigrants poisoned us and our streams with pigs and diseases, so you are now poisoning your own youth.

"Next a medicine man, *Hilis-ha-yah*, goes out on the north side and a spokesman tells all the visiting campers, 'We have now come to the quiet time. Please control yourselves and your children. No loud laughing or talking. Now is a very special time to allow communication with the Great Creator.'

"Two men are the dance masters. One selects the first dance leader, and the dance commences. During the dance the two men go around and see that no unnecessary talking happens. They kinda focus our attention to honor the dancers. The dance songs are antiphonal. The leader sings, and the larger tribe answers back and forth.

"'Ho! Ho!,' and then the answer, 'Hey! Hey!' When the chant and dance comes to an end, everybody hollers four times just as Tookebudche had hollered four times in the original vision.

"Meanwhile, the women are beautiful. They adorn themselves with turtle shells with tiny rocks inside. They tie them above their ankles and move their feet to keep a line. My sister still has a set of those turtle shells.

"We practiced all kinds of ceremonial movement to help us work through our problems and find our true relationship with sacred creation. One of my favorites was the *Drunk Duck Dance*.

"See, we recognized that we had all kinds of problems with alcohol since our bodies couldn't assimilate the drink very well. I struggled a bit myself. We knew that we had to dance our unpleasant experiences into the open. We had to bring the negatives to the surface or they would do us in. We didn't over-emphasize these toxic experiences, but we didn't ignore them either.

"We also knew it was good for couples to dance. By dancing together in ceremony we could see visibly what was wrong in the way they treat each other. And by dancing together, eventually they discover the love of their youth.

"If you had couples in marriage therapy dance close to the earth, it would help them. It might put you out of a job. First, the man and the woman hold hands. Then, three couples up front raise their arms into arches, and those behind wobble like ducks as they promenade through the arches, laughing and learning all the while.

"Well, there you have some stories about dancing. To such dances my elders took me when I was lost in my sorrow over the loss of my father. I danced and danced. I cried and cried. Then, I danced through the protective shooting as my father neared his journey to the other side.

"I danced until I overcame the powers of the witches. I danced through my thinking I might have shot the wrong person. I danced over a long period of time, several dances, until my inner world calmed down. I danced until I reached beyond."

"From our area in Oklahoma, Buffalo Bill Cody invited Ponca, Pawnee, Creek, and Otoe Indians to dance as part of the show, and he gave us a way to express ourselves in this European-American Civilization that was being forced on us.

"He is a bridge walker from our old world to the modern day, and, maybe the likes of you will build a bridge to a new time that can hold the best of both. Seems like we will need it the way our prophecies indicate Mother Earth is headed.

"Well, us Indians don't generally perform ceremonial dances for entertainment, so we created something called *fancy dancing*. My healing as a young man led me into another form of dancing that I want to tell you about now. Fancy dancing has become central at our Pow Wows, though they are not deeply spiritual, they are nevertheless important. They are half spiritual and half athletic.

"In 1938, at the Indian Exposition in Anadarko, Oklahoma, I entered the Fancying Dancing World Championship Contest. My name was not Bear Heart then. I hadn't been on that vision quest yet. My Indian friends called me *Buckskin*. It is good to have many names so you don't get stuck thinking about yourself in one way. Fancy dancing takes a lot of stamina and intense training.

"You have your full costume on, and the powers-that-be judge you on your body movements—especially your head and how smoothly you turn around as you move back and forth. I ended my dance on the very last beat of the drum with both feet on the ground, and then I leapt high in the air and landed on the ground with the splits.

"Quite a sight to see.

"We had a pipe dance, a chicken fluttering dance, and a feather-picking contest dance. In the feather-picking dance, the officials dug a hole and put a feather in it with just the little end sticking out. Then, I would dance and, without skipping a beat, I'd try to pick up the feather with my mouth.

"Much of this dancing was in Osage County, Oklahoma. At that time the Osage tribe had quite a bit of money because they were smart enough to pool all of their resources together. One Osage elder called out to me, 'Come over here.'

"He had dug a hole and instead of a feather, he had stuck a twenty dollar bill in the hole. 'Pick it up, and it is yours.'

"Boy howdy, was I going to pick up that twenty-dollar bill even if I had to use my hands. But I was able to perform the dance and pick it up with my front teeth.

"Now, there was much teaching in this particular dance. At first glance, it is just a young man seeking to get some money.

"But, if you look closer, you will see that Andrew Jackson's image is on the twenty-dollar bill. That was the man who committed genocide against my people. In effect, he killed my great grandmother. Yet, here I was dancing to get the twenty dollar bill with his image in my mouth. Later in life it caused me to think deeply about making money.

"Money can leave a bad taste in your mouth if you don't watch it.

"Anyway, the officials took the best fancy dancer from all of the pow wows, and I was one of them. All that season we danced time-and-again. I won the World Fancy Dancing Championship, and the prize was a trip to Madison Square Garden where I performed as the feature dancer for the whole shindig.

"During my performance there was another dancer, a Russian ballerina, who attended our fancy dancing for her own entertainment. Her name was Lisa Parnola. She had never seen an America Indian dancer and was impressed with what she saw.

"Afterwards, she came to me and told me how much we had in common and asked me to dance for her. I showed her some of my steps.

We kinda had a shine for each other, and she invited me to come back to Russia to perform with the famous Russian ballets.

"I told her I couldn't because I was still in school and needed an education if I was to get along in the white man's world. Besides that, Russia was still under communist rule at the time. I didn't want to get into the big contest going on between these world powers. I am glad I didn't go down that road. Staying near my tribe opened the door for me to study with the elders.

"But I will tell you this. Lisa Parnola invited me to come to her ballet performance in New York City the next night and gave me tickets. At the end of her performance the crowd clapped and clapped, so she came out for an encore. You know what? For her encore she performed my Indian steps I had showed her, and, boy was I proud about that.

"I guess you could say all of this dancing carried me through the dark clouds of my youth to the most important ceremonies of my life: vision questing."

6

BEAR MOUNTAIN: VISION QUEST

"Are you at a point in our walk so you can hear about vision quests?" Bear Heart asked a simple question that had an ominous feel to it. There was a *you-will-never-be-the-same* if you go much farther with me quality about the question.

To prepare for this exploration, he told me briefly about his first three vision quests, ones that were linked to moving through his father's death, all before his twentieth year. But there was another wound I have not mentioned that figured into his thirst for larger vision.

Just before his father, Nathan, died, he had a life-changing accident. He was fixing his mom's iron bed frame with a hammer, and an iron fleck flew into his left eye and put it out.

Eventually, he received an excellent eye prosthesis so that many people did not notice; nevertheless, he struggled as he moved into manhood with the limitation of one good eye. Did the loss of a physical eye open the door for larger spiritual vision? Was I slow to recognize his prosthesis because he displayed such a wide angle of spiritual vision?

During another learning expedition on the flanks of the Sangre de Cristo Mountains, he asked me about any quests I had been on. Reluctantly, I told him about my Rattlesnake Island quest, the one with tornadoes, Oreo cookies, and no elders. Throughout that telling, he laughed and laughed, sometimes clicking his teeth, almost grinding them. I wondered if he had false teeth to go along with one eye.

Then, with compassion for the stuttering of my boyhood quests, he indicated that we often need several warm-up quests before our deeper identity begins to clarify in a later crying for a vision.

Our conversation was relaxed as we walked through the woods until we came to a log where we sat down to munch a bit on trail mix and then turn ironically to the subject of vision fasting.

"We Indians have gone on vision quests for thousands of years, much longer than your anthropologists propose. I read the other day that evidence of quests over ten thousand years ago has been discovered on one of our sites near the Black Hills.

"It is in our blood. Originally, the questing was done for the safety of our tribes. Young warriors or tribal leaders went out for several days without food or water to commune with the Great Presence. They were seeking strength and guidance in a world where challenges with other tribes for hunting grounds was common.

"Some tribes relied entirely on deer, turkey, fish, and buffalo for protein, so having access to land where these critters were plentiful was crucial. Hence, tensions between tribes arose with some frequency.

"Aho, don't get it in your mind that indigenous people were perfect. There is struggle even when you are part of the sacred web because people are people, and we make serious mistakes. But the struggle increases tenfold when you live with the mirage that you are special and apart from the trees, waters, and wind.

"The Creeks came from a tradition that included raising corn and other crops, so it was different for us. We weren't so dependent on hunting and fishing as others, so we didn't have to compete for hunting grounds as much as some.

"But we had our red stick warriors as well, ready to go to war. We found ourselves in bad, even evil places at times: out of sorts, out of step, out of balance. Our quests focused on seeking a return to harmony with our surroundings. Our crops, our hunting, and our life depended on how closely we were attuned to all of the spirits of the land. We knew spirits dwelled even in blades of grass or what you call weeds.

"These quests were completely practical and necessary for us to learn how to converse with all the creatures, both predators and prey. Our visions told us where to hunt, where and when to plant, and how to be friends with every aspect of the sacred web.

"We found that we had to enter a certain state of mind in order to gain the transmissions necessary between the seen and unseen. We couldn't just tune in through our everyday modes of thinking and feeling. We needed to go out from where we lived day-to-day and open ourselves to the beyond. That's not easy.

"Today, vision quests are a bit different in that we go out to find direction in our lives in a very different set of circumstances. Such quests last from a few hours to four days.

"You know, *wascina* have to start out slowly and be patient. They can't quest the way practiced Indians can. If you fool around with the powers of the wild, you might fall and break a leg or worse. I say *practicing* Indians because our people have by and large drifted away from the ancient ways.

"Some folks romanticize the ways of indigenous peoples as if we all still practice deep spiritual ways. Not so. Like the dreaded smallpox, the *wascina* virus of consuming has infected us as well. There are very few practitioners. The ways of ancient wisdom are preserved by those who practice.

"You go to reservations, and you will see there are a limited number of folks actually connected to the *Red Path*. So, I am teaching these ways in the hope that you and others will actually continue to practice the spiritual wisdom. It doesn't matter what your DNA lineage.

"What matters is your persistent honoring of these ways through doing them. Blood is important, but much more so is your practice, which is your lineage.

"Anyway, back to the actual experience of questing. The length of time that you go out is not the focus. Several questers go out at the same time, each to a different solitary spot. I teach people to find a personal power symbol like an animal or plant. After the questers come in, they consult with an elder to be given a name, one that fits their inner spirits with Creator's purpose.

"People ask me why we fast from food and water. Let me insert here that white folks (*wascina*) usually need water, though sometimes it helps if you do without. You have to be really experienced before you can fast from food and water. You can get in trouble if you don't have proper guidance.

"You might even run into a tornado on a lake somewhere if you eat cookies the way you did. Well, the purpose of fasting is to empty yourself so you can receive something from above, something to motivate you, to inspire you, and to guide you in a way that you are meant to go.

"As you know, folks run around all over the place and don't really know who they are or where they are going. As we say in our tribe, folks in America run around like chickens with their heads cut off.

"While I am a traditionally trained medicine man in the Muskogee Creek tradition, I have gathered the traditions and practices from many of my fellow medicine men to forge a way of questing that works for me and those who go out with me—even beginners.

"My defining quest came when I traveled to Bear Butte, South Dakota. By that time I was in my mid-20s and had already quested three times. Yet, something stirred within, telling me to go again to gain greater insight, and this time not in Oklahoma. I knew that Black Elk himself was still alive and living in the area, so that was an attractor.

"Anthropologists speak of our quests as if questing is a rite of passage only for young adults. Not so. We go on quests at many different junctures in life. Crazy Horse went on thirteen vision quests, and only toward the end did he receive the name, *Tasunke Witko*.

"His name illustrates how mainstream professors are far off the mark. They often translate his name literally as *His-horse-is-crazy*. That is a little closer to the bone of things than just Crazy Horse. But it is still a gross distortion. The name more accurately is translated *Prancing Horse*, or *Spiriting Horse*.

"See what I mean? Your academics continue to find ways to disrespect my people. If you think of a man as being crazy, then you don't have compunction about killing him.

"Prancing Horse's spiritual power was such that he could ride into battle with nothing but a breechcloth to cover himself. He came so close to government soldiers that they could smell the smoke in his hair and feel his breath. Sometimes, he would just prick them with a knife instead of killing. Such brazen courage and behavior meant he was crazy, or so thought the *wascina*.

"It is little known that Prancing Horse—as I prefer to call him—made an adjustment to the white culture. He was even promoted to sergeant in the U.S. Army, but many white soldiers, including officers, remained convinced that he was just another crazy red devil. They trumped up charges, false charges, and led him away to jail. But that wasn't enough; the soldiers stabbed him in the back with a bayonet even as they were taking him to jail.

"Anyhow, enough of that. I wanted to go to the holy place of some of my Lakota and Cheyenne brothers and sisters as a part of my reaching out to various tribal traditions. By this time, I had teachers from a number of different tribes, and one of them, a Cheyenne, offered to put me out on the mountain to quest.

"Let me tell you a bit about Bear Butte. It has been a sacred site for many tribes for thousands of years. Your scholars say over 10,000 years, but, really, much longer than that. Technically, Bear Butte is not a butte at all, but rather a small mountain near the Black Hills.

"My Lakota fellows call it *Mato Paha* or *Bear Mountain*. My Cheyenne friends call it *Noaha-vose, Giving Hill*. When I arrived for the quest, I saw why they call it that way because from a distance it resembles a sleeping bear.

"I approached the sacred ground with deep reverence because I knew Red Cloud, Prancing Horse, and Sitting Bull had all quested there."

As Bear Heart talked, I wondered about the place described. Bear Butte itself is small compared to the neighboring Rocky Mountains, themselves available to the various tribes. The Native people could quest nearly anywhere, and I asked myself, "Why choose this one mountain as being the Mt. Kailash of North America?"

I was curious about the same thing in regard to the Comanches I grew up with on the Llano Estacado. At the height of their influence, the various Comanche bands held sway over all of the land from Santa Fe, New Mexico, through Texas and Mexico all the way to Guatemala.

They could have chosen nearly any one of spectacular mountains in Meso-America like Pico de Orizaba at 18,491', Popocatepetl at 17,802', or Istaccihuatl at 17,159'. Yet, they chose an inverted set of mountains, red rock canyons, highlighted by the sparsely visited Palo Duro Canyon not far from my family land.

The answer to such unusual choices for questing lies within the network of spirits dwelling in such sacred places. They call to people because they offer an opening into the vast unknown; the land itself becomes a bridge for walking into mystery. The intimacy of a specific web of eco-fields yields visions, not the height of the mountain or the depth of the canyon.

I have used the term, *eco-fields*, several times thus far in this narrative. It is time to delve into its meaning so we can understand better how vision quests work.

After Bear Heart's passing, I returned to graduate school to study the relationship between quantum fields and ancient wisdom, a fertile confluence. In that extensive research, I discovered a branch of quantum fields called eco-fields.

I have written extensively about that research in another book, *The Mother Tongue: Intimacy in the Eco-fields*. It is enough here to remark that this newer science is making clear that there are matrixes of eco-fields that are alive and talking to each other all of the time.

They exchange information and meaning in a technical way, 24–7. In retrospect, I am clear that Bear Heart and other wisdom holders knew of such exchanges in their personal experience and through tribal traditions. Through the passing of generations, people were attracted to these webs of eco-fields at a profound level of information and meaning exchange.

Communities of eco-fields vary greatly in terms of possibility and impartation of wisdom. What we might assess as a vacation site in our usual culture is not necessarily a vortex of visions, or, as quantum physicists describe, a window of nonlocality.

Places of power reveal themselves only to those who have ears to hear and eyes to see.

Now, back to Bear Heart's vision quest.

"When you go to Bear Butte, you will see that almost every tree and bush are draped with colored pieces of cloth strung together in what we call prayer ties. As I made my way up the mountain, I passed many offerings made by my brothers and sisters through the years. I put out my flags and my own prayer ties, 405 of them. I tied that number of prayer ties because I had been guided by my Cheyenne elder to know that there are 405 spirits within Bear Butte that connect with the questers to give visions.

"When I put you out on a mountain, I will have you tie that same number. I continue with this practice in an honoring of Bear Butte. Where you vision quest will have different spirits and numbers of spirits to guide you. But always tie 405 ties as a way to connect with the grandmother mountain.

"That's one way we can honor and connect with Prancing Horse, Sitting Bull, and Black Elk. With your ties, you make a vision circle that includes them.

"After a time of fasting on Bear Butte, it appeared that I would not have a vision. Then, I heard a rustling in the trees, and I could tell that the weight of the steps of the creature was much bigger than a deer. It was ominous and raised the hair on my neck. Out of the woods, a bear came to my vision circle. I am not talking about a visionary bear, though that would have been something in and of itself.

"I am talking about a bear that is a real thing in the world of five senses. Yes. I could see him, even with one eye. I could smell him. I hoped he wouldn't taste me, even though I would have tasted better then, than now—I am old and stringy these days.

"Well, a very large black bear ambled over to my circle and stood up on its hind legs, a position of possible attack. He must have weighed 350 pounds and stood at least seven or eight feet in his upright stance.

"At first, I felt afraid, but then I gathered myself. I stood up and faced him. He moved closer and knocked me down, gently for a bear that size. I got up. He knocked me down again with a mighty paw, and again I rose and faced him, looking him in the eye. I braced for him to knock me down a third time.

"Then, I sensed that he wanted to talk to me. Maybe he knocked me down to get my attention. I felt that English just wouldn't do. Maybe, because I was more comfortable and natural in my own language, I talked to him in Creek.

"*Puca Nokose!*

"*Grandfather Bear!*

"I addressed him respectfully as my elder and teacher. I told him that my father was of the Bear Clan and that I wasn't going to fight him. But I wasn't going to run either. He turned his head and listened to me. Long moments passed when a silent language in a long ago tongue passed between us. Slowly, he turned and walked away.

"I sat down in my circle, shaken but not shaky. It seemed to me that my life turned in that encounter with Grandfather Bear. I didn't know fully what the message was. That's the way with questing. We know little, but there is still a little light.

"Time passed. I gathered my ties and returned to the Cheyenne elder who had put me out on the mountain. It is important to have an elder who guides you. You found that out when you got caught in that tornado and had no one to assist you in the language of Spirit. That's why you wandered away from the path into the desert of intellectual abstractions and other gobbledegook for so long.

"My Cheyenne teacher told me, 'You have the heart of a bear that respects strength, and you are not afraid to stand up to him. You will be called Bear Heart.'

"And I took this name openly as my own. Some people still call me *Mark*. Some family members call me 'Chief.' But mostly I like to be called by my spirit name. It's natural for members of the Bear Clan to have names related to the bear. There are names like Bear Paw or Bear Foot, but, as far as I know, I'm the only one in my tribe that has the name, *Bear Heart*."

"If you are named after a bird or animal, it's good to know something about your namesake. For example, I learned that the Bear is aware and psychic. He knows and distinguishes various things in the forest. He has somewhat poor eyesight in that they don't discern the yellow-red-orange color spectrum as well as humans.

"But otherwise, they see well enough. They have exceptional hearing. Their sense of smell is unparalleled in the animal world, much greater than the best of bird dogs. They are great tree climbers. Although the bear is big and strong, they can run through the forest at 40 mph and never break a twig.

"One thing I know from my experience in the vision circle: the bear is not only big and strong but also gentle. The bear helps me that way, I hope.

"When a bear goes into the water and then comes out and shakes, all the individual sparkles of water reflect the sunlight. When he shakes his head, the bear is sharing his powerful mental processes with all living things, including us humans if we know the language.

"The bear teaches us about taking care of ourselves before we get sick. Every winter the bear goes into his den and hibernates. While in hibernation, his heart rate can drop from 40–50 beats per minute down to 8 beats per minutes.

"Unlike other hibernators, my grandfather bear doesn't have to wait to bring up body temperatures. Grandfather can awaken and arouse quickly. They teach us resilience and readiness. This hibernation is a healing period that allows Grandfather to function better when he comes out.

"He shows us that there is time for everyone to rest and not overdo it. As you know, most in our cities don't follow that wisdom. The bear is protective. He moves in and out, though the mind, body, and soul, to see that everything is on the up-and-up. His presence can be reassuring and fill us with confidence that we are on the right track. These are a few of my learnings from Grandfather Bear.

"Before long, it will be time for you to go on another vision quest."

Though the bear is not my totem, he will always be my grandfather because of this story and many visitations. When Bear Heart comes to me in the night, in many ways the encounter feels more like the archetypal bear spirit reaching out to impart its wisdom.

As I was writing this book, Bear Heart appeared to me in the form of a beautiful woman who was visiting our sweat lodge for the first time. How, you might ask, would I recognize him in such a different form of a living and breathing woman who was brand new to our community?

She came up after the sweat and surprised me with mysterious words, "I have a gift for you from the Bear. Ever since I arrived today, I have had an overwhelming urge to give you one of my most prized possessions."

She then lifted a leather cord from around her neck, and out from under her blouse came a bear claw with the hair still on the top. The leather cord wrapped itself around the claw in a circle with a brilliant but small piece of turquoise sewn into the leather as if the claw had a one blue eye. That's how I knew Bear Heart was present—the claw had one eye.

She continued speaking in a soft voice, "I have had this claw for some time, but I knew it didn't really belong to me. This morning when I woke up from a dream, Grandfather Bear told me to wear it though I don't often. It bothers me. It is too powerful.

"I asked Grandfather why I was to wear it but got no answer until I saw you and heard your chant. Then, I knew our relative the Bear had sent this so you can walk tall."

At first I was going to refuse the gift, but when she placed it around my neck, I could feel the bear's presence. "Don't get puffed up with the gift because she is so pretty," Bear Heart laughed, "Judith will have something to say about that."

The gift-giver stepped back and placed her hand over her heart. Moved, I thanked her as best I could, and I never saw her again.

When I want to stand and walk tall, I wear the claw of my relative the bear.

Even when Bear Heart walked with me on Earth's plane, there were times when he spoke with a voice that sounded more like the bear on his vision mountain than like the regular guy he was much of the time. The bear voice was the utterance he used through the woman visitor that day.

His memories mingle with his spirit voices from the stars in such a way that I scarce can separate them as we shall see as the story continues.

7   MEETING AN ELDER UNDER A TREE

Last night ancestral Bear Heart shocked me awake with an unusual garb. His hair was long and down his back, longer than when I knew him in a usual, historical manner. Around his head, he donned a red bandana with stars emblazoned across the front, like a crown of stars. He had a necklace made of bone hanging around his neck. There was a design, but I couldn't tell what it was.

He wore a vest with cave art symbols sewn down the front, similar to one Reginah said he sported most of the time in his later years. She said he would walk around in his underwear displaying his prized vest, which presents quite a visual.

That vest was gifted to me after he made the great journey to the ancestors. In his appearance last night, he wore a similar vest with two colored stripes down each side of the front with symbolic marks, perhaps a forgotten language, spaced evenly from top to bottom.

As I write, I pause and walk into my bedroom closet and fetch the vest; I put it on to support my nighttime experience with him. "Maybe," I tell myself, "Wearing the vest as it exists in current space and time will assist me in remembering the encounters last night."

Creatures surround him; ears, birds, and hummingbirds. He stands ankle deep in a stream as he speaks with a playful voice:

"Tell them about our first meeting at Ghost Ranch. They know about my Bear Heart vision as a young man. They even know a little about you, now. That's enough of our growing up days. Tell them how we got together. Get on with it."

Judith and I were living at 1212 Kipling St. in Houston early in our marriage. Our psychotherapy careers and practices were going well, but my clients were asking disturbing questions. They wanted to know what direction they could take after their psychological crisis abated. They aspired to meaning and purpose beyond problem solving. They wanted community, something beyond group therapy.

I did too, but I couldn't guide them where I had not been.

One Sunday morning I talked with Judith about transcending the confines of a usual therapy practice, and went on to moan about my persistent thirst for something more. I didn't know what.

After leaving my work as a pastoral minister, my spiritual practices waned since they lost meaning. The rituals of organized religion lacked earthy connection, but I had found little with which to replace them. I took courses in Buddhist vipassana meditation. I went to workshops with people like Swami Muktananda and Huston Smith. I sat mesmerized with Ram Das. I studied with Rollo May and Fritz Perls.

Still, I felt disconnected. I sensed intuitively that my experience of estrangement was a virus of current civilization, but I had no notions about a cure.

My Eastern religion meditation teachers assisted me in a practice that allowed me to disconnect from the vagaries of my ordinary mind. But such spiritual practice often disconnected me from the juice of life.

Many of these approaches saw connectivity as a distraction from enlightenment and just fed my split from natural life. They seemed too much akin to the abstractions of Western Civilization and the war with the flesh in the Abrahamic religions.

I was tired to the bone with this war that split me off from the flow of the river.

Then, in a flash, I recalled moments with *Nahuatl* speakers in childhood, the aroma of juniper after rain, and my hikes to a waterfall where I first encountered an ancestor spirit. An intense longing to return to such primordial connection and a sense of relatedness with sensual creation grabbed me.

"I need to find a Native American mentor who can reconnect me with the heart of Nature," I blurted out to Judith.

I continued, "I have been looking all over hell and half of Georgia in the Eastern traditions and in psychotherapy, and the direction I seek may be right under my nose."

Judith smiled with my use of the phrase *hell and half of Georgia*, one my mother, Juanita, used when I was a boy given to roaming about lost in the neighborhood.

I had no tribe and few nature connections beyond pollution-choked trees in urban parks, zoos, and public golf courses. Professional organizations were dry as a bone, competitive, and hierarchical. I had been a patient in group therapy and a student in supervision groups for psychotherapists; both were helpful but of limited coherent and intimate value.

There was little exploration of the deeper moorings that might be called spiritual and, to my dismay, professional meetings were held in smoke-filled conference rooms set in hotels with few windows. My profession of psychotherapy was clearly unhitched from the natural order; humans in the mental health paradigm lived as if nature was a far-off vacation.

Then, from Carl Whitaker, an esteemed mentor, I heard about an organization of psychotherapists called The American Academy of Psychotherapists. It was different, he said, and might assist me. Following Whitaker's lead I researched the organization and discovered it was founded in 1955 by Rollo May, Carl Rogers, Jules Barron, and Albert Ellis.

These innovative scientists and therapists, like me, hungered for gatherings to push their boundaries beyond the mainstream norm into a domain that May called *love* in his monumental book *Love and Will*. Whitaker's descriptions of psychotherapy as both science and art interested me, and so I applied for membership.

After a lengthy application process, I was accepted to what I hoped could be my tribe. Soon, I attended my first AAP Summer Workshop; it was held in a remote retreat center in Monteagle, Tennessee, an auspicious place set in a mountain forest.

Rosa Parks had attended a civil rights retreat there in 1961 just before the Montgomery Bus Boycott, and Johnny Cash was inspired by the forest setting to write and sing a popular song called *Monteagle Mountain*.

In this new tribe, I met people I considered to be the most innovative psychotherapists and scientists in the field. A strong communal value encouraged participants to conduct creative workshops for each other that pushed the edges of our clinical practices.

What we taught each other was not ready for prime time with our patients since our inclinations and imaginations wandered into areas too vulnerable for public practice. We became our own laboratories for experiments.

Two gestalt psychologists—Joan Fagan and Irma Lee Shepherd— impacted me immediately with a process called *environmental theatre*. These two women embodied the Divine Feminine and inspired me with their offerings at our various summer conferences.

These new forms of therapy were conducted outside usual office space, deep in the heart of Nature where human control was lessened.

With these experiences nudging me, I walked across the bridge from merely human intimacy to a larger intimacy of humans within the mosaic of a specific eco-field.

But still I hungered for grounding with an ancient wisdom to match Fagan's and Shepard's science.

Through these creative explorers, I connected with a number of different Native American elders as potential guides in the direction for which I intuitively yearned. Yet, the right fit did not come easily. Several possible Native American wisdom keepers appeared, but the energy between us just didn't resonate.

In the early 1980s, members of AAP who lived in Santa Fe, New Mexico, hosted a summer conference to be held at Ghost Ranch, a retreat facility near the legendary village of Abiquiu. The theme of this workshop was *Bringing Out the Shadows*, an exploration of the unknown within and without.

I knew about Ghost Ranch from Ansel Adams who exulted, "...the skies and land of Ghost Ranch are so enormous and the detail so precise and exquisite that wherever you are you are isolated in a glowing world between the macro and the micro."[1]

His words whetted my appetite to attend.

But more significant, by attending, I now had the opportunity to follow Georgia O'Keeffe to Ghost Ranch where she lived. Her life trajectory of artistic brilliance had begun in the Palo Duro Canyons where I grew up.

Not long after she arrived at Palo Duro Canyon in 1916, a short distance from West Texas State College where she taught, she wrote a friend. "Last night I couldn't sleep till after 4:00 in the morning—I had been out to the canyon all afternoon—till late at night—wonderful color—I wish I could tell you how big—and with the night the colors grow deeper and darker ...I'm so glad I'm out here—I can't tell you how much I like it."[2]

When I first experienced her paintings as a boy, I knew she had connected with the emotions, drama, and slashing reds and purples of Palo Duro. The spirits and living energy forms of the canyons coursed through her artistic creations, or, it might be said, these living systems of eco-fields actually were expressing themselves through her.

She painted what I experienced, and, although she didn't know it, she became my model of feminine inspiration. Truth be told I had a crush on her. These beloved canyons in Northwest Texas formed an intimate and primordial base that held us both in an indescribable intimacy. It was a triangle, a sacred pyramid, but she, of course, knew nothing about my point on the pyramid.[3]

When I heard that AAP was going to Ghost Ranch in New Mexico where O'Keeffe lived, I knew I had to go even though it meant leaving my clinical practice at a crucial time. I wasn't so much interested in the workshops being offered as I was in this mysterious landscape I had seen in her paintings that were cousins to my beloved Palo Duro.

In a fashion, I could not name, the opportunity seemed connected to an opening, a balm to heal my deepest longing to return to the natural order of things. The iron box of my tangled emotions had been opened in therapy, but what I now needed was a retrieval of my soul, which had been misplaced along the way.

When I arrived at Ghost Ranch, my bed was in a bunkhouse with exposed concrete floors and a short walk to communal showers and bathroom facilities. The beds had mattresses that lay loosely on a web of wire that substituted for box springs.

It had a church camp feel to it, mainly because the Presbyterians had bought the ranch from the Pack family in 1955, over O'Keeffe's stern objections. She said she didn't like the Presbyterians very much as neighbors; they were too stiff. Maybe, I mused to myself, a delicate unease was *predestined* as might be advocated by the theologian, John Knox.

I walked over to her house, hoping for a chance to see or even visit with her. Perhaps, she would be the guide for whom I searched since she was a mongrel like me.

At last, this would be the one who could assist me in reconnecting with Mother Earth. In my fanciful mind, her being my guide was a done deal because I knew the world needed to open to the Divine Feminine, and what better woman to offer that initiation?

But, alas, she was not home, nor would she return while I was there. The ranch hosts told me that she spent much time in Santa Fe where she would die six years later at the age of ninety-eight. During that six years, Judith and I dropped by her house from time-to-time hoping for a conversation and peering through the cracks in her front gate, but a connection never happened with this extremely private genius.

I kept coming up empty in my search for a fellow soul-traveler.

Participants in the summer AAP workshop at Ghost Ranch arrived in the mountains of New Mexico on a Sunday in July. At an elevation of 6,378', it offered a welcome retreat from Houston heat.

It was the custom at such events to invite local people to entertain us. For example, at one of the workshops in Appalachia, we had clog dancers and, in Bar Harbor, Maine, a lobster fisherman.

A senior psychologist, Darrell Dawson, was the host of the AAP Summer Workshop that year, and he had arranged for Bear Heart to come talk to us about Native American healing. Such an arrangement was not central to the agenda, but rather a potentially interesting option for those who might be attracted, but not to be taken too seriously.

Bear Heart was scheduled to come on Wednesday after two days of the participants' steeping themselves in an exploration of shadow psychology. Following Jung's directives, we had plunged into domains of personal, cultural, and, little did we know, Nature's shadows. We were in for a major surprise with what Jung called a golden shadow, the far reaches of Nature's potential through humans.

I woke up on Wednesday morning before dawn and took a walk past the front gate where there was a simple sign that said *Ghost Ranch: Visitors Welcome*. A cow skull with horns on the sign and an iron sculpture of the same cow skull on the gate caught my attention.

Walking along I saw a woman dressed in black; I wasn't certain she was from this world. On a barbed wire fence, hung the remains of a snake, maybe a diamondback rattler. Off in the distance there was a geological formation called Kitchen Mesa because it looked like a place you might cook, and it reminded me that I was hungry.

I was seeking connection with the spirits of the land and sublime enlightenment, but the smell of bacon and hash browns took precedence.

At breakfast, I was laughing and enjoying both the food and my friends when a host of the workshop came scurrying up to the table, a worried look on his face.

"William, you know this guy Bear Heart, don't you?"

The tone of Darrell's voice alerted me to something being out of joint. "Yes, I do. I have met him, as I recall, a couple of years ago."

Actually, I couldn't remember too much about Bear Heart, or even if Darrell was referring to the same person I had met since my search had put me in the company of many indigenous wise persons. If I had met him, Bear Heart hadn't made much of an impression on me.

"Well," Darrell continued looking at his watch, "It's 7:30 a.m., and he is already here. We have him scheduled to speak to us in the cafeteria as we eat our noontime meal. He's just sitting out there under a tree. I asked him to come in and have breakfast, but he just nods and says nothing. I explained that he wasn't scheduled to speak until our noon meal, but he still just nods. Will you go out and talk to him? Someone said you'd know what to say to get him back on schedule."

My friends at my table looked at me, and I wrinkled my brow. I really didn't know what to do with such shamanic unpredictability given that, like most psychotherapists, I ran my life as a slave to the clinical hour.

I finished my breakfast, put my dishes in the collecting area, and ambled out to the area Darrell mentioned. Sure enough, sitting under a large cottonwood tree was a man, likely Bear Heart, though I still wasn't sure I had met him.

Like Darrell said, Bear Heart sat cross-legged with his back against the tree. He wore a black Stetson with an eagle feather and a hat band with a silver heron, a white shirt, a turquoise necklace, a large silver belt-buckle, neatly-pressed Levis, and older but shiny boots.

He looked to be in his late 60s, but he was a curious mix of youthful vitality and ancient lines in a classic face. I was forty at the time, so someone in their mid-sixties seemed very old. I didn't speak as I sat down, and, for a while, I leaned against the tree myself. Such was not my usual urban behavior, but the scene inducted me into a mild trance of peace and quiet.

After a while, I broke the silence: "They were expecting you at noon today to give a talk."

Quiet, then a reply:

"I am here now."

"Do you plan to speak at lunch?" I asked him knowing already that the workshop schedules weren't high on this man's agenda.

"I believe I will just stay here. If anyone wants to talk to me they can come on over and have a seat beneath this grandmother tree. It is a good spot. I will send out a beam of light, a filament from my belly button to the various folk. It carries an invitation if they are so moved. Those sensitive to light will get the message."

Now, I was faced with a decision. It was a little after 8:00 a.m. by this time, and I knew I was scheduled to lead a demonstration of ecopsychology. It was a planned part of a seminar, and I didn't want to shirk my responsibilities.

On the other hand, something was bubbling inside. Just sitting there looking at the scarlet sky and iridescent colors of the surrounding mesa in the presence of this man seemed like a once-in-a-lifetime privilege and gift.

Before long, my co-leader for the 10:00 a.m. seminar came by and whispered in my ear so as not to disturb Bear Heart. He asked me what on earth I was doing sitting under a tree when we had work to do.

I didn't know how to explain, so I whispered instructions for him to explain to the participants that I would not be at the seminar and to accept my apology. I scribbled a note to tape on the seminar door which he stuffed in his pocket. Then, he directed his attention toward Bear Heart and asked him if he was going to speak at noon.

"I plan to sit here, and I am happy to talk with anyone who wants to come by. I will be here until there aren't any more folks wanting healing. So far, I have this one fella here, Taegel. You are welcome to join us."

The expression on my colleague's face changed. To my surprise, he did want to join us. He hesitated and then opened up and asked for help. Bear Heart directed me to go over to his faded red truck and get a medicine chest that was a converted tool box.

It was painted red. I also fetched a bundle wrapped in a Pendleton blanket from his truck; he called it an eagle bundle. Inside the blanket, there was a beaded pouch that contained a sacred pipe, a focal point of his healing powers.

An aura of light surrounded this unusual man as he held eagle feathers lightly in his hand and fanned across inflamed areas of the body of my colleague. After a few minutes, I looked up to behold eight or ten of fellow psychotherapists in line, waiting their turn even though no instructions or announcements had been given. They had been attracted by the scene of tree, shaman, feather, and my friend lying on the grass.

There was a palpable silence even though AAP gatherings were usually rife with raucous dialogue.

Bear Heart gently helped his first client up from the ground and sent him on his way. Then, he spread the Pendleton blanket on the ground and reached into the medicine box for herbs.

He also had a piece of bear fur on which he placed his sacred pipe. I had been mesmerized by the proceedings and was shocked when I looked up. The line of people waiting to be with this modest shaman now stretched to include forty or fifty people and snaked around a corner so I couldn't see the end of the line.

The next person, a prominent analyst from a large urban area, told Bear Heart about trouble with her heart. She had had one surgery and felt vulnerable about another. He placed his hand on her heart and began to sing a song of healing:

> *Ah ma maya tomah,*
> *Ah may maya tomah,*
> *Hey ya nah, Hey ya nah*
> *Hey ne yo weh*

His singing came from a resonant place that seemed to move up and down my chakras as he sang boldly through the scale, starting higher and going down and then up again.

At the low end, I could barely hear his guttural words. He sang and sang. Time and space warped. We moved from one position to another within the time/space continuum, skipping from the top of one wave to the top of another, tip-toeing the troughs, pulled by an unseen hand within the gravitational field.

When I looked up, tears were running down the face of the woman lying on the Pendleton blanket. Several people in line knelt down and touched their foreheads to the red dirt as if pulled into a vortex, swirling with ancient notes of the haunting song.

Before he went to the next person, Bear Heart took a drink of water which had been brought spontaneously by one of the persons standing in line. He dusted his hands together and asked me to fan him with an eagle feather, explaining that energy from the woman's heart problems passed through him and needed to be sent into the Earth to be recycled and sent back to her in a refreshed form when she was ready.

He also asked me to fan myself and explained that the energy could leap over into me since I was close to him and the energy exchange. "You are my medicine helper for the day," he said in a whisper that inducted me into an energetic space strange and yet familiar.

And so he worked tirelessly with each person. I looked up, and the line was even longer, maybe sixty people. I marveled. I considered these sophisticated professionals standing in line to be the *crème de la crème* of Western psychotherapists and mental health scientists.

I knew many of them. I had read their books. I had been in workshops with them. Yet, as they came one-by-one, I heard vulnerabilities not usually divulged in professional or even private settings.

They had access to the best medical facilities in the world. They talked to excellently trained therapists and physicians about their issues. Yet, here they were standing in the hot New Mexican sun to sit at the feet of this seemingly simple man.

Later, many of them told me that these moments under the cottonwood tree were among the transformative experiences of their lives.

At noon, I expected us to pause and go to lunch, perhaps to hear Bear Heart expound on what he was doing. I invited him to eat, but he told me that our Creator was moving in our midst and that we must proceed. We did not need food to fill the space important for spirit at that moment.

After each person, he and I would go through a ritual of cleansing and renewing. We used feathers, chanting, singing, herbs, and spring water. Confiding in me as a co-worker, he made a few comments on each situation. Some of the people in line ventured in to eat lunch, but some did not. We paused to catch our breath.

In the pause, I pondered the name of the place of our retreat, Ghost Ranch.

European Americans routinely in history have given negative names to sublimely powerful natural spots and to medicine people. Our mainline culture treats power places much the same way it treats minorities. As I write, I am looking at a beautiful horizon of mesas a few miles across the Blanco River Valley where I live.

We have been gifted with this view—my tribe and me—and it has inspired, shaped, and expanded us for over two decades. Each time I look at it with awareness, I lift my spine because it seems like the backbone of this web of eco-fields. Its backbone becomes my backbone.

Even so, the European-Americans who settled this valley named it *The Devil's Backbone*. Does associating a place of heart-stirring beauty with the devil seem as strange to you as it does to me?

The split in Western Civilization between humans and the natural order has paved the way for an exploitation of and suspicion of natural areas. If you name something evil, it opens the door to exploit for personal gain, to desecrate, and even to destroy.

While 'ghost' stops short of devil as a description, it had planted in my mind the notion of a questionable place. Ghost Ranch? In modern media the term is most often used with frightening movies with an aim of scaring the viewer.

Instead of being evil, I propose connecting with that energetic element may be our only hope. Is the *ghost* dangerous at times? Yes! But worth the connection.

Under the cottonwood tree, we were the cosmos in human suits We were Nature being aware of herself. Nature healing herself. Nature laughing with herself. Nature welcoming home her wayward human parts. The *ghosts* were not in us so much as us—body, mind, soul— coming together as one. The hungry inner ghosts were being fed by the sacred landscape.

Shadows grew long. The air cooled. My colleagues disappeared to their dorms and cabins. Bear Heart and I sat under the tree watching the sun set.

The two of us had ventured out onto a bridge between worlds, and I didn't want it to end. Not yet. Every event in my life had been preparing me and now pushed me onto the bridge.

The push was part and parcel of a larger pattern, a purpose, not just for me but also for our species.

I intuitively knew that all of us are part of this great return of humans to a conscious immersion in the natural flow of possibility wherein our species recognizes its humble participation in the circle of life.

"When can we meet again?" I asked matter-of-factly as if I had not just seen the globe turn on its axis. Just as offhandedly, Bear Heart took my AAP name tag and scribbled a telephone number on its back, and said simply with a chuckle, "This is a fine day. We did some good together."

Just like that I pivoted into an exploration of the unseen and of shamanic guides to take me beyond where I had ever been before. I had tasted a sacred intimacy as a natural person, and I hungered for more.

8   SHAMANIC SNAKES

On the flight back to Houston from Albuquerque, I puzzled over this unusual man whose office sprawled under a cottonwood tree and whose co-workers were the surrounding creatures in a given eco-field.

Questions came from every quarter: "How did he develop into the healer of healers? What kind of training did he have? What did he mean by ghosts, ancestors, star visitors, and spirits? What kind of relationship could we have so that I could fill in the glaring gaps in my life and work without giving up rigorous science?"

After being bombarded by questions, I settled on one as primary: "How can I be connected to the natural order like this man?"

The model I had at the time for such a relationship with an elder like Bear Heart was Carlos Castaneda and Don Juan, whose story may be fact, fiction, or a little of both. From the cottonwood tree narrative in the previous chapter, you might think we were headed in that direction. But, not so, even though there was some of that romanticizing on my part; indeed, such a flight into fantasy faded quickly in the heat of our walk on a path of consciousness.

Early on, Bear Heart clarified, "We have come together because we both have been selected by a Greater Power. My spirit guides tell me you have been called. I know some things because I am older and because I come from the Creek medicine ways. You know some things because of your education and life experience, and grit in your teeth from High Plains sand storms.

"I am not here to make you Creek. You are not here to make me a psychotherapist or a scientist. We are here to serve the Great Spirit at the meeting place of our two rivers where we and others can awaken to being aware."

He lingered over the second syllable, *psychoootherapist*, punctuating the word with his laughter and ever present elbow, gently nudging my ribs. You might think I mainly got sore ribs out of this venture from the way I describe our encounters, but the jostles went both ways.

Because Bear Heart lived in northern New Mexico and I, in Houston at the time, we settled into extended trips to be in each other's presence.

When he came to Houston, he stayed in our home located in a cultural creative hotbed in the center of the city called Montrose. Living together in close quarters allowed us to get to know each other as a pair of sometimes comical and sometimes insightful men. Specifics in our layered stories began to float to the surface of daily life.

After his vision quest at Bear Butte, Mark was on his way to identifying himself as Bear Heart. Back in Oklahoma after traveling the world through his fancy dancing, he attended Bacone College, an institution that had its origin in the Muskogee Creek Nation's Tribal Council.

The Creeks partnered with A.C. Bacone, an itinerant educator, to create a small college friendly to the indigenous mind. Originally called The Indian University, it would play a key role in Mark's life and, to a lesser degree, the emerging Bear Heart.

The story of the making of a Muskogee holy man who could attend to the needs of scores of our cultures' key psychotherapists and scientists would come to me in dribs and dabs. The heart of the story would not be found in mainstream memes, but in backwoods and backstories, in ripples on the surface of a pond generated with a stone thrown from a mysterious hand.

Frankly, I was challenged to jump from one of the turns of the concentric circle of ripples to another. Our mutual stories jumped around, and it bothered me. Then, I realized he was inviting me to make quantum leaps of awareness through our various stories. In a moment, I will tell you a doozy about snakes, but first I want to puzzle with you about what title to give Bear Heart.

One night around a fire, I asked Bear Heart how he referred to himself, "Do you think of yourself as a *medicine man*?"

After stirring the coals, he answered me: "Following the lead of my teachers, I don't use titles very much. Some people have called me a medicine man. Some younger folks from the 1960s called me a *guru*."

He overemphasized the last syllable, as *kangaroo*. Smiling, as always, he continued, "You know European/Americans used many terms like 'witch doctors,' 'fetish men,' 'medicine man,' and, more respectful, 'medicine elders.' Recently, the term 'shaman' has been used, and I believe that is a term that comes to us from Siberian tribes, maybe the Tungusic peoples."

"So, some of the folks outside my tribe that I work with call me by a variety of titles that honor me. Inside the Creek tribe, I sometimes am called *Hilis-ha-ya*, which might be translated as a medium of medicine. Medicine power comes from linking humans with larger Nature to bring about balance, beauty, and harmony."

"The Great Mystery, *Ofunga*, or *Wankan Tanka*, moves through us and seeks a balancing so that we might all live together in the natural and orderly flow of life. Most all of us live in restricted flow. My work is about releasing the dams that block the flow of the rivers of energy. You do that by learning how to let Love move through you and into you no matter where you are."

Through the years, Bear Heart guided me in questioning titles. Questioning any fixed point in the flow led to awakening and expanded awareness. Early on a shaking loose from titles was strange to me because I was acculturated to seek out titles as a form of advertising my competence and also as badges of honor.

Bear Heart, on the other hand, didn't like to present himself in a manner that detracted from the Larger Love flowing through the sacred web of eco-fields.

However, when he published his book, *The Wind Is My Mother*, he and Molly Larkin used the subtitle: *The Life and Teachings of A Native American Shaman*. I suspected he agreed to that subtitle reluctantly, given his warning me about the seduction of titles.

To check out my perception, I emailed Molly questioning the subtitle of the book, and she laughed, "The publisher wanted to use the term shaman, and we explained that shaman is not a term used by Native Americans. They said if we use the term shaman it will increase sales, so Bear Heart and I agreed to it."

Upon reading Molly's response, I got a good laugh because it underlined that we all have to make compromises to live in this culture, even on something as important as a defining book, the only book Bear Heart wrote. If Bear Heart were around in the flesh, it would be my turn to elbow him in the ribs and poke a bit of fun. "Hey," he might retort, "we're all human!"

While I have continued to use academic and clinical titles to identity myself in our dominant culture, I have followed his inclination not to use spiritual titles. Before I met Bear Heart, I ceased to use the title *reverend*, even though I was ordained as a young man in the United Methodist Church. The title just didn't seem to fit me in my twenties since I wasn't all that *reverend*.

Bear Heart often kidded me about being "Dr. Will." A favorite phrase of his was, "You can have a double Ph.D. and not know much about how things really work."

He was right about that observation. He had many stories about me that poked fun about my attempts at integrating the two worlds of— shall we now say *shaman* and scientist. I had a few stories about him, as well. That is why I chuckle at Molly's email about the subtitle of his book. On more than one occasion, he laughed at people who advertised themselves in various publications as a "shaman" or "guru" or "lama" or "medicine man."

At the bottom of Bear Heart's and my conversations about titles was a questioning about not only titles but about the practice of Western rationalism to name things. To fix things. To live with the illusion that once we have named something, we understand it. Especially, ourselves. The thing is not the thing named. The map is not the territory.

Nothing is fixed.

Once we swim where the rivers of shamanic wisdom and the newer sciences meet, we can know that there is actually no such thing as a *noun*. Everything is a verb; everything is in motion, whether we like it or not. Much of the time, we don't. We try to fix things in order to be safe and end up adding to our suffering.

To be in harmony with Nature is to move with Nature in elegant acceptance that we can't stop the movement even though we try. To be in motion is to open the possibility of awakening to what is. To move with the motion of the fields around and within stimulates a larger awareness.

Much of our unhappiness arises in grasping, trying to hold on. We ride for a moment on a wave of joy, and then harden our beliefs about that wave thinking we have found the truth. We try to clamp onto the wave only to find that we grasp nothing.

The truth moves on, wave after wave, some full of pain, some full of pleasure. Then, we find ourselves paddling like crazy, all the while telling anyone who will listen what our truth is about; only it no longer exists. Working in a shamanic domain meant being sensitive and aware of subtle and great changes, wave after wave.

In the writing of this book, I sent 1.0 versions to Reginah WaterSpirit, Bear Heart's spouse, since I value her response and needed her to check for accuracy. When she read the above paragraph, she wrote this response:

"Every once in a while I would be awakened in the middle of the night by Bear Heart's singing of *Ole Man River*. After many episodes of this annoying habit of his, which I thought was selfish and rude, I had an insight when I spontaneously started singing the song myself. I checked and noticed that I was uptight and caught in a great stress. My stress came from doing my very best to hold on to old paradigms. I was clutching ways I had become accustomed to and depended on as if these ways would save my life.

"Then, I began to listen to the words I was singing, words I had heard in the middle of the night many times from Bear Heart.

Ole Man River, that Old Man River, he just keeps rolling along... you and I we sweat and strain, but Ole Man River he just keeps rolling along.

"That was a turning point. I became more willing to let things change and say, 'Thank you!' Nowadays I find myself singing the song when I am holding on too tight, and one time I woke myself up singing it during my dreamtime."

It was beginning to dawn on me that the bear walk emphasized learning how to give up straining and resisting in order to roll with the river. A principle quality of nature-based consciousness arises from knowing how to listen to fears without allowing them to dominate as we will now see in the doozy of a story I promised.

One day while driving on the Gulf Coastal Plains in my 1979 popup VW van, Bear Heart asked me to pull over. I had been asking him about his initiation as a shaman, pestering him, really. He had told me that he studied with two principal elders over a fourteen year period: Daniel Beaver and Dave Lewis, both Creek *Hilis-ha-ya*.

"So you want to know something of my training, is that right? How are you about snakes?" He reached back and stretched, leaning his head against the back of the platform seats in the rear of our van. I replied that I had had a few encounters, but they weren't my favorite creatures.

"The Kickapoos in your fine state of Texas use snakes rather than dogs for guards. These people are actually very friendly as a tribe to snakes. They allow snakes to come into their living area and give them food they like, just like they do with members of their families.

"In my tribe, we were always told that snakes are our little brothers so we should never be afraid of them. Respect them? Yes. Know their danger? Yes. We learned that if you let your fears run you, you will attract their attention in a negative way. The proper thing to do is to honor them."

Bear Heart rested for a few moments and glanced to see if I was still with him. Then, on he went, "Snake stories are at the heart of most cultures, and you can know a lot about people and cultures by the way they treat our relatives that crawl along the ground. I never did connect much with the Genesis treatment of the snake as evil. At a certain point in my training as a *hilis-ha-ya*, my teacher took me to a little canyon in Oklahoma, what you might call an arroyo."

"Now, notice that I don't use the term *medicine maker*, the way some might. The medicine is already in the web, put there by the Creator. We just learn how to connect with it in the vibration of the web and allow it to pass through us.

"My teacher and I were standing on the south side of the rim rock. Now, I knew this place to be the home of rattlesnakes. In our part of Oklahoma, we have quite a few timber rattlers, some diamondbacks, too. But the timbers are the ones to watch. These guys get big and are considered very dangerous because of their long fangs and high venom output.

"It was pretty warm that August day, and I could see a lot of snakes, some under the edge of the rim rock and some down in the dry creek bottom in a nest.

"My guide invited me to this challenge to see how I was coming along with waking up to what was around me. He wanted to know what kind of connections I was making. I knew this examination was big. This test, he explained, was not necessarily a final exam, but close. It could be final, he laughed.

"Now, I was certain that he was going to have me walk through the den to see if I could master my fears, that is, to put the fears to the back of my mind so that I was not broadcasting them to the snakes. That's important because you always have fears. You need to respect your fears but gently place them aside. This was a test to see how aware I could be of my inner world and those big boys on the ground.

"I walked slowly with my shoes off, concentrating on my breathing and singing a medicine song for the snakes. When I was about in the middle of the den, my teacher called out, 'Do you see that big granddaddy over there by that rock yonder?'

"I nodded, 'Yes,' because I didn't want to speak, which might've excited the den.

"Well, go over and touch that big medicine snake on the head. Touch him four times," drawled my teacher in a tongue mixed with Creek flavors and Oklahoma twang.

"Very slowly I tippy toed through the snakes like they were tulips. I can tell you I wasn't singing like that guy Tiny Tim. I was singing my medicine song and sliding my shoulders down my back so as to lift my spine and letting my bare feet bring energy up from the ground.

"My terrors flowed on down the river. My awareness was heightened to the nth degree. My life depended on each aware step. When I reached the grandaddy, I paused and sent him a message that he was my friend, that I respected him, and that I was in training to help other humans to learn to honor the snake presence in our lives.

"I told him that I would honor him by opening myself to the great healing and power of his tribe. I didn't speak this information out loud but in little energy packets."

Bear Heart looked up to the sky and then down at the dirt around us, allowing me to soak up the moment.

"After a long and suspenseful hesitation, I reached down and touched this very large brother on the top of his head. Four times. Not once did he rattle. I walked out, very carefully with each step, until I got to the other side.

"That's the big walk of medicine power. My teacher, David, showed me the energetic power of singing. In a way, the singing had put the snakes in a trance. Then, the touching four times not only honored the grandaddy snake but also snapped the family of snakes out of their trance. That is why the trip out of the den was especially difficult because they now were returning to usual awareness.

"Another thing: when you go to help me lead vision quests, you will need to make friends with the chief snake. If you are on the bad side of the snake tribe, you will be in trouble. You can see that medicine means you are fully awake to everything inside you and out there. You have to go through your fears to the other side.

"If you learn from your fears, they will quieten.

"If you fight them and disrespect them by giving them too big a place in your awareness, then your fears will get out of control. They are like unruly children who seem to want to rule. But they really want to know if you are in charge, or like you say, if you have a larger you. When they know you have enough consciousness to hear them out but then put them aside, they will relax.

"Someday, you are going to be an elder in a vision quest, the one others turn to. Somebody is going to discover snakes close to humans. There will be several *someones* who want to kill the snakes. They are not bad people. They are just acting out of what they have been taught. They think they are protecting, but they are really putting the encampment in danger.

"Why? Because the chief snake will take note and send messages to all of the snakes in the area that you are typical *wascina* who are their enemies. Then, you got real trouble. So, don't let yourself fall into that trap."

We sat for a long time in silence while I let his teaching story soak in through the layers. It moved through what I had been taught about snakes. It moved through the Adam and Eve story. It moved through the snakes I had seen killed on fence lines of my boyhood.

It moved through the practice of some of my friends in college who gassed snake dens at Sweetwater, Texas, as part of their infamous snake roundup. It moved to a memory of my college mates who as a prank placed a rattlesnake in bed with me when I was asleep, its mouth taped shut. Then, it dawned on me that there was an invitation embedded in Bear Heart's story.

I spoke to my respected friend, "If you are suggesting that to engage in shamanic work I will have to make first-hand friends with a timber rattler, I can tell you right here and now that it will never happen.

Not in this life time. I've already had a large diamond back in bed with me, and I don't plan to go down that road again."

That rebuttal brought peals of laughter from Bear Heart, as if he knew something that I didn't know about myself. He said nothing more, and I thought that was the end of it.

Fast-forward your video camera of perception by three decades. In this scene, Bear Heart has long since moved into the ancestral domain. Our spiritual community, the Earthtribe, is camped out on Deer Dancer Ranch, a 600-acre wildlife preserve where we ceremonialize on a regular basis.

It is late afternoon as Judith and I sit in front of our tents relaxing with nuts and fruit to finish off our evening meal. Marlan Curry, a long time tribal member, comes crashing through the woods, shouting, "Dr. Will! Dr. Will! There's a big rattlesnake over by my tent."

At that instant, time and space collapse into my training with Bear Heart. He suddenly is present with me, a visitor from the stars, smiling at my statement that I will never have anything to do with rattlesnakes.

He reminds me about my aversion to Timber Rattlesnakes, what with their neurotoxin and hemotoxin mix aimed at both the destruction of blood and nerve cells. I call on his wisdom, not primarily as he was decades ago, but more as a current presence.

This is a time I need my ancestor.

Judith and I walk at a slow pace toward Marlan's tent, and I hum the snake medicine song as I walk, the one Bear Heart sang to the snakes in Oklahoma. An anxiety flooded my awareness zone; it stemmed from the big snake that had visited my bed in college. I hummed the snake song and quieted the terrified college student inside coming awake to the feel of the snake.

The anxiety calmed down and left me with a respectful fear. I knew rattlesnakes are among the most venomous snakes in North America, and they deserved caution. As the years passed, I reflected on this axial moment. It assisted me in knowing the difference between anxieties that stem from past experiences and respectful fears that seek to alert me to danger.

When I arrived at Marlan's tent, I saw a medium-sized snake. Believe me: medium in the Timber rattlesnake world is big to most of us. Because I had seen such snakes from time-to-time in this wildlife ranch, I had studied them carefully to be prepared for situations such as this one.

Timber rattlers are very large, up to 6' and heavy, weighing up to 10 lbs. They age to twenty years and are an endangered species in Texas. Mainstream people in Texas view them as enemies. Recently, I saw a bumper sticker in our little village that read: *Real Women Kill Their Own Snakes.* Such an attitude has pushed these lovely creatures to the brink.

Judith and I shooed the campers to the background and squatted down and began singing the snake medicine song Bear Heart taught me. Soon, the snake sister relaxed and stretched out. Ordinarily, I have a snake handling tool with me, but I left it at home, likely an unconscious forgetting.

I looked around.

There was a shed not too far away where we stored tarps for our sweat lodge and also some tools. I walked slowly away from the snake, never taking my eyes off her and found a hand rake. Quickly, I bent the teeth open. Returning to the snake, I continued to sing and placed the widely bent teeth next to the narrow place that separated the large body from the diamond-shaped head.

To my great surprise, the snake voluntarily placed its neck between the teeth and wrapped its long body up the handle of the rake until the rattles were near my hands. Since I knew that this type of rattlesnake is territorial, I knew I had to relocate it at least five acres away, what with forty campers in tents all around. The protective need was both for the campers and the snake.

My path to a near-by stream took me through the campsite carrying the snake on my rusty rake. Sister snake was perfectly calm. As I walked, up came Alan, a man with considerable experiences with snakes.

"What a beautiful creature," he remarked and walked on by. The snake remained calm and relaxed, although I had to stop and rest from time-to-time with the weight of my fellow traveler straining my forearms.

Then, as the snake and I continued to move through the campsite, other people came up to see what the hoopla was about. When someone approached who led with their culturally induced anxieties, my snake sojourner would rattle even before they were within a few yards.

The sound of a timber rattle going off near my hands constituted quite a startle. Each rattle jolted me, heightened my awareness, and enlivened me! Later, campers 100 yards away told me the sound of the distinctive rattling was so loud, it jolted them out of their tents.

As I moved away from the fear evident in various spectators, my new friend calmed down. The snake read the eco-field, tuning into judgement or negativity. It obviously was awake and aware and sensitive. After a while, I came to a stream flowing with life and potential prey for my new relative. So it was that I found a place for this young adult to live, at least until we broke camp the next day.

Later that evening, as I settled into my chair in front of my tent to meditate, ancestral Bear Heart came to me, "You remember that day you told me you would never handle snake medicine? Well, you didn't touch the snake four times, but you did OK for a mongrel. Although it took you a very long time, it is better to be awake and aware later than not at all. The chief snake received your respect and honor.

"Next time, you need to touch his head to wake him up from your song. If you can't bring yourself to use your hand, you can use a stick. But do it very gently and respectfully."

It had taken me over thirty years to become fluent enough in snake language to make even this small intervention. The intimacy was fleeting. The vision, reassuring. Together, they pointed the way in distinguishing between anxiety and fear.

Incidentally, don't try this kind of snake handling at home.

9

WAITING, WILLING, AND WATER

This shamanic learning process I was experiencing was unlike any of my academic education or stints in psychotherapy either as a client or practitioner.

There was logic, yet not like Greek philosophical logic. There was a kinship with science, yet holistic, not reductive. There was some sequence, yet Bear Heart and I wandered in circles. There was discernment, yet very little judgment. There was decisive action, yet a focus on waiting.

For Bear Heart, waiting implied something much stronger than patience. Patience was fixed.

Waiting coiled before striking.

Waiting relaxed into a whirlpool and allowed a pull downward to the bottom before pushing off.

Waiting did not fight the current.

Waiting did not lose energy in resisting.

Waiting saw what was coming, accepted, and then allowed it to go by without doing harm.

Waiting was intimately tied to a visitation from the future.

The future was not out there in a linear sequence but imbedded in the present, as was the past.

Waiting quietly in the circle of life embraced all in a converging.

A close partner of waiting, is willing. When I asked him what the most important shamanic quality is, he replied, "First, show up. Just show up. Rain, 100-degree heat, sleet, or snow: Show up. No excuses: Show up."

One day as we were driving along, Bear Heart asked, "What do you know about songs and their significance."

By now I knew the rock bottom answer, "I am not sure to what you are referring, but I am *willing*." Willing was the magic word in our process. There was something about the tone of his voice that told me we were about to launch into a very important dimension of our walk together.

"Songs!" I said to myself, "I had sung in the choir in high school, so how difficult could learning a few songs be?"

Once again, I would find myself on a very steep learning curve.

"Let's jump into deep water by my teaching you the water song we often sing in the sweat lodge and other places," he smiled, sang, and then continued.

"This is the song that *wascina* often ask me to sing when there is a drought. They ask me to perform a rain dance. The song is not about bringing rain. They don't understand that the singing of the water song is not an effort to tell the Great Mysterious what to do. See, that's where Western Culture goes astray. These songs are prayers, but they are not an effort to inform our Creator, as if the Power of the Universe needs for us to relay information that is previously unknown. Funny humans, that we are."

He waited for me to respond, but I had learned to wait.

He continued, "*Wascina* culture has missed the point of the Indian's relationship with water. We don't tell water spirits what to do. We sing in order to harmonize ourselves with the living nature of water. Even during floods we know that there is an underlying intelligence in the living entities you call weather systems. We don't think we are bad people when floods or droughts descend.

"We do know that we often have slipped out of harmony and balance, and the sour notes we sound with our poor choices close us off to being present with whatever is happening.

"Our songs and prayers are to bring us humans back into a pure relationship. Even if our experience is unpleasant as with a tornado, we know that the big challenge is to shift so we can be in harmony with what is. If it comes our way, we meet the challenge, knowing others go free."

Over his mild objections, I tape recorded the water song because he sang in a tribal language. As soon as he finished singing, I asked him what the words meant. He told me that it was important to sing the song without knowing the meaning of the words.

I needed to learn to wait on deducing meaning after experiencing the sounds. He instructed me to feel the song move through my body and to allow the sounds to unblock my inner turmoil.

Once in a right relationship with the weather spirits, I could have varying amounts of influence that depended on what was needed within the larger web. The songs, he explained, made me part of the weather spirit team rather than a controlling influence.

In my research into eco-field science, I would later discover that sounds we put into quantum fields are information-and-meaning carriers that all elements of the environment receive and relay. Most elements of the sound system of fields have phonic ears, with the exception of humans dominated by current civilization's noise.

"We've known for a long time that chronic noise is having a devastating effect on academic performance of children in noisy homes and schools," says Gary Evans, an expert on noise, crowding, and other forms of environmental stress. Research confirms what we know intuitively: the sounds in a given landscape are crucial in every facet of life, including learning.[1]

With research like this in mind, I carried the tape recording of the water song with me on a journey Judith and I had planned. We flew to Loreto, Mexico, located on the Sea of Cortez for a week of solitude and respite from the concrete city.

I also needed space from the intensity of what I was experiencing with Bear Heart, and Loreto was an excellent spot to sort through the jolts to my world view.

Plus, I just couldn't seem to learn this ancient song in a noisy urban environment. A block to learning at the sapient level sent me in the direction of considering whether certain conditions are necessary for tuning into the wisdom of such a song.

Did I need silence with background waves on a beach in order to connect with a water-inspired sound? I could read emails with television in the background, but linking into these treasured phonics required something more. Maybe a spaciousness near great water would assist.

The Loreto village was founded in 1697, by Jesuits, who were guided to fresh spring water by generous indigenous people, as the monks traversed scorching desert terrain in heavy black robes. The township is located on the east coast of the Baja California Peninsula. As you look at the map, it is about ¾ of the way down the eastern shore of the peninsula with stunning views of the Sea of Cortez.

Once there, I wandered the beaches where the desert cacti meandered down to hold hands with emerald waters and offered inspiration for my learning the water song.

Had the sea itself heard the chords many times before? Or maybe the sea actually sang the song and relayed it to receptive students.

Each day I spent extended time singing the challenging song calf deep in water, looking at the cloudless sky. After an hour or so, I found I could sing the song while in water, but not back in my room. It seemed odd. It was as if the water itself conducted the song much like it might conduct electricity.

Loreto is interesting because of a desert/sea interface. The village only gets about six inches of annual rainfall, so it appears to be in a perpetual drought. It seemed an inhospitable location to learn a song about water.

Since I was not learning very fast, I questioned myself. Then, a thought came. Is the absence of water necessary in order to know water? I puzzled about such matters as I had one foot in burning sand and another in the sharply cold sea.

Toward the end of the week, I had completed the first stage of ingesting the song, and, to my great surprise, it rained. Not a big rain, but a rain nonetheless. It crossed my mind in a fleeting way that there might be an energetic connection between the singing and the rain, just as Bear Heart had suggested.

But—dominated as I was by the rigid cause-and-effect of mainstream culture—I quickly dismissed the possibility. I did not know yet about the importance of correlation in quantum physics. The whole notion of a link or correlation between singing, clouds, rain and even all forms of moisture seemed, frankly, preposterous. Still, I couldn't deny what had happened.

I sang; it rained.

Later in the week, Judith and I wandered by the site of an ancient spring which might have been the attractor force in the forming of the human village. I sang a bit to synch myself with the waters. And, off balance, I nearly fell into the bubbling water as if there was a bridge between the sounds of the song and the water itself.

Still, I made no definite affiliation between song and waters.

After a week, we left Loreto without my being convinced there was a correlative power available in song. I just couldn't link my singing with an interactive relationship with water because in my psychological training that was "magical thinking." Clinically speaking, magical thinking was a cognitive behavior to be avoided at all costs because it was a signal of immaturity.

One of my doctoral professors defined magical thinking as "the fallacious attribution of causal relationship between actions and events." Children and immature adults lived in such magic, or so I was trained. The marriage between science and ancient wisdom wasn't going that well for me.

Penetrating the fortress of Western Civilization's reductive epistemology is not easy. I was beginning to see that I was hard-headed and not that quick a study when it came to a dimension of experience outside the domain of the science of psychology.

I had treated many families where children thought they were the cause of things going on in their world that was simply not true. An eleven-year-old girl thought she was the cause of her father's heart attack and suffered greatly because of such magical thinking. I knew there were times when magical thinking had to be overcome.

On the other hand, I was discovering that many more of my clients were suffering precisely because they had lost the ability to see the magic in life. Depression, taught Jung, often stemmed from the repression of the sublime.

How easily I had fallen into the trap of mainline culture's view of reality that eliminated the magic and enchantment of our beautiful blue planet. I had spent so much time confronting the unaware use of magic that the mystery of the unknown had drained out of me.

The next time Bear Heart and I met, he mentioned that I should be wary of the powerful tools he was teaching me. I needed extreme wakefulness and patience that comes from waiting, he emphasized. As an example, he said that the water song was a tuning fork into the latent moisture present at any given moment, and I needed to be sure I knew what I was doing before I engaged it in any ceremonial way.

He went on to offer instructions about amping up the song by singing it in the presence of medicine circles that connected humans with ancient trees. The song carried sounds that humans had learned from the clouds and wind currents themselves, *weather spirits*, he called them.

He noted that when you sing this sacred song, you are stating an openness to be a conduit between heaven and earth. The trees, clouds, and even humidity know the sounds since they gave them to humans in the first place. Once you sing, the weather and water spirits pay very close attention. You don't always get what you want, but you do get attention.

"You had better know how to ride before you get on a spirited horse," he laughed.

He went on: "Before you sing the song, you need to cry out to the weather spirits of the area, 'Here I am. I am willing to be an opening for the moisture that is needed at this moment in this place and all other places. I confess that I don't know what best suits this place. I don't know what is best for the whole of creation.

"I know that you, the weather spirits, have a job to do and that you are directed by a unifying wisdom that has an infinite exchange of information between its various parts. I know that the relationships with all of the needs of Earth are complex.

"Yet, I want to tell you that as I look around at the plants, the animals, and the soil, they all seem thirsty. Very thirsty. So, I am willing to be an opening if it fits the will of our Creator."

Bear Heart continued to explain that he would let me know when he thought I was ready to use water songs in a shamanic manner. For now, he explained, I needed to rest into waiting and learn patience, but the virtue of patience and the skill of waiting continued to elude me.

A couple of months passed. I was eager to share what I was learning with a nucleus of psychotherapists and health care providers wishing to move beyond the limits of their current paradigms. Looking into the shady corners of my motivation, I had an inner battle.

On the one hand, I was smitten by possibility and wanting to show off what I was learning to my colleagues. On the other hand, I didn't believe fully the experience I had of singing in Loreto actually interfaced with the rain. It seemed preposterous. I had a war going on between my rational and intuitive sides.

While walking one day in a green area of teeming Houston, an oak tree seemed to speak to me. The inner feeling of connection startled me, but the message persisted in asking me to bring a circle of humans to start a new kind of friendship between our species and the trees. Struggling to overcome my skepticism about receiving such a message, I said simply, "I am willing."

I didn't say, "I believe in this approach." I just said, "I am willing." The willingness practice enabled me to proceed as if the message was sacred guidance.

At first I thought of hosting my learning circle of professionals in the famous Rothko Chapel, a site-specific structure that houses fourteen of Mark Rothko's paintings. The architecture of the building itself is a work of art that grew out of vigorous debates between Rothko, and noted architects—Philip Johnson and Howard Barnstone. The chapel doubled as a place of meditation and colloquiums that drew scholars from around the world to discuss issues affecting justice and freedom throughout our planet.

While I was deeply moved by sitting in silence in the building, something about the fourteen large paintings and four alternates didn't feel right for our gathering.

I was aware that, after a long struggle with depression, Rothko had committed suicide in New York City in 1970. Maybe, that energy lingered. On the other hand, I once had attended meditation in the Chapel with Buddhist monks where we chanted in a beautiful way, and a gathering seemed perfect in such a potentiated locale. Further influencing me was the fact that Judith and I lived in a townhouse designed by Howard Barnstone, and we loved his work.

Still, sitting in front of the paintings on a very hard bench, I was uncomfortable in a number of ways. Soon, I was pushed outside by what felt like an unseen hand. I was reluctant to leave air-conditioning, given Houston's tropical climate, so I didn't succumb to the nudging without a struggle.

Outside of the climate-controlled space of the chapel, I breathed more freely, even though Houston's humidity was formidable. Sitting on a bench, I looked at a distinctive sculpture by Barnett Newman known as *Broken Obelisk*. The stunning piece of art stands in front of the chapel in a reflection pool designed by the architect, Philip Johnson, and is dedicated to Martin Luther King, Jr.

I had been part of a civil rights task force in 1969 when John and Dominique de Menil offered the sculpture to the City of Houston as a memorial to Dr. King to stand in front of Houston's City Hall. Still wrestling with its undertow of racism, the city turned it down.

Now, the sculpture graced an outdoor meditation area with benches that would hold our group well. The sculpture and attendant pools must be the place for me and my students to gather! Or so I concluded in my usual, daytime state of mind that moved quickly through my neural system like the urban traffic around me.

That night other messages conflicted with my day time reasoning. I entered a shamanic journey, one I was learning to use in order to seek guidance. In the middle of the night, the veil seemed thinner. My questions slept on the pillow beside me. Much as I loved the area around the sculpture, I came out of the journey knowing that the reflection pool and sculpture did not have a feel for the place to launch one of the first training experiences with my fellow professionals. My reluctance was complicated.

Under the cottonwood tree at Ghost Ranch, I was secure and bold in these trans-scientific practices in the awareness that few of the people in that remote setting were from Houston. I could be as far out as I wished, distanced as I was from my daily colleagues and referral sources.

There was no danger to my professional reputation in the mountains of Northern New Mexico. Yet, here I was in Houston now inviting fellow professionals into a training experience that stretched me out on a limb. As I looked around at the people near-by, I concluded sitting near the famous sculpture might be too public. I wasn't fully out of the closet where I hid my integrating the paradigms of the ancient world with newer sciences.

Still, I kept chanting, "I am willing."

The next day I strolled just west of Broken Obelisk and Philip Johnson's reflection pool until I sat at the foot of the oak tree that had called out to me some days before in a Mother Tongue I was just learning. Its limbs reached out until they almost touched the ground some fifteen feet from the massive trunk. A major limb jutted out from the trunk about four feet off the ground and then curved down to the soil where it sent roots for nourishment.

Gingerly, I sat on the limb to see if it would hold my weight. It gave way ever so slightly and sent a shiver through my body as the limb swayed as if hearing a distant music. In this moment, I knew we needed to gather near this tree.

While meditating with the assistance of the rocking limb, I noted how my considerations of a gathering place had taken me from the air conditioned, existential angst of the Rothko Chapel, to the sculpture dedicated to human rights and justice, to the arms of a majestic oak, itself the sculpted scripture of nature written over time.

It came to me as I sat in the arms of the tree: there are no real human rights or justices unless said rights are placed in the folds of our tree brothers and sisters.

More to the point: humans have no rights apart from the rights of Nature.

Everything else is an illusory exercise in futility. There is no life, liberty, or the pursuit of happiness apart from the well-being of our environment. I didn't have such wisdom yet, but the power of that truth was reaching out to me through the limbs of the royal oak.

At last, I was now settled on a place. The time we set to gather was before sunrise, a choice based on the significance of the early morning and avoiding Houston's heat. Surprising to us all were the bonds we had with the grass, the trees, the soil, and the morning star.

What I had to say paled beside the simple exercises of connecting in a felt-sense with this marvelous green space in the heart of a teeming city.

Bear Heart had been a bit surprised when I told him I was taking our teachings to a circle of my fellow psychotherapists so soon. Pleasantly surprised, I thought. He suggested I take it slow so as not to overwhelm the participants or get beyond myself, a disturbing tendency he had noticed in me.

"Especially don't get beyond yourself," he repeated, gently. "The Sacred Web will know if you are claiming more than is actually within your circle of awareness."

Toward the closing of our time together on that fateful morning with the training group, the sun peeked just above the tree line to the east. Light shown through the bamboo cane that protected the Broken Obelisk and separated us from early meditators. Inspired by the moment, I suggested that I teach the group the water song, the one I had just learned in Loreto, Mexico.

Remembering Bear Heart's caution that the song was powerful beyond my understanding, I looked up to the sky to make sure that there were no clouds nearby. I breathed a sigh of relief. There weren't; it was crystal clear. No threat of rain.

So, we launched into singing. Or, rather, I launched into singing since no one else knew the song. I sang and sang, and rather impressed myself with how well I was doing. Maybe, I thought to myself, I was further along in this primordial process than I thought.

Then, to my utter surprise, we were drenched with water. We looked around. What had happened? Had a sudden storm moved in off the Gulf?

After a few minutes, it dawned on us that the Rothko Chapel area had an extensive outdoor watering system that was on a timer to go off at 6:30 a.m., and we were sitting right in the middle of the system.

We laughed and laughed. The participants were very generous in their patience with me even though most everyone was dressed in their professional attire, and my arrogance meant they would have to return home and change clothes.

Yet, we all marveled at what had happened.

In that moment, we were transfused with certitude that singing and water were linked together in a mode of correlation beyond our ability to reason. Could such a connection extend even into mechanical systems that watered the park?

Such appeared to be true even for beginners. The next time Bear Heart came to stay with Judith and me, I had decided not to tell him of my *faux pas*. I was considerably embarrassed at my inability to learn the art of waiting. Then, as we sat around our evening meal, the whole story poured out. Bear Heart—ever on the lookout for humor—leaned back in his chair and roared, laughing so hard that tears ran down his cheeks.

Finally, he said, "You are better at *willing* than *waiting*. But you are really good at being all wet."

Some years later Reginah WaterSpirit, his medicine helper and spouse, sent me a DVD of one of his important teachings after he journeyed to ancestral domains. The crown jewel of this particular teaching by Bear Heart was the telling of the above story.

She said that he loved to tell that story wherever he went, and did so with love and humor, sometimes mentioning my name, sometimes not. And most times that he and I spent any time together, he would comment on the power of sprinkling systems.

"That's what happens when you become a backsliding Methodist: they keep sprinkling you to get you back from your heathen ways," he winked.

For my part I have loved knowing that my main claim to spiritual fame was being all wet.

Through the years, I have reflected on the influence of sound in general within the system of eco-fields and in particular on the significance and influence of ancient sounds on the flow of observable events. Evidence has accumulated that strongly suggests our conscious interaction with the material world influences the shape of reality that emerges moment to moment. Quantum physics has opened the door for the influence of consciousness in any given circumstance.

Here is a quantum situation: a scientist conducts an experiment at the point of wave/particle interaction testing the interaction between the visible world (particle) and the invisible domain (wave).

You are well acquainted with the world of waves. When you listen to the radio, watch television, or cook in a microwave oven, you are using a variety of electromagnetic waves. The types of electromagnetic waves differ from each other in terms of wavelength. Wavelength is the distance between one wave crest to the next.

In introductory quantum physics, we are taught that particles (the material world) behave as particles or waves depending on whether or not they are being observed. *Observed* is the wild card in the game of the real world we take for granted, and observation is a description scientists use because they are sometimes embarrassed to note the power of consciousness.

In other words, the consciousness of the scientist influences the collapse of a steep wave of possibility into a particular observable reality; namely, a particle.

Let's be clear: this description is not science fiction or the soft science of a psychologist. Wave/particle interaction includes our conscious participation and describes a basic building block of 21st century science. Quantum physics has brought us around the circle to the primal resonance of the indigenous mind. Sometimes, as I swim in the waters of eco-physics at the fork of the river of indigenous wisdom, I recall T.S. Eliot's words:

"We shall not cease from exploration, and the end of all our exploring will be to arrive where we started and know the place for the first time."[2]

In both these paradigms, the power of consciousness as the matrix for the interaction and linkage of the material and trans-material world becomes explicit. That is the value of the newer sciences: making explicit what has been implicit in many wisdom traditions. Every generation needs its own story, and the story of 21st century physics and, especially, eco-field physics appears as one of our most promising narratives.

It may be the story of our day.

Back to the role of sound and singing with water. In quantum physics, the movement between the domain of unseen waves and the sensual reality of particles happens when steep possibility waves collapse into particles under "certain conditions."

Our consciousness can, under "certain conditions," influence weather when sound interfaces with clouds of possibility. That truth confronts us in both 21st century science and shamanic traditions. Water and sound are close friends.

Water takes sound into itself and spreads the information within the sound across vast distances instantaneously. Whale songs offer us a good example that can stretch us around this interaction between ourselves and water spirits. Part of what makes whale songs fascinating is their evolution between seasons.

In any given area, in any given period of time, all humpback whale singers will perform nearly identical versions of a song. A whale song is most commonly sung during the mating season and only by males, but the songs undergo surprising transformations between years.

Sometimes a song will only change subtlety—slight variations in tone or volume. Other years, the song is unrecognizable from the year before. Hymn sections may completely disappear, and new themes arise. Regardless of the scale of change, however, all singers within the same geographical region will adopt the same adjustments.[3]

Then, boom!

The song changes, and immediately all the singers in the area change to that new tune. By immediately, I mean in an instant. And that is not all. According to one researcher, humpback whales, across the globe in the Indian Ocean and in other areas far removed from Hawaii will switch to the new song. Again, in an instant.[4]

Slowly, it was dawning on me that my research in eco-physics and my relationship with Bear Heart were bringing me back to a web of intricate interconnectivity beneath common sense reality. I was being introduced to a matrix of consciousness, a ground of being, that had its own root language, a *Mother Tongue*.

And, I was still in the kindergarten of achieving anything like literacy.

10   INITIATION, INTIMACY, AND RELINQUISHING

Where is this strange walk with bears taking us?

That question pounded after I learned the water song and got doused by a sprinkler system. Bear Heart responded by offering another challenge which I will address in a moment.

It was dawning on me that Bear Heart was guiding me through a series of initiations. When linked together, the learning moments constituted an ancient initiation of primal consciousness. Each experiment aimed at enlarging my awareness, choices, and practices by connecting more energetically to the sacred web. At times, I actually found myself vibrating as if lying on a prodigious spider web.

Or lying on the inside of a piano listening to the music of the spheres.

Eventually, I would see this pathway as part of a toroidal movement of Consciousness Itself. David Bohm, esteemed physicist, coined the word, *holomovment*, to describe a cycling out of a primordial grounding of love, a rising up through chaos and confusion, and a forming of islands of coherence.

These points of coalescence in the cycle of primordial love show up in history as individuals, communities, and civilizations. Whatever their expression, organizational forms of consciousness don't exist forever. Like us, they are born, live, and then die in order to live again in another form.

Why do they die?

When individuals, communities, tribes, nations, and civilizations lose their vital connections with the possibilities and fires of compassion, they eventually shatter. Then, follows a crash and sometimes a drifting down into the ground of being to be renewed, only to be born again in another form.

Everything and everyone has its day in the visible world and then moves on to make room for new creations.

Such reflections circled around to the question: Where was this path leading? Or, even broader in the present tense: where is the Universe going?

I once heard the astrophysicist, Brian Swimme, respond to that very question like this: "The Universe is unfolding from a beginning flaring forth to a state of consciousness whereby every part knows every other part in its fullest."

That description fits these shamanic visions and laboratory experiments. The visions and experiences were, indeed, coaxing us with an unseen nudging toward increased intimacy in the web of eco-fields we call Mother Earth.

If walking with bears takes us across a bridge, the other side is more intimate.

Together, Bear Heart and I were walking this initiatory path of consciousness toward a provisional description of intimacy:

Intimacy is deeply and warmly felt in the heart area in such a way that past and future converse in the present. This convergence is so strong that we experience a profound connectedness with all aspects, humans and other-than-humans. It is a willingness to make yourself known in relationship and to know the other.

The two of us were micro-experiments in the intimacy of consciousness that could eventually lead to macro-experiments in lodges of love. We wondered if we might be part of a creation of tribes within Mother Earth that might contribute to mid-wifing a sustainable and regenerative civilization. Only the Great Mystery knows how such experiments turn out. As for us, our task was to wait and to be willing.

Difficult?

Yes, *and* the lessons in consciousness were about to get more demanding.

The next steep hill in the initiatory pathway required not only the skill of willing and waiting, but also *relinquishing*.

One spring evening Bear Heart, Judith, and I sat in a restaurant that overlooked Buffalo Bayou in Houston. As usual we were laughing at our foibles and admiring a thatch of trees that hung over the muddy waters when Bear Heart suddenly stopped in mid-sentence, paused, and then spoke, "I want to tell you about a time in my life when things just fell apart."

I thought he was going to retell the story of the death of his father, but this shattering of his life was different. His willingness to talk with this level of vulnerability was a bit unusual, so he had our attention. Our trust in each other was growing.

He started out with halting words, "On May 11, 1964, Mother's Day, my wife, Edna, and I received word that our beloved son, Nathan, had died in a plane crash as a soldier serving his country. This was a year when America's involvement in Vietnam had increased. President Kennedy had been assassinated the year before, and your Texas man, Lyndon Johnson, was trying to figure out what to do. Anyhow, Nathan's plane hit a wire while landing in the Philippines, and the ensuing crash killed 84 soldiers, including our beloved son. It seemed so senseless."

"Yes," I thought to myself as Bear Heart paused, "It was senseless. The Gulf of Tonkin Resolution a couple of months after Nathan's death would allow Johnson to wage all out war against North Vietnam. Thousands of young men would die deaths for something called the domino theory. Turns out the theory was only a figment in Johnson's considerable imagination."

Bear Heart continued, "A smoke screen war was going on while me and my family tried to grieve. You know what? Nathan ordered an orchid for Edna for Mother's Day from Hawaii before they took off on that dark day. The beautiful orchid was delivered a couple of days after he died.

"The arrival of such a beautiful flower just seemed to anchor that experience. It smelled like an orange or maybe a lilac, and every time I smell that smell the feelings come back to me. In some ways, the orchid helped, but, in another sense, it just stuck with me. I had a very hard time in moving through it. My whole family seemed caught in a spasm."

Bear Heart paused and took a long swig of water.

"Finally, after some time passed, I asked a couple of elders to help me with this undigested grief that just sat in my stomach. I told them I was completely helpless to let go. They told me it was deeper than letting go. I had to reach down into the depths and *relinquish* my beloved son to the beyond as an ancestor."

Our food arrived, and Bear Heart interrupted his story. I was completely surprised with the date of 1964 that he just mentioned because he had told me about the passing of his son several times. The impression I had received previously was that the crash had happened fairly recently to the time of his narrative.

His roots of grief went very deep and were still raw in his telling, as if it happened recently. I wondered what approach the elders were going to take with him. It was two days before he returned to speaking of Nathan.

Early one morning we walked from Judith's and my house in Houston to a park near the Rothko Chapel. As we sat under a large oak tree where the sprinkler had doused my training circle when I sang the water song, he tip-toed into how the elders helped him.

"The elders told me I would need to purify my inner, medicine council. You know, to cleanse what was going on inside. I would need heat and sweat to loosen and assist in the purification, so they took me to an *inipi* that I will never forget.

"It took a lot of heat to jog loose my innards. Once out of the sweat lodge, they drove me to a river bank that had a sandy shore. I didn't know exactly what they were doing when they dug a hole about five feet or so deep.

"They told me to take off all my clothes and to enter the hole in a standing position. They sang songs about the compassion of our Creator as they slowly covered my body. Only my head was visible. Before they left, one of them whispered in my ear, 'We put you in this hole because we love you and want you to be purified. You need to go back into the womb.'"

As we sat on an oak tree limb that spread close to the ground, Bear Heart paused and drifted back to being buried alive. Quiet. Then he proceeded.

"At first, I struggled to see if I could move. Then, I just felt helpless. When little ants crawled across my face, I was scared. Really scared. Then, I found myself apologizing to Nathan for times I wasn't that good of a father.

"I apologized to myself for letting myself down. Time passed. Tears came. I asked for forgiveness. The forgiveness I asked for was not from our Creator. I knew our Creator always forgives and doesn't need to be asked.

I was asking for myself to forgive myself. I asked for the power to forgive a government that involves itself in insane wars. I needed to feel helpless so I could open to the vast love and forgiveness of the Great Mystery."

Silence returned in the telling as if we both needed to let those words sink in. My head and heart were spinning because I knew I had a long list of grievances I needed to relinquish.

"The sun beat down even though it was a pretty cool day. A sense of release started to settle in. I wasn't ready to relinquish. As I completely experienced my lack of control in the sand and settled into being forgiven, I started to feel thankful.

"I was thankful for Nathan, sure. I was thankful for all the good things in my life. I went on and on with my list of gratitude. I was lost in that experience when, finally, the elders returned. They said nothing, but dug me out. I can tell you that was some sense of liberation. They toweled me off. Then, we sat in a circle, drummed, and sang. After a while we sang the pipe song, and then passed around the sacred pipe. I knew this was a most important part of the relinquishing."

"What is the *this* you mention here?" I asked, wanting to be sure I followed this last part of the process.

"Being in the circle of life after being born again. They were teaching me that everything is in the eternal circle—everything, including Nathan and my feelings of loss. And the politicians who make war. And the faulty runway that caused the crash. You haven't relinquished what you are holding onto until you can be fully present in the circle with your bare feet on the ground with people who fully love you."

He paused again for a long while, and then added the punch line, "To relinquish in this way you need a tribe of people and all living things. You can't do it just by looking inward."

The two of us stood up from the tree and stretched. We walked at a snail's pace down tree-lined streets covered in a shroud of silence. Not complete silence since cars were honking and roaring by. But we said nothing. I didn't talk much for a couple of days as pieces of my life floated to the surface.

In my journal, I compiled a partial list of toxic memories: a junior high friend I hit for no good reason; the expression of my daughter's faces when my first marriage crumbled; a racist assumption I made about a golfing friend; an insensitivity about a colleague's loss of his father; and the walling off of my father's spiritual gifts. These were a few memories in my iron box that needed the purification and relinquishing Bear Heart described.

Years passed before I realized there was a definite pattern for purification that resulted in relinquishing. It was simple.

Embrace and express love to each and every incident that comes into my awareness or vision circle.

Apologize first and foremost to that aspect or sub-self within that bubbles to the surface. In some instances, that is enough. In other situations, an apology to the person or part of the environment in the relationship may be necessary if they are open to hearing an apology.

Relinquish what you are holding onto. Usually, people think of asking for forgiveness, but I was learning that forgiveness is a profound relinquishing of what you are grasping. Forgiveness is not about convincing our Creator to forgive us; but, rather, a willingness to relinquish what we hold onto that doesn't allow the forgiveness, already there, to flow through freely.

I also was learning that I needed to find grace and forgiveness from other channels of the Creator other than the person I harmed. If I went to the harmed person and offered an apology and then expected them magnanimously to make me feel better, things usually got worse.

Relinquishing meant doing the work on myself before I offered an apology. If I had relinquished, then the apology was clean and forgiveness encompassed the field around us.

Thanksgiving then follows naturally.

Most important is the circle of community where there are witnesses to the moments of relinquishing. This circle does not consist only of humans but of all creatures great and small who are present, along with any ancestors who want to visit.

In a bear walk, it is not enough to have human witnesses. You need all creatures listening and watching. Not to be ignored, Bear Heart taught me to take off my shoes and walk on damp grass in order for a full relinquishing to occur.

I wondered if this process was cross-cultural with indigenous people around our beautiful blue planet?

In 2010, I was teaching in Hawaii when I was introduced to the ancient practice of *Ho 'O Pono Pono*. We were teaching on the west shores of Maui when an indigenous Hawaiian elder led us in chants. She was a friend of Morrnah Simeona, a well known wise person and keeper of the ho'o pono pono tradition.

Afterwards the elder spoke briefly about this practice. *"Ho'o,"* she said, "in English is something like the *"to"* in an infinitive. "Like to speak," she said. *"Pono* is the verb that combines with *Ho'o.* Literally, it means *to pono."*

"What?" I asked, "Is *to pono."*

"It means to purify yourself of the mistakes you have made. It means to renew and realign yourself in order to restore harmony which has been disrupted by your choices or other conditions. It means to purify and release yourself from what Morrnah called karma, errors you might be carrying not only from this life but from many lifetimes. It means to be cleansed."

This brief conversation, along with research on the subject by several graduates students in The Wisdom School where I taught, prompted me to delve into Morrnah Simeona's teachings. The prayer process of Ho'o pono pono sounded very much like Bear Heart's teachings. Perhaps, I thought, I could gain some clarity by co-ordinating the two approaches, a collaboration of ancient practices.

Simeona's practice can be summarized as applied to any situation in four simple prayers:

⁓ I love you.

⁓ I am sorry.

⁓ Please forgive me.

⁓ Thank you.

This ancient Hawaiian prayer practice collaborated with Bear Heart's teaching for purification that resulted in relinquishing. Notice that Bear Heart and I emphasized additional steps.

⁓ Link with community and the web of life in ceremony.

⁓ Take off your shoes and walk on the skin of Earth to a new day.

Lest I forget, Bear Heart emphasized another very important step:

⁓ Fasting.

11   FASTING

Driving from Albuquerque to Santa Fe, I glanced at the Sandia Mountains on my right, east of the freeway. The Pueblo name for the mountains is descriptive: *posu gai hoo-oo*. Try saying that phrase out loud. It means water slides down into valley.

Have you ever noticed how sensual and descriptive and alive indigenous names for persons and places are in contrast to our dominant culture? I like the Spanish *sandia* also, which translates as *watermelon*, a description that refers to the reddish color of the mountains near sunset.

As I drove, the sun dipped below the horizon on my left and—true to its name—painted the mountains a brilliant shade of watermelon highlighted with red, oranges, and purples.

Full of anticipation, I was on my way to meet Bear Heart in Santa Fe for a vision fast.

It was dark thirty by the time I reached Cerrillos Road in South Santa Fe. I found a cheap room for $30 at the Silver Saddle Motel which I learned had been built on old Route 66 in 1958, the year I graduated from high school and the year of my first vision fast. It seemed fitting that this quest, a couple of decades later with Bear Heart's guidance ,would include a correlation with the first.

Bear Heart explained that fasting—*i-ilawi-cita* in his native tongue—was necessary in order to make space for a fuller form of spirit to enter my inner world. Other than that cryptic statement, he said little about how or when to start the fast.

Steeped in scientific inquiry as I am, I carefully researched the experience of fasting. After all, I questioned nearly every thing my new friend was teaching, even though my trust was inching forward. Since I was teaching part time at a local medical school as a clinical supervisor, I spoke extensively with medical colleagues who offered interesting information.

Simply put, fasting is the willing abstinence of food, drink, or some portion thereof for varying periods of time. In a physiological context, fasting can be seen as occurring when the last meal was eaten 8–12 hours prior. You start to get substantial benefits as early as eight hours after the last meal, hence the first meal of the day is called "break-the-fast."

What are the benefits?

There is growing scientific evidence in research that shows that intermittent fasting has substantial health benefits. Upon a Google search of "fasting for health," I get a surprising 33-million hits. It seems there is a renewed interest in this ancient practice.

Let's get one bugaboo out of the way in terms of benefits. Weeding through my conversations with colleagues and reviewing the literature reveals that fasting is likely not a useful weight-loss tool.

There are, however, many other benefits. Aware and informed fasting may see improvements in blood pressure, cholesterol level, and insulin sensitivity. Some research even indicates that informed fasting may reboot the immune system, clearing worn-out immune cells and making room for new ones. This research goes on to state that fasting might protect against cell damage caused from aging and chemotherapy.[1]

Does fasting slow down the aging process as some suggest? Maybe. Such research may explain the energetic vitality in spiritual seekers who regularly utilize fasting as a spiritual practice.[2]

Our brains seem to crave the experience of fasting as if to link us to a more nature-based heritage. Mark Mattson, the current Chief of the Laboratory of Neuroscience at the National Institute on Aging Research, underlines this point:

"Fasting does good things for the brain, and this is evident by all of the beneficial neurochemical changes that happen in the brain when we fast. It also improves cognitive function, increases neurotrophic factors, increases stress resistance, and reduces inflammation."[3,4]

Such research is encouraging, but, as you might imagine, I looked into the risks as well. At the time, I was teaching with Jim Chappell, M.D., a dean at the local Medical School in Houston, and he said, "William, as your friend, I strongly advise you to be careful. You could die of fasting from water for three days."

Bear Heart laughed out loud at that "medical fact" when I reported it to him. "Maybe for *wascina*," he said, "but I have gone longer, much longer."

I checked him out on this one. Despite such a helpful rule of thumb in medical circles, some people have survived without water for as long as ten days. Three weeks without food. Jim's warning, however, alerted me to the power involved in spiritual fasting and also to the possibilities I needed to consider for myself and for others in my newly formed spiritual community.

It is, I concluded, imperative to watch closely the balance of your physiological system when engaged in serious fasting. Hence, the need for elders whose knowledge base includes both ancient wisdom and modern science.[5]

In 2002 Boston marathon runner Cynthia Lucerno died from drinking too much water that had depleted her body of sodium. According to the *New England Journal of Medicine,* 13% of the runners in that marathon suffered from what they called "water intoxication."[6]

In the Spring of 2015, on our annual vision fast, we had one quester fall into a state of electrolyte imbalance. She was well versed in the physiology of the body. She was well acquainted with many features of vision questing. She had been mentored extensively. Even so, she found herself in a state of considerable vulnerability.

Here's how it happened. Late one afternoon, she closed her eyes to rest as she sat in her vision circle. When she came back into fully awakened reality, she was thirsty and sun burned. In response to that condition, she drank much water. Soon, she drifted into the aforementioned water intoxication, meaning the water washed the electrolytes out of her body through urination. When we brought her in from her vision circle the next day, she was in a vulnerable state.

She didn't want to drink Gatorade because of its high sugar content, so we made sure we had other electrolyte supplements for her under the supervision of a nurse.

If you combine the intensity of usual fasting with the immersion of a group of vision fasters into the wild heart of Nature, you are entering a powerful domain that has potential for enormous benefits. Such spiritual fasting requires a watchful eye.

Basically, I was ignorant of fasting when I arrived in Santa Fe on my initial quest with Bear Heart. I knew that fruits and vegetables contain three essential electrolytes: calcium, potassium, and magnesium. I have always been a chump for chips, so I had plenty of sodium. I also noticed that Bear Heart ate his share of various snacks. When I asked him about it, he replied, "You can change what is bad for you into what is good for you in your attitude when you are eating."

Such transformation was largely beyond me at the time, and now, too, for that matter, though aware eating with proper breathing does wonders for digestion. I never did settle in myself as to whether Bear Heart had alchemical powers to transmute processed foods into organic delights. Could he change Twinkies into broccoli with an attitude adjustment? Not likely, but who knows?

Outside my door at the Silver Saddle Motel in Santa Fe was a metal chair, the kind that has been painted several times and rocked back and forth. In the evening, I settled into the chair to contemplate the Sangre de Christo Mountains just to the east. Already I had been fasting for a day, but I chose to eat bananas and other fruit to assist in balancing my electrical system.

By the time I arrived at our meeting place the next day in a Santa Fe residence, I had been fasting for two days. I was feeling the effects of the absence of food and water. Space was opening up in my inner landscape. I was slowing down.

My interest in talking in usual conversation was fading. My tongue seemed a bit larger. Earlier, I had daydreamed about food, but now a strange indifference even to the fantasy of my favorite breakfast of waffles and eggs didn't hold much power. I found it easier to unhitch from my usual patterns of inner dialogue. Busy mind chatter drifted into the background.

I probably should not have been driving in such a trans-ordinary state. It likely was not the best plan to begin the fast before I reached the visioning landscape, but I was both hard headed and ignorant of the powerful process.

Because of the geographical distance between us, I had not really had the kind of practical guidance I needed to know about such things. When Bear Heart and I talked in terms of preparation, we conversed mainly about spiritual matters. We had been preparing for this quest for nearly two years, yet the practical ins-and-outs of how fasting would unfold had been neglected.

As Bear Heart and I continued to work in the founding of the Earthtribe in years to follow, we saw the considerable possibility available in preparation with an ongoing community.

I took Bear Heart's teachings to a growing council of elders within the tribe we were forming in Houston, and we integrated the ancient teachings with what we knew to be the best in psychology and physiology. With the Sacred Mystery, we were co-creating a version of this ancient pathway that fit our mongrel natures.

In the Earthtribe, we consider vision fasting to be a three year process. When a person begins to feel the call to quest, she attends a vision encampment, usually in the Spring of the year. She begins the process by supporting others who are questing.

That is important because in the Earthtribe, we feel that the painful estrangement from Nature so prevalent in Western Civilization has produced humans who think of themselves as being the center of things. Our industrialized and informational culture is narcissistic at its core. Thus, we teach that the vision fasting journey begins by moving to serve others in their quest.

The link between *me* and *we* begins.

Ours is not a workshop approach to vision fasting. Bear Heart taught me that respect for the process is the best signal that you are in a traditional lineage. We seek to be respectful by moving ourselves into a three-year pathway, which even transcended Bear Heart's practice. We likely needed an extended version because we didn't have him to guide us after his journey to the stars.

At the end of the encampment week for the potential vision faster, there is a *Stake Ceremony*, a ritual downloaded into our midst years ago to assist in our quests. In the Stake Ceremony, the tribe chants and drums in a circle. If a person senses the attractive nudge of Spirit to quest, then she comes forward and asks permission of Mother Earth to drive a stake in the ground.

Each year there are usually eight stakes put in the ground. Sometimes more, sometimes less. At the moment of driving the stake in the ground, the quester enters the second year of the vision fasting journey.

The new quester then chooses an elder to be her mentor the following year. During that time, she meets at least once per month with the elder to explore spiritual, emotional, and physiological aspects of vision fasting.

Then, the next spring the seeker actually goes out to fast in a vision circle, a circle whose energy has been building. After the quester comes in from the actual fasting and circle sitting, she moves to the third year.

In the third year she returns to supporting and serving those who are questing, as well as continuing to integrate her transcendental experiences into everyday life. There develops a rhythm between focusing on loving the other, moving deeply into loving within the inner system of selves as related to the eco-fields, and then, to complete the cycle, serving other humans who are seeking their return into the heart of the natural order.

Meanwhile back in Santa Fe and my personal fasting story, I did not have an ongoing tribe in which to engage in vision fasting. The Earthtribe had not yet been formed. Bear Heart had assembled mostly indigenous elders to be part of this particular quest.

These strangers offered some support, and were experienced in the questing process; they assumed I was as well. I wasn't. They knew each other in that they gathered from time-to-time, but they did not have an ongoing tribal affiliation, at least in regard to vision questing. Theirs was an intertribal affiliation that spanned several states.

Some of the medicine people who were part of this encampment met regularly with Bear Heart in an ecumenical gathering of tribal shaman and elders. He knew some of these people from being invited to the Voluntary Controls Program at the Menninger Foundation in Topeka, Kansas.

There he met physicist and biopsychologist, Elmer Green, Rolling Thunder, Yogi Swami Rama, and Doug Boyd, who would later chronicle some of these events in his book, *Rolling Thunder*. I was excited to meet these persons who had participated in Menninger's ongoing twelve-year research project that concentrated on "physical fields and states of consciousness."[7]

Although he was not present in this particular vision quest, Elmer Green's influence could be felt. I knew from various professional articles that he had been able to demonstrate extraordinary bioelectric states in the laboratory.

At the Texas Institute for Child and Family Psychiatry, we had an extensive biofeedback program for our patients. It was aimed at shifting brain waves from beta to alpha and even theta in some cases.

Drawing on the results of the Menninger research, we were teaching our patients to shift their consciousness from ordinary to trans-ordinary states (TOS) by learning methods of profound relaxation.

In these states, a free flow of the energy of fields could move through the body with fewer constrictions. Trained in these early forms of neuro-science and biofeedback, I knew my consciousness was shifting considerably through my fasting. But what I was experiencing thus far was minor compared with what was to come.

Along the way, as we drove to the visionary eco-field, one of the medicine persons asked me if Bear Heart had taught me essential shamanic songs, songs like *The Pipe Song*, *The Honor Song*, *The Water Song*, *The Calls the Spirit Song*, *The Healing Song*, *The Snake Song*, and on the list went.

I mumbled a reply in an effort to cover up my ignorance, and he asked me again.

"I only know a few of those songs," I replied, somewhat embarrassed. I failed to mention that I was so inexperienced with shamanic singing as inadvertently to turn on sprinkler systems.

As we drove higher into the mountains of Northern New Mexico, perhaps close to the Colorado border, in a place called Wild Horse Canyon, I wondered what I had gotten myself into. I didn't know the songs. I was a mixed blood among shaman with lineages that reached back through the millennia.

To top it off, in this larger group, my access to Bear Heart was limited. It seemed I was on my own. Maybe, I fretted, this whole pathway was a mistake. The fasting was impacting my neural system, and my thinking wasn't all that clear.

I would soon learn my trepidation was justified.

12   CLEANSING THE WINDOWS

As we moved deeper into the practice of vision questing, conversations with Bear Heart amped up the importance of cleansing ourselves of toxic waste that accumulates over the course of living, in general, and working intensely with people, in particular.

Those involved in the service professions become deeply connected to others through a serving and compassionate relationship. In that connection, there is an exchange of multilayered energy, and the two of us agreed it is important to purify oneself or else become an ambulatory toxic waste station.

Such a necessity for purification is especially true in a polluted environment generated by Western Civilization. Just driving on a freeway often involves a transfer of highly charged, chaotic energy into our systems, not to mention carbon pollutants, smog, and ground-level ozone.

The stress of everyday living creates intense contractions within our musculoskeletal system so that the flow of energy in the form of electrical impulses hits the dams created by the stress-induced clinching.

Before we know it, we are uptight in a high loop. When the flow encounters the dams, there is a physiological pooling on one side and a trickle on the downstream side. Within the flow is a current of lactic acid which then remains in the pools because we don't have adequate release and cleansing practices. Eventually, the acid irritates the nerve receptor cells; these irritations become inflammations and the seat of much of our pain and disease.

Cutting-edge science is now telling us that many diseases, including heart difficulties and various forms of cancer are intricately connected to inflammation, a process that leads to cholesterol-clogged arteries. Such a documented proposal means that inflammation sets the stage for heart attacks, strokes, peripheral artery disease, and even vascular dementia, a common cause of memory loss.[1]

So, yes, there are immense benefits to purification ceremonies such as sweat lodges and fasting, the process which I have found to be the most effective in the release of contractions. But the larger hill to climb is the release of humans from the bondage of a stress-dominated culture.

About the time Bear Heart and I were discussing stress, inflammation, and purification, our clinic at The Center for Creative Resources in Houston was on the graduate rotation of various universities for training psychotherapists, psychiatrists, family physicians, teachers, and pastoral counselors.

Our office setup included a closed-circuit television system that linked a team of senior therapists and their students with a treatment room where a trainee or a seasoned therapist would see a client.

The client signed a release to be part of the training, so it was a very effective form of therapeutic education. While the client gave up the privacy of meeting in seclusion with a therapist, she gained multiple perspectives from the larger treatment team watching in an adjacent room through closed circuit television. Such an arrangement was not for every client but worked well for many.

On some occasions, I would work with a client while Judith headed a team that included graduate students in an adjacent room. Through our televised system, the trainees observed as I engaged the client with the aspiration of learning from both useful therapeutic moments and mistakes. We also videotaped the session for future study and clinical research.

One day in the treatment room, I talked with a woman who had been through a severe trauma. As part of the treatment, I had her lay down on a ceremonial blanket on the carpeted floor and breathe through her feelings.

Utilizing a light trance induction of hypnosis, I took her briefly back to the trauma and then to a place cherished by her in Nature. In her mind's eye, she let go of the suffering, anger, and pain associated with the trauma and invited a healing presence to enter where the wound had been for so many years.

Through an indigenous breathing technique I had learned from Bear Heart, I invited her to expel the toxic waste of the trauma. We also engaged an integration of therapeutic tools that drew on Thought Field Therapy (TFT) and Emotional Freedom Technique (EFT).[2]

Both were aimed at allowing various energy fields to pass through the client and release tension and stress in favor of a more relaxed state. After an extensive active imagination or shamanic journey in which she had moved through a cave and a tunnel into another reality, she returned to her ordinary state of consciousness and sat up, holding her knees to her chest.

She reported that she felt much better. A knot in her stomach had disappeared.

While she rested, I told her that I would consult with the training team in the next room and that she could take this time to rest and collect herself, integrating the healing experience into her more usual ego state.

I left the room and walked briskly to the office where Judith and the trainees were watching by our closed-circuit television arrangement. When I opened the door, Judith and the five other professionals were white as sheets, like they had seen a ghost.

It turns out, they had.

"What is going on here?" I asked, a bit alarmed at the vulnerability in the room.

All six of the people pointed at the closed circuit television monitor. I looked up at the screen, and I could see my client sitting where I had left her, holding her knees to her chest.

That aspect of the scene was perfectly usual. However, along the floor was a complete outline of her discharged energy. Was it an energetic representation of her trauma? Or was it some other phenomenon?

I squinted and rubbed my eyes. A perfect outline of a ghost-like body would not go away. My client continued to pull her knees up to her chest and sat in the middle of an out-stretched energetic form that had been expelled during the therapy.

At least, those were my first thoughts.

Judith said that during the treatment session they could see the energy pouring off her body like a dark mist. As it left her body, it shaped itself into a coagulated form that looked like her but flowed out on the floor.

It totally bumfuzzled the interns.

Was it an electromagnetic outpouring from her body? Was it a bridge between the wave/particle domain described by quantum physicists? Was it what ancients called "spirits or demons?" Was it a visitor from another dimension?

In any case, the form on the floor propelled us into a reality beyond our current paradigms.

Immediately, I went back into the treatment room and invited my client to return to her chair, which she did. She was completely unaware of the form-like mist that had issued out of her welcome release and purification.

When I asked her if she noticed anything different where she had been sitting, she said, "No." I told her that we had observed an expulsion of toxicity and that we were examining the tape. After I affirmed the excellent and courageous work she had done, we scheduled another appointment, and she left. She paused at the door with a quizzical smile on her face and thanked me.

Then, I returned to the observation room to examine the monitor more fully in order to make some sense of what was unfolding in our midst. On the monitor was the continued outline of an energetic body on the floor.

We discussed what it might be. Did it have something to do with the camera? Was there some technical miscue we were overlooking? We made adjustments in an attempt to eliminate hidden variables in our technology. We turned the camera on and off. We wiped the lens. We doubted what we were seeing and sought some explanation within a more rational paradigm.

About that time, Jack Jensen, M.D., an orthopedic surgeon who practiced in the office next to us, entered the discussion. With his assistance, we eliminated more variables.

We even changed cameras. Still the energetic body lay on the floor. While we could not see the toxic form of her release with the naked eye, we continued to observe it with various cameras and camera angles. It remained outlined on the floor of the treatment room for over 24 hours until it finally dissipated or departed after I burned sage and juniper for purification.

In the discussions we had with our team, we explored the reality of leftover energy within our treatment facilities. At that time, I had been involved in the practice of psychotherapy for more than twenty years and was still a relatively young man.

Just think, I intoned to my graduate students, how these energy forms have gathered in my office over time. And think of all that energy moving into and through all of us, all outside our awareness.

We should, I kidded, get hazardous duty pay. For several weeks we discussed with our students the importance of purifying ourselves when there is a discharge of energy in a therapeutic transaction.

I still have the videotape, and I look at it when I doubt the necessity of purification. I propose that any deep listening by any person to another who is in crisis leaves a residue of emotional and energetic energy both with the interior and the exterior eco-fields.

The questions our students raised with us boiled down to one: how do we cleanse ourselves of leftovers in our transactions? I suggest that addressing that question is a central one in a culture beset with fear, angst, shame, addiction, environmental degradation, an avalanche of negative news, and a variety of traumas.

Another dimension of our undigested energy globs comes into awareness through tensions and conflicts we experience in relationships. Both partners in an intense conflict lose energy in the exchange during which there is a "deposit" of unwanted energy in the other. Astonishingly, there are few models of conflict resolution taught in a typical academic setting that pay close attention to purification of toxic waste.

In Judith's and my work, we use a variety of approaches to move through tensions in our marriage and in clinical work. Hal and Sidra Stone have provided us with a most useful map that attends to purification.

They call these moments of conflict—negative bonding patterns—because of the presence of negativity during the relational exchanges. Hal and Sidra are spot on: much of our bonding in mainstream culture is in negativity. Take an ordinary weather forecast. More often than not the forecaster seeks to evoke fear with continued reference to "getting hit" with a storm.

A trailer might suggest that we will need our umbrellas for the morning commute even though the forecast for rain is spotty. We subsequently are bound to a negative narrative about the upcoming day.[3]

At the core of tension in intimate relationships in negative bonding, according to this model, is a power imbalance. One partner hits (emotionally and/or physically) the other from a power side of the personality (often an internal critical parent).

The damaged partner experiences hurt and vulnerability and then shifts into a power gear and returns the hit. Soon, there is a cycle of hitting and hurting. Resolution, however, is not complete until the negative energy deposit has been scrubbed from the system.

What is crucial in purification?

Not just emotional and spiritual release but most important, physical sweat!

Sweating increases an almost magical chemical we call endorphins. Toxic elements such as alcohol, cholesterol, and salt are excreted through the medium of sweat. According to recent studies, sweating reduces the incidence of kidney stones by flushing out the kidneys.

Sweat contains antimicrobial peptides effective against viruses, bacteria, and fungi. These peptides are positively charged and attract negatively charged bacteria; they also enter the membranes of bacteria and break them down. Sweating unclogs pores that can cause various skin problems. No wonder hot yoga has become popular, along with Zumba, bicycle spinning, and myriad exercise regimes.

All good. But there was more I needed—exercise-type sweating was only a first step. Much more was needed in the hyper-complex world in which we live to rid the system of an everywhere negativity.

The *inipi ceremony*, sweat lodge, offered the deep cleansing I needed. The benefits astounded me, and I wanted to share the experience with

Judith. Such an occasion presented itself during the sweltering days of a Houston August, circa 1980.

The only place we could find to conduct the ceremony on short notice was a vacant five-acre lot north of Houston, near a subdivision; not the most auspicious place for a sublime experience.

In the hot afternoon, we built the lodge with traditional willows cut from a near-by drainage ditch. We covered the thatched roof with blankets and draped black plastic over the top, a grudging nod to the petroleum industry. Bear Heart didn't like to use the plastic, but it was all we had. Tarps and hides of the type he usually used were not available.

We entered the lodge about sunset with sweat already dripping off our bodies from Gulf Coast humidity. About an hour and a half later, we emerged from sitting on the rich dirt, from looking into rocks heated to a red glow, from smelling the pungent fragrance of a variety of herbs, from hearing deeply moving utterances of a dozen pilgrims, and from the smoking of a sacred pipe.

We crawled out of the lodge on our hands and knees feet first to symbolize a breech birth. Bear Heart told us that children and pilgrims born through breech birth had powerful medicine.

Upon emerging from the hot lodge, I couldn't believe how fresh and cool the air felt. Even sweltering Houston felt cool after this ceremony! Toweling off, my skin breathed in a way that opened the microtubules of my cells to reach out and mingle with the energetic pulsations of life all around.

I lay down on the cool ground, with my belly button connected with the rich soil of Mother Earth. With each deep breath, toxic waste poured into the ground. It would be returned to me recycled, said Bear Heart, after it was purified.

I loved this cycle because it underlined a sustainable use of energy whereby the negative had its place and then was returned in positive form.

After a brief ceremonial meal of fruit, Judith and I opened the doors of our 1979 VW pop-up van. Before I turned on the engine, we sat in a most profound moment of intimacy.

"What just happened?" Judith asked with a voice indicating we had been through an experience unlike anything she had ever known.

Over three and a half decades would pass as we purified ourselves in this fashion once or twice per month. Such a cleansing practice was challenging and a lot of trouble. I kept searching for a purification process that would take its place. I found many helpful ones, but none that penetrated to the depth of my cellular structure and the domain of sub-atomic particles like the sweat lodge did.

But what of people who do not have a sweat lodge ceremony available to them?

Recently, I received an email from an enrolled member of an indigenous tribe in a nearby state. She was in desperate need of a cleansing ceremony, but, to her surprise, her tribe did not have a regular sweat lodge ceremony in the entire state.

Her tribe taught that she needed this purification each month; yet, there didn't seem to be a regular practice available. If need be, she wrote, she would drive ten hours to enter the sweat ceremony with us. Her email set me to thinking about those persons who don't have a tribe that engages in this practice.

Allow me to break down some of the components of the ceremony which can be engaged for purification when the whole enchilada is not available. As I proceed, you will see how this ceremony touches aspects of ourselves not inherent in jacuzzis, commercial saunas, or other sweat inducing experiences.

We crawl on the ground and sit with our bare feet on the soil. There is considerable scientific evidence that such sitting allows the electro-magnetic field to pass through the soles of our feet in a process called "Earthing." Earthing in and of itself can enhance our cleansing and provide vigorous steps towards wholeness.⁴ I make it a point to walk bare-footed on the exposed ground nearly everyday.

In sweat lodge ceremonies, we stand in a circle with the fire heating up the rocks. A simple ceremonial linking with friends around an out-door fire will release much that needs to pass through us.

We chant, drum, and sound the conch outside in richly nourishing eco-fields. As such we join with all aspects of the environment as rela-tives. The trees reach down and draw pollutants from our bodily systems and even assist our breathing.

We breathe in to the count of 13 and out through the mouth to the count of 8, starting with a concentration on the head, then to the heart, then to the solar plexus, and then to the genitals.

We dance together in five rhythms to the sound of drums and other music. We engage in body drumming, acupressure, acupuncture, myofascial release, and other body therapies.⁵

Our civilization has produced cleansing practices that are distor-tions of the purification process. Bulimia (compulsive vomiting) and an-orexia (compulsive fasting) are examples, especially with young people, of an intuitive urge to cleanse ourselves.

By the same token, chronic constipation is common in the main-stream and speaks not only to diet but to a blocked civilization. All of these adjustments in life deserve our awareness and compassion. They are largely memetic symptoms of a culture gone awry.

The wisdom of the sweat lodge ceremony offers a profound cor-rective. No wonder such ceremonies are present in many cultures un-der different names: Mexican temezcals, Scandinavian dry heat saunas, Afghanistan rock heat, Irish/Celtic sweats, and so on. There are many different forms of sweat lodges available in different locations.

A word of caution. It is very important for sweat lodge facilitators to be properly trained. As we proceed, we will see how a long-lasting spiritual community called The Earthtribe grew out of Bear Heart's and my work.

Through the decades, a particular form of healing has evolved, and those forms will be addressed as we proceed. Sweat lodge guides in the Earthtribe receive eight years of training as part of a rigorous commitment to respecting the power of this process. Before engaging in a sweat lodge practice, it is a good idea to inquire as to the lineage and training of the leaders.

What is the purpose of this cleansing?

For our personal benefits solely?

Or for a much larger endeavor?

The windows of our perception are cleansed so we can see clearer. See what? See beyond ourselves to all creation. This intimacy is at the heart of who we are as natural humans, and we cannot rest until we have those connections.

It is the aim of our Earth walk. Releasing the contractions of muscles, emotions, and mind tangles lies at the heart of purification with an eye toward more intimate and aware connections with our surroundings.

The purpose of such cleansing that leads to relinquishing is the co-creation of a regenerative and sustainable civilization. As we delve into the creation of compassion and nature-based communities, we turn to a partner of purification and fasting: vision questing.

I was about to discover domains of perspective, power, and vulnerability just beyond my experience, or even my imagination.

13   SEES FAR

An envoy of cars drove some three hours north of Santa Fe on Highway 159 toward our vision encampment, following the spine of the Sangre de Cristo Mountains.

In the distance, about 70 miles away were two peaks that stand alone, not part of the Sangre de Cristos, and across the Colorado line. The Ute Indians call them *Huajatolla* (pronounced Wa-ha-toya), which translates as "Breasts of the Earth." Official maps call the mountains, *The Spanish Peaks*; such a pedestrian naming is in contrast to the indigenous linkage of the living mountains with breasts.

I figured we were about two hours northwest of Raton, New Mexico.

When I feel vulnerable, I call up measurements in my mind to keep me connected with the side of my brain interested in linear matters. That's the side of me that hits the brakes when I go too fast on the freeway and pays the bills on the first of the month. These mental gymnastics present only an illusion of control; in this case, a comforting illusion.

Snow still covered the Huajatolla since the West Peak is 13,626' and is the easternmost mountain over 13,000' in the USA. Better than the measurements as a comfort was a sustaining energy emanating from the Great Mother's bosom in the form of the two peaks. The snow at the apex appeared as nipples of nourishment.

Our parade of cars left the tiny pavement of Highway 159 and wound on a bumpy, dirt road to an encampment. When we arrived about midday, some questers were already hard at work building a large *inipi* or sweat lodge.

Others were preparing their vision circles. One quester came from a tribe where the tradition was to dig a hole for a descent into Earth's skin for his quest, and the sound of his digging attracted my attention. I sauntered over to assist him.

The scene of his digging reminded me of holes I had dug intuitively in the Llano Estacado as a boy. As children, we called our holes, forts. Many days and nights I spent lying in such holes looking up at a spreading pear tree which dropped its bounty into the hole for me to break my boyhood fast.

Sometimes, when I ate the pears green, I paid the digestive price. Fallen and rotting pears attracted honey bees, wasps, june bugs, hummingbirds and butterflies.

The hummingbirds and butterflies followed me throughout my life and became my allies. Beyond the pear tree limbs were the vast stretches of blue sky dotted with cumulus puffs, as if smoke from a sacred pipe.

These were textured memories that floated to the surface as my new friend toiled with his vision site, but I decided not to dig a hole for my quest. For one thing, I didn't have time. But just seeing what this quester was up to connected me with the significance of being down in Earth's crust, seeking a vision.

Bear Heart had taught me how to build traditional sweat lodges, so I joined in the cutting and lashing of willows for a vision lodge that would follow later in the day. Since the practice of sweat lodges in North America has been preserved by Northern and Southern Plains tribes, the lodges most often are built with white willows which grow readily on the plains especially along arroyos.

On this day, a shaman in our circle used the bark of the willows, which we shaved off, for temporary pain relief and other forms of healing. The drug we call asprin is made from acetylsalicylic acid, a by-product of willows, and I felt a debt of gratitude since the high altitude and fasting had given me a headache.

Little did I know or even imagine at the time that the Earthtribe would sprout from this vision quest and that hundreds of sweat lodges would be built over the next three and half decades. We would learn that the eco-fields would tell us what materials to use in building the ceremonial huts when willows weren't available.

Years after this powerful New Mexico, encampment, the 600-acre wild life preserve ranch on the Gulf Coast of Texas, Deer Dancer Ranch, would share its yaupon saplings with us for building the framework of sweat lodges.

Later even still, we learned that the Comanches used these same yaupon saplings in the spring of the year when they journeyed to the edge of the Comanchera east of the Balcones Fault. They nibbled on the poisonous berries to provoke vomiting, a practice they needed in order to cleanse their systems after eating dried and sometimes stale buffalo through the winter.

We in the Earthtribe came to like yaupon lodges and also juniper frames since willows weren't available. Near our homestead in the Texas Hill Country, we built a juniper lodge out of saplings that lasted for over a decade. It was the stoutest lodge I ever experienced.

Once, when Judith and I were invited to teach one of the first courses at Wisdom University in 2005, we felt called to build a lodge in a redwood forest in Northern California. We were stumped about how to proceed because there were no saplings, only giant redwoods. At our wits' end, we consulted the caretakers of the land. They suggested we talk with the redwoods, which we did.

Talking with redwoods was quite an experience in and of itself. John Steinbeck wrote, "The redwoods, once seen, leave a mark or create a vision that stays with you always. No one has ever successfully painted or photographed a redwood tree.

"The feeling they produce is not transferable. From them comes silence and awe. It's not only their unbelievable stature, nor the color which seems to shift and vary under your eyes, no, they are not like any trees we know, they are ambassadors from another time."[1]

After an extensive conversation with the redwoods, we noticed that professional arborists had been trimming certain shooters at the edge of the trees' circumference to give them breathing room. The tree specialists showed us how to trim around the bottom of selected giants for their benefit, and we found that these trimmings made a spectacular lodge.

We had a sense from the trees that they appreciated our giving them a haircut, and our lodge experience over a period of days confirmed their generosity.

The extreme droughts of our climate change era have birthed other forms of creativity in building lodges. We have designed lodges that can be built with milled cedar that can be transported from place to place. In the Earthtribe, that has been our practice in recent years in order to avoid cutting willows and other saplings struggling for life during extended periods of little or no rain.

Currently, we are experimenting with sustainable bamboo. I located a local patch of bamboo, and the keepers of the land gladly allowed me to cut back what they considered to be unruly invaders.

At first, the bamboo was challenging likely because the shoots didn't like the label of trash trees given to them by locals. Also, the bamboo didn't bend easily. After soaking a few days gently in water and after

I apologized for the derogatory words directed toward them, they slowly gave their permission to grace us with a beautiful framework.

Ordinarily, Bear Heart engaged in what he called *healing lodges* for our Earthtribe. A warrior-like endurance in these healing lodges is not the focus, though they can be really hot. Earthtribe lodge experiences usually do not last more than an hour and a half since people who come to the ceremony may be quite vulnerable and are new to the process.

Even though we have been practicing these ceremonies for decades, we are sensitive to the needs of the most vulnerable persons because the experience is, indeed, powerful medicine. The ceremony is not to be engaged without the presence of trained elders.

The lodge on this vision quest in New Mexico was an anomaly. Mostly full-blooded native shaman were in attendance, and they had grown up with this practice. Bear Heart mentioned to me that I needed to brace myself for a different kind of experience, but I didn't really know what I was in for.

We entered the lodge at 5:00 p.m., a fact I knew because they asked me to remove my watch and put it on the earthen altar in front of the lodge, sometimes called *unci*.

The rock carriers invited me to doff my bathing suit and explained that this particular, shamanic lodge required us to return to our "birthday suits." It was about 60 degrees F and quite pleasant for a spring day, so I gladly stripped and put my cloths in a pile outside.

Sweating nude was a bit odd to me but interesting. Occasionally, we sweat in the nude in the Earthtribe, but our usual practice is to wear bathing suits or other loose clothing. Since we are hybrids and not pure bloods and since it is a new experience for many of the participants, we go slowly.

All of the rocks in this particular vision lodge I describe were volcanic extrusive and simply called "sweat lodge rocks" by the elders. When the rock carriers brought in the rocks, they were glowing red. Bear Heart announced to us that, since we thought we were advanced in our shamanic training, we would need to burn through our pride.

The heat was intense; our arrogance was large. His intent was to stretch the strongest beyond their endurance in order to call forth our warrior abilities. This approach was very different from the healing lodges, which focused on working with vulnerability.

Many layers of skin peeled off as the fiery rocks burned through my resistance. When the first door opened, I saw it was already dark outside. By the time we completed the other three doors, I had reached a complete openness but was hanging on by a thread.

I barely noticed that seasoned medicine people crawled out of the lodge until there were only a few of us left. For at least half of the lodge, I lay on the ground breathing in the searing heat so that my lungs felt on fire. On several occasions, I made a move to leave.

This ceremony completely humbled me. I cried. Death hovered. I thought of Thomas Aquinas' line: "humility is truth." That virtue never appealed to me, but here I was lying prostrate before the powers.

Years later, cancer visited my loved ones. Aging grabbed me by the shirt. Massive storms—energized by climate change—washed over me, sent swirling waters into our houses, and left me agog. This intense ceremony prepared me to engage the mighty forces of Nature by lying on the ground and acknowledging the mystery; how little I know; how fragile we humans are.

Still, Earth's arms seemed to hold me steady. The cool soil nurtured my fears until they quieted.

At last, the final door opened, and I dragged myself out of the lodge, coming out feet first as Bear Heart instructed. I lay on the ground, shivering. Later, I learned that the temperature had fallen precipitously below freezing. I picked up my watch from the altar and was shocked to see it was after 11:00 p.m.

We had been in the lodge for over six hours.

Something nudged me on my left ribs as I lay near my clothes with little interest in putting them on, and I heard Bear Heart's gruff voice, "You still alive?"

Then, he laughed, poked me again with his big toe, and continued, "Best to get up and go find your vision site."

Stumbling, I found my clothes and put them on as best I could. Looking around, I hoped for some help in locating my vision circle. Some eight hours before, I had selected a specific landscape for my prayer ties that looked toward the breasts of the Mother in the distant peaks.

Chest high juniper bushes, spring sage, and Thompson's yucca outlined the place I had chosen for the vision site. It had been easy to locate my site in the late afternoon before I had crawled into the sweat lodge. But now, as midnight approached and the temperatures plummeted below freezing, finding my way seemed a monumental task.

The walk from my site to the lodge in an afternoon of sunshine was only about 30 minutes, a pleasant meander in the bright warmth. But after the intense sweat lodge, I now realized the inky traverse over strange mountainous terrain—lighted only by a half moon and my jiggling flashlight—presented a major challenge to my trans-ordinary state of consciousness.

Somehow, I brought in my usual state of surviving to shake hands with this shamanic state to form a partnership in finding my circle.

Or so I hoped.

Looking around for help again, I saw I was all alone.

On another vision quest, where Bear Heart and I worked together in the Sierra Nevada Mountains, a woman selected a site on a ledge overlooking a small canyon. Disoriented, she took a tumble that resulted in minor injuries.

Coupled with the experience I described above and her fall, I knew beginning vision questers needed more assistance. This help was especially crucial for those who were not accustomed to this form of rugged meditation.

As the Earthtribe would unfold over the next three decades, we linked each quester with one or more supporters whose task it was to know where the vision site is located, to accompany the quester to the site, but not to interfere with the privacy and value of solitude.

In our emerging version of this practice, the quester is settled into their circle, and then the supporters respectfully leave. The vision supporters learn much in expressing love and guidance without drifting into a co-dependence so rampant in our culture.

I also would learn how to support questers energetically without being physically present. Through the years, Bear Heart and I would smoke the sacred pipe in meditation at 10:00 p.m., midnight, 2:00 a.m., and 4:00 a.m. He was a resolute holder of vision space during those times.

For decades thereafter, I held the space in the way he taught me, but, as I pushed into my elder years, I saw the need to train other pipe carriers to offer a distributed mode of support.

Nowadays, I join the circle in the tipi at 2:00 a.m. to 4:00 a.m., and, often Grandfather Bear joins us from his place in the Milky Way to co-create an *eternal now*. This point in nonlocality offers support to the questers.

Back in time and in New Mexico, I trundled toward the vision site with a view of moonlight on the mountain breasts. Earlier, I had used them as a visual to guide me to my circle, but, in the dark, I could see only faint outlines.

I knew I was in trouble.

A moderate state of hypothermia hovered. I was shivering and confused. I put on my jacket with an awareness that I needed to increase my body temperature. My training and preparation told me that my body temperature was plunging toward 95 degrees F, close to a danger zone.

Strangely, I observed and diagnosed myself while at the same time being submerged in vulnerability. My walking labored as I stumbled along. I shined the flashlight on my fingers, and they were an odd, blueish color.

I blinked, and talked aloud, placing one foot in front of the other, the way I might have when stopped by a policeman to check if I was driving under the influence.

At the bottom of my resources, I let go and grasped for Spirit's hand.

Bear Heart had told me the quest was a little bit of death, a training experience for the real thing. In the 1970s television series, *Sanford and Son*, Redd Fox often thought he was dying of a heart attack and uttered a humorous phrase, "Oh, Elizabeth, this is the big one; I'm coming to join you." As I walked, it felt like I was on the bridge to the big one.

At long last, I saw the sleeping bag I had put down in the afternoon, a green one that had a stale smell. I lifted the string of prayer ties at a door into the circle; a door is what we call the place where the two ends of the string of prayers meet.

Without further adieu, I collapsed into the bag and zipped it up. I knew seasoned vision questers sat cross-legged, stayed awake, and meditated to raise their body temperature. Not so with me as a novice.

In the face of the larger forces of Nature, I was completely humbled. That trait never appealed to me, yet here I was lying on the ground next to death.

I ducked my head into the bag and breathed, feeling the warmth slowly regenerate me. My clothes were soaked with sweat, so I wiggled them off until I was naked against the stiff green material of the moldy sleeping bag.

After a few moments, my nose surfaced like a river otter swimming in a stream to gain fresh air. Then, with my lungs full of the fresh mountain air to sustain me, I ducked down again to allow my breathing to be a mini-heater. This procedure went on until I returned to a more stable state, near equilibrium.

Most of the night I lay awake. As my body temperature slowly returned to normal, I pulled down the edge of the sleeping bag to gawk unabashedly at the stars. In the last moments before first light, I drifted into a light sleep.

Suddenly, I was awakened by a growling sound. As I adjusted to the first light, I looked directly into the eyes of a ruby-throated hummingbird. It had a bright, startlingly red throat, a black mask that stretched around its head, and a bright green cap.

Although it belonged to the smallest bird tribe on the planet, it hovered in a sublime, cloud of power. I caught fleeting glimpses as it flew away and then back as if to speak with me in a tongue I had lost long ago.

To my amazement, the winged messenger flew backwards, and then forwards. Up and down. Tears welled up from an inner point forgotten, an essence that had been asleep since my days on Rattlesnake Island on Lake Conchas.

My eyes opened wide.

I knew that this was an turnaround moment when the wheel of life rotated like the old tractors from my family land. I basked in an instant of transparent clarity. The humming bird's long beak seemed to reach into and perform mysterious, open-heart surgery.

Unspeakable joy poured forth with exhales of deep breaths. The rotating wings beating over 50 beats per second whirled around my head in speeds that lifted me up where eagles dare to fly. Sacred doors opened, and I slipped through into a nonlocal eternity.

Everything spread before me as a movie of what was to come, for myself as a small part of Earth herself.

I knew I was seeing myself return to a natural identity. Years later, an Earthtriber, Mary Sue, would have a vision and acquire the name *Sees Far*. That name describes my experience. I knew I was part of a Great Returning, an impulse of the Evolutionary Spirit herself. I had glimpses as if through a smoky mirror. Through the smoke I could see Earth Herself was headed toward a mighty balancing, a movement toward a new equilibrium.

And what role would humans have, if any?

14   LODGES OF LOVE

Lying there in my circle in Northern New Mexico, I basked in the arms of a sensual and yet firm Love radiating from the high desert landscape. In the distance, I could see the *Huajatolla*, the breasts of the Great Mother Herself.

I felt profoundly nourished by Her, yet a bit chastened at my naiveté regarding the risks involved in the quest. In spite of it all, I was immersed in a qualitatively different sense of relatedness.

Somewhere, I heard about a person who grew up in institutional religion in the USA. Then, later in life, immersed in an African natural area, she heard the singing of young people, children of the forest. Her heart opened. Touched by grace, she called it.

Asked about the two experiences later, she replied, "When I was growing up in the church of my father, I was offered a glass of water for parched lips. Upon hearing the forest sing through the children, I swam in a sea of love and became water itself."

Both experiences concerned water, but the latter shifted cellular identity.

So, it was for me as the sun peeked over the Mother Mountains. This experience was not my first mystical rodeo with the Numinous, but it was qualitatively different. Different in that the sacred within the actual landscape sought me out.

Yes, I positioned myself by traveling to this eco-field. Fasting helped. Ceremony purified my inner environment and made space for a larger and more sensual Love. That was my part, but, beyond my effort, I was keenly aware that my surroundings were actually interested in me.

"Why?" I asked.

Then, it dawned on me that the systemic array of eco-fields wants humans to wake up so we will cease our destruction and get with the program. A strong message reverberated: you must humble yourself before the powers of Nature.

Was this the key message from the tornado of my youth?

At a primal level, I felt microtubules of my cells fluttering and flowing out like the tentacles of a jelly fish into surrounding water. They were receptacles to a presence reaching into my body through the hovering hummingbird.

I had been sought out and physically touched by the sound of tiny wings, and I knew this presence was none other than the Creator of our Universe. If I had to project a gender assignment to the Divine at that moment, it would most definitely be Feminine.

The reality of that touching, coming from a physical landscape, formed the core truth of my life. I would continue to question many aspects of my experience. I would continue to doubt when life's turns took me into dark alleys. But the force of that connecting went deeper than questions and doubt.

After that astounding encounter, even the questions would turn me toward the sublime.

What if my physical surroundings have an interest in my being larger in my perspective and, paradoxically, humbled by the mysteries of forces at large in Nature?

What if an evolutionary impulse wants to connect me with the natural web in such a way that we humans cease to be its apex?

What if we all are rising out of a sea of consciousness and that consciousness seems, at least in some moments, loving?

And what if in this domain of seeing, feeling, touching, tasting, hearing, smelling, and intuiting the physical world is reaching out to us and through us to all others?

To revisit Jung for a moment, what if archetypal presences outside our psyches utilize the sensual and material to invade and unfold us through dreams, visions, and synchronicities in the interest of evolution itself? [1]

I don't know how long I stayed in the vision circle. Hours? Days? I was not in chronological time. I "lost" my Timex watch, never to find it again or to buy another.

I swam in eternity, or nonlocality as we say in field physics. You know about Einstein's space/time continuum. Because the physical world consists of three dimensions, and time is one dimensional, space/time must be, Einstein surmised, four dimensional. Most 21st century physicists now consider all of our existence to be embedded in a 4-dimensional space/time continuum. [2]

The encounter with hummingbird opened a portal beyond usual length, width, and depth. Then, I moved into Einstein's 4th dimension of the space/time continuum. And even beyond these Einsteinian dimensions, some quantum physicists now hypothesize many more encounters with reality, perhaps as many as ten dimensions. Superstring Theory in newer physics posits that the Universe exists in ten different dimensions. Beyond Einstein's four dimensions, the fifth and sixth dimensions open worlds where possibility arises with increasing clarity.

According to superstring physicists, if we relearned the Mother Tongue and mother perception, we likely could see possible universes unfolding. We could learn more effectively to participate in the manifestation of possibility, especially if we could give up the illusion of our being separated from and better than our surroundings.

As masters of the fifth and sixth dimensions, we could travel back in time or go toward different futures. Seven through ten dimensions take us deeper and deeper in participatory possibility. Does this paragraph taken from scientific inquiry not fit well with many shaman in general, and Bear Heart in particular?[3]

I wasn't thinking about such matters in my vision circle. I was experiencing them, only to reflect later. I swam in nonlocality, a trans-ordinary sea of waves. Wave after wave of love had me holding on to vestiges of ordinary life in the first three dimensions just so I could find my way back to the vision encampment.

And I needed the help of ordinary reality to decipher such a return. To stride back I needed a firm hold on length, width, and depth. One foot in front of the other.

But back to what? To whom? I longed for continued resonance. I knew that much, but I knew little about nature's community building.

Even so, my story was now embedded in the natural order through the gift of hummingbird. What I had sought as a young man at Rattlesnake Island on Lake Conchas was now coming to pass. What was missing in my sojourn into institutional religion, in my doctoral work, and in my psychotherapy practice was now apparent.

The implicate was becoming explicate. My heart and mind overflowed. I longed to share my emerging story and amplify this natural affinity with infinity in community even if I didn't know what that meant.

Time passed in my circle as my fast continued.

I waited for someone to bring me back to human connection. But no one showed up. Finally, I rolled up the long string of prayer ties that constituted the boundary of my vision circle. Gratitude swelled as hummingbirds swirled around me as I packed up my smelly, sleeping bag. Looking around, I gathered my flashlight and a small backpack. I didn't need much stuff.

Despite the fact that I had been in a serious physical crisis during my stay in the vision circle, being embedded in this web of eco-fields was full of psychic resources. I was at the Great Mother's breast. There was enough. I was traveling light; and yet, there was plenty.

This particular vision encampment didn't offer the kind of support where someone came ceremonially to usher me back into the encampment community. I wrinkled my brow, thinking it didn't seem very tribal. I made a note to find a way to re-enter the human world that worked better.

Although still in a trans-ordinary state, the return to the encampment was not difficult. What seemed beyond my reach in the dark of the night after the massive sweat lodge, was now easy. Well, not exactly easy, but doable. All I had to do was follow the sounds of conchs, drums, and singing coming from the vision village.

It was a little like leaving my car in a parking lot on my way to a Friday night football game. On such rare occasions that I attended these games, sounds of bands with school songs and cheer leaders in the distance created goose bumps on my spine and arms.

Such was the case as I neared the vision encampment, only these sounds in New Mexico were different from Friday night football sounds and lights. These were sacred notes from shamanic domains. My inner scientist was delighted; he was experiencing all ten dimensions of the Universe. Or was it unlimited and parallel multi-verses?

Along the way, I met an elder I recognized from the six-hour sweat lodge. I didn't know his name; he didn't have a name tag. But his eyes and hugs came from a place beyond names, a point of being that exists outside rationality and hotel conferences.

He had a red bandana folded neatly and tied around his forehead. His indigenous ears were big, as was his nose. His bottom lip protruded out from his top lip so that his mouth appeared perpetually open.

Around his neck were leather medicine bundles from many vision quests. Cradled in his left arm was a drum which had chevron designs painted in an ochre color as if straight out of a pre-historic cave.

We said nothing as we ambled along, but then I had the urge to tell him about my hummingbird awakening. I opened my mouth to speak, and, to my surprise, he held up his hand as if to say *how*, in a Hollywood rendition of "Indian" encounters.

Only, he was instructing me with this firm gesture to treasure my experience in silence. He did clarify his hand signal, "Save your words for the elder council."

I have thought about this encounter through the decades, and each time I contemplate how he engaged me with compassionate detachment. He was able to connect with and, at the same time, not be drawn into my excited energy. He had no need to talk since we were speaking a lost tongue with our surroundings that filled the space.

Back in camp and under a squat juniper, I sat quietly eating a banana and washing it down with cool water. The electrolytes coursed through and lifted my body as I returned to more usual functioning. After the warmth of the sun gave way to lengthening shadows and a returning chill in the air, an older woman came to usher me to a circle where Bear Heart and other elders sat.

Even in camp chairs their spines were straight, and a smoky haze gathered behind their heads from a ceremonial fire. Seated on a red blanket, I gathered myself, closed my eyes, and took a nice and easy breath.

The sound of a hummingbird buzzed around me with such force that I opened my eyes to see if he had returned to place his beak in my heart once again.

Bear Heart invited me to tell what I had "seen," meaning what had come to me through any number of channels of perception. After I told the elders some of what had transpired, we sat in silence for an extended period.

Finally, Bear Heart spoke, "You will now be called for a leg of your journey, 'Fuswah-enhales-wah,' which means in the Creek language, bird or winged medicine.

"You carry the medicine of wings, and you will be able to heal others and help mend the sacred web with your connection with wings, wind, and starry sky. Wings take you to the stars.

"People will be drawn to the sounds of wings and the fresh air of the sky without even being aware of the magnet that pulls them into your presence. Don't get too excited by their attraction because it is not to you that they come but to the lure of wild things."

He paused, lifted his eyes to the sky, and sang,

Qui-nah yo-we-noh, yunnah hey,
Qui-nah yo-we-noh yunnah hey,
He yah wannah, hey ya-nah
hey nay yo weh!

This was a song sung to the eagle, a close relative of the tiny hummingbird.

He then reached into a leather bag and extracted a sacred pipe, and spoke again, "We gift you this pipe to be carried on behalf of a community of people who will come to you for their own healing and for Grandmother Earth.

"Many lodges will come from these seeds planted here these few days. This is part of a much larger prophesy. Way beyond what you or anyone can see from where we sit today. The ancestors are way out in front, over there beyond pulling us toward them, toward a point that we can only glimpse in moments like these."

In our future times together when we would return to the city, I would argue strongly with Bear Heart against my role in co-creating these lodges of love. My reluctance stemmed from failed experiments in earlier communities that revealed my own limitations.

My previous attempts at spiritual community didn't work out well. But in this moment, in the vision encampment, and in this state of enhanced consciousness, the statements from the elders seemed completely congruent with their visionary experiences and with the prophesies of their tribal fore-parents through the millennia.

Strangely, everything seemed possible; everything I could imagine; everything on the far side consensual reality.

An elder spoke:

"Look. You can see. There is a string of light coming out of our bellies that stretches into the beyond. On the other end, the ancestors are reeling us in, pulling us toward a point when the tribes will become our Mother's tribe that reaches around her belly. You can go kicking and screaming or you can glide, but either way you are going toward a Love that knits us together."

A feeling unlike anything I had ever felt before stirred in my solar plexus and moved up to my chest; I had a willingness to take the next step by relinquishing a white-knuckle hold on the life I had built.

15

TREE SITTING

Our vision encampment woke up the next day to chant, to blow the conch, to drum, and to meditate. Sadly, the time came to leave.

In a profound daze, I crawled into my rental car, a maroon Chevy, to drive back to Albuquerque via Taos with a plan of hopping a plane to Houston. The dirt road, which was not much more than a deer trail, led out of the encampment. It twisted and turned, and challenged my driving skills which were not yet up to par; they were stored away in a practical ego that seemed far, far away.

I was flying by the seat of my pants or, more accurately, by the seat of my soul; I was soaring high on winged medicine.

The primary ego functions in my inner council that pay the bills and drive my car had been gently ushered to the edges to make room for a much larger identity inspired by the wilderness. These primary selves had not had the microphone for some time, either with internal chatter or to link with the cultural world.

In the language of the vision encampment, they had not had their turn with the talking stick, so they were not activated. These sub-flows of my interior were not entirely pleased with the new developments in my visionary life. My inner conservatives thought the whole Bear Heart enterprise quite odd and, perhaps, detrimental to my professional career, my finances, and maybe even my marriage.

On my way out of the small canyon, I felt lost in the simple act of finding the highway. The road I drove on wound through desert brush, and had divergent trails. Turning off the ignition, I rolled down the windows, took a robust whiff of the late morning air, and contemplated which fork to take.

Off to my left in a pinyon pine, a brilliant dot of blue appeared. A bird with predominately azure plumage and a reddish brown breast stared at me intently. Then, it flew off to another tree with its feet extended in a landing motion to the next branch. With tactile flare it seemed to invite me to follow.

This elusive guidance was not from the invisible world but the very visible. Such a fusion of the invisible and visible seemed to be a hallmark of primal wisdom.

It was gradually dawning on me that this eco-spiritual approach did not invite me to escape from the material world in order to be spiritual. It entreated me not only to honor the world all around me but to notice that my surroundings displayed an inclination to participate in my direction.

Could it be, I asked myself, that the way to enlightenment is not to push away from the sensual but rather to embrace the beauty of trees, spring water, and colorful birds? I had tried many approaches that encouraged me to be suspicious of attaching to the world. Now, here was an opening that told me it was through aware connection that l would find love and liberation.

This path told me the human problem was not attachment but not enough aware attachment.

Open all senses to the subtleties around and specific messages will come through, so these experiences seemed to be saying. Everything in the material world was emerging out of a deeper consciousness of Spirit and moved with energetic and connective vitality.

Later, I would realize that I was enmeshed in the neural pathways of the extended brain of Earth Herself, and what I was experiencing was the electrical firing of the electro-magnetic field coursing through the synaptic linkages of the bird and me.

So this is what prayer feels like, I thought, as I watched the blue bird. Prayer in musty buildings guided by dusty books didn't work for me. But intimate linking with my feathered friend?

This felt like prayer.

As I looked around, the trees, the birds, the insects, the grass, the sky, and the mountains all seemed not only to radiate wisdom but actually to function as a brain.

One day, I would call these surroundings an eco-field. Later still, I would call this connective tissue exchange within a neural system an *eco-brain*. A phrase came to me, a catchy one: my ego-brain is actually an eco-brain.

Starting the car, I followed the flashing blue, saying to myself, "This must be Winged Medicine, this affinity with Infinity through a tiny bird. That's why the vision gave me the name, *Fus-wah-enhales-wah*."

The fear of not finding my way on the animal trails suggested a much larger anxiety which had coursed through me like a virus from mainstream culture for much of my life. In this moment of alliance with the blue bird, my anxiety was now disappearing, or, at least, fading as I experienced myself in an infinite context.

A vision song would eventually come to me:

The blue bird comes
And I let go
Of all those fears
I cherish so.
I am no longer so depressed;
Instead I'll dance my vision quest.

Astonishingly, the blue bird led me directly to a numbered highway, and I was sure I had discovered some sort of spiritual GPS system. I mused that I now had powers beyond common sense, reason, and even imagination in connecting with a natural order underneath the disorder of my ordinary life.

Being in a trans-ordinary state allowed me to speak a Mother Tongue understood by the eco-field and its creatures such as blue birds and hummingbirds.

I was beginning to think I was special.

Later, a profound shock hit me as I learned that much of my life would continue in a state of hazy fog. My usual life patterns allowed only glimpses into the dimensions of possibility described by Super String physicists and backwoods shaman. Literacy in the Mother Tongue of the eco-fields was a long way in the distance for me, maybe not even in my lifetime.

Even so, I seemed to be held in the hands of a Great Mysterious on that beautiful day. I was a neuron firing together with the blue bird and the mountains until we wired together in profound community. Neurons that fire together, wire together, as they say.

And in one glorious sequence of moments we were wired through a common language!

Before I knew it, I was on the outskirts of Taos. When I was fasting during the previous days of questing, images of food came on occasion. In my vision circle, food had lost its central place in my awareness. But, as I passed the village sign for Taos, I could almost smell the sausage at a restaurant called Michael's Kitchen and Bakery, which I knew was just down the road.

I first came to Taos when I was four years old in 1944, so I had watched it grow over many visits from a rustic village to a posh destination with cultural buzz. As a child and as an adult, I loved this little spot and visited frequently.

On a summer trip in 1974, Judith and I noticed a brand new breakfast place opening called Michael's, and we became regulars when in the area. So, now, some years later and coming out of a profound vision space, I hankered after my favorite dish.

Once inside the restaurant, I was seated alone in a wooden chair with a hard bottom that put added pressure on a back sore from days of sitting on the ground. My mouth watered as the waitress brought out a plate of pancakes sprinkled with powdered sugar, bananas, pecans, and orange slices.

Boy, had I been waiting for this!

The sugar and sausage beckoned to initiate me back into mainstream culture. The ingredients seduced me with a carbo high. To my surprise, I could eat only a few bites. My visionary soul was still close to the surface and simply did not want the same food craved by my usual set of selves.

The sugar and visionary highs didn't mix well. Had I been freed of carb compulsions? Not really, but freedom from these addictive urges would increase in frequency. But not so close that I could regard myself as liberated.

Not wanting that plate of food was just the first in a series of adjustments as I sought a new equilibrium in making room for an identity as Winged Medicine, *Fus-wah-en-hasles-wah.*

Judith and I lived and worked in the Montrose neighborhood of Houston in a townhouse on 1212 Kipling Street. The culture shock between the distant mountains and the inner city was jolting. An assignment given by Bear Heart to assist in next steps in the journey rattled around in my head, or, more accurately, in my heart.

"Find yourself a tree and sit," he said, "Eventually people will be attracted to explore. When that happens, let me know, and we can talk about having a lodge gathering. We are called to establish lodges of love, and your vision tells me you are hearing such a call."

That dictum made perfect sense in the ambience of the New Mexico encampment, but, in a teeming city, I questioned its validity.

Trees were everywhere in a subtropical Houston, famous for its plethora of plant life. A few blocks away were several parks and a university rife with ancient oaks, but, for some reason, I was attracted to a small magnolia tree near the parking lot of my office.

At the office location of 1107 Marshall street, the tree was handy since it was just a couple of blocks away from where I lived. For the next period of time—maybe a year or so—I sat under the tree nearly every day. Waiting. Waiting the way Bear Heart had taught me. Well, not exactly to his specifications. Much impatience and doubt accompanied my waiting.

Marshall Street was a side road that ran east to west, and the corner street was Graustark, which ran north and south. Eventually, I used the north/south/east/west axis as a way to practice the first four directions of a cross-cultural Medicine Wheel. Sometimes, my sitting was noteworthy but, most times, boring and hard on my back. I didn't feel very spiritual, mostly grumbling to myself.

People driving by occasionally honked while I held my breath until the exhaust fumes faded. Walkers glanced at me and sometimes offered a greeting.

In the beginning, there was little or no attractor force being generated as Bear Heart had promised, nothing magnetic or magic. No one ever showed up at the tree, which was a big disappointment since I had imagined an alluring power that would immediately provide potential lodge participants.

Slowly, however, conversations about an Earth-based spirituality gained traction, but not at the tree as I had imagined. Mostly, my fellow psychotherapists, clients, students, and academics noticed something different in my demeanor and asked questions.

Some of them saw me sitting at the tree and were curious. The presence and wisdom of not only this small tree but also the urban forest seeped into my being, and percolated through my relationships. The magnetic language of the urban forest filtered through my conversations. It didn't fit my magical expectations, but was effective.

Eventually, the trees in this system of urban eco-fields caused an epistemological crisis in my worldview with the raising of simple questions.

Could plants actually figure into and influence all of life, including the therapeutic process in my professional practice? Could they be my co-workers?

During this period of my clinical practice, a number of professionals noticed that I worked well with people who were labeled with serious psychiatric diagnoses. Disorders like schizophrenia, borderline disorder, bi-polar disorder, various phobias, severe addictions, and acute depression were common with some but not all of my clients.

The more I worked with people who engaged in these monumental struggles, the more I learned from them. It dawned on me that carrying a serious diagnosis sometimes meant that the person had an opportunity for larger possibility. The emotional suffering seemed to be soil out of which brilliance sometimes emerged. This potential increased if I could learn how to get out of the way and allow natural healing to occur.

Truth be known, the academic and mental health community knows little about the healing of schizophrenia and other serious diagnoses, most of which may be diseases of Western Civilization. Chemical disturbance within the neural system often is a by-product of a more basic estrangement of culture that manifests in the individual.

Many indigenous peoples of the pre-1492 Americas embraced persons with these idiosyncrasies through ceremony in such a way that they tended to find their place of usefulness in the tribe.

Bear Heart and I had talked about such cases that he believed could be knitted together within the ceremonial fabric of a nature-based community. But I had not seen his tribe in action at the time, so I had my doubts.

Even though skeptical, I ventured into experimenting with correlating some of my clients with the sacred web of plants and engaged the hypothesis that their internal system would do better if connected with various life-forms outside the human network.

Even before I met Bear Heart, I had selected an office that brought the outdoors inside through a large floor to ceiling window; I liked to sit near this plate glass window that looked out into a beautiful courtyard with a majestic, native pecan tree and ivy ground cover. In the distance, I could see the magnolia tree where I sat and meditated each morning.

I hung a potted plant overhead with a hook on an air conditioning vent so that it dangled above my head as a connector with the plant world. Even though I didn't really believe at the time that the surrounding eco-field was the principle source of healing, I still felt enlivened by the plants.

So, now you have a backstory for me to tell you about a client I will call "Jonathan." Typically, he sat near the door where he could escape any intimacy such as eye contact that might occur.

On the day I have in mind for our story, he was going on and on in a completely nonsensical expression of himself. I sensed he was listing in a direction of increased schizophrenic gibberish, if not a psychotic break.

Gripped with my own vulnerability, I abruptly sat forward in the chair to move closer to see if there was something I could do or say that might move him in a more creative, sane direction. As I lurched forward, the Danish modern rocking chair I sat on slipped out from under me; it had rockers made of stainless steel runners that easily slipped on the carpet.

I threw my arms up in the air to gain balance and hit the potted plant hanging over my head. It subsequently pulled loose from the hook in the A/C vent, fell a few precipitous feet, and hit me in the head.

Then the ceramic bowl broke, cut my head superficially, and dumped garden soil and plant roots, first on my head, then onto my lap, and finally to the floor.

Completely bumfuzzled, I started to laugh and laugh until I myself was near hysteria. Wiping the debris from my face, I finally looked up to see what Jonathan was doing.

I expected him to be in a tizzy. Clinical terms were not on the tip of my tongue at the moment or even now as a description. To my great surprise, he was sitting up straight in his chair and the schizoid look in his eyes was replaced with a clarity I had not seen before.

For the next forty-five minutes, he talked with adult and aware acumen. He made concrete plans to move out from the apartment behind his parent's house, spoke of the possibility of a job, and wrote me a check for the session, an activity he usually left to his mother.

Harry Golishian, a well known senior psychologist in the Galveston/Houston area, was my supervisor at the time, and I couldn't wait to tell him how the plant had helped mend my schizophrenic client. The two of us participated in grand rounds at a local medical school, and Harry told the story with great relish as part of his presentation.

In the middle of the story, Harry started to laugh and said with a wry smile, "Hell, William, somebody in the room had to have some semblance of sanity. It certainly wasn't you. There is only so much craziness that can go around in a system at one time."

It was not exactly the success story that I had imagined I would achieve with this stellar group.

A month or so later Bear Heart came to spend time with Judith and me for a few days to assist in the unfolding of my tree sitting. Like my senior psychologist supervisor, he started laughing before the story was completed. Unlike Harry, he had a completely different take on what happened that reached outside the therapist/client relational system.

"Plants have intelligence but not like ours," he started out, "The real messages were coming from the pecan tree and the ground cover ivy, as well as the magnolia tree where you were sitting.

"They could see you were not getting anywhere with your client. They had compassion for you and Jonathan and set up a council to see how they could assist. Your friendly little plant volunteered to sacrifice its comfort in its house and fell on you to wake you up to a much larger view of things.

"I can imagine that big pecan tree is still telling all of her neighbors about the good doctor who finally figured out how to help his client."

These comments sent me into research mode to address how such a nested communication might take place.

In a more extensive research project reported in my book, *The Mother Tongue: Intimacy in the Eco-field*, an eco-field is defined as a space configuration in which there is a network of information and meaning exchanged between all aspects of the ecosystem, under the knowing umbrella of a specific landscape.

Hold that definition for a moment and consider your brain as a tuning device into fields of information all around us. Neuroscientists have been tracking the brain. The research has moved our understanding from a gray mass in the skull, to locating neural cells in the heart, in the intestinal tract, and in other parts of the body as well.

There is, for example, a long neural cell that extends down the spine, or say some researchers.

Some biologists such as Rupert Sheldrake even suggest that our brains extend into the fields around us in what he calls morphic resonance, a kinship with all forms in our surroundings, even trees and potted plants.[1]

We have within our brains roughly thirteen trillion neural cells. If you look at a neural cell under certain conditions, it looks something like a jelly fish with thousands of wispy tentacles called microtubles, waving out from the cell as if to connect with all that surrounds.

Stuart Hameroff, M.D., professor of Medicine and Director of the Center for Consciousness Studies at the University of Arizona, gives us solid clues about how our bodies tune into fields for the exchange and expansion of consciousness through these microtubules.[2]

Microtubules are part of the cytoskeleton of all cells. They are hollow cylinders about 270 angstroms in diameter. An angstrom is a unit of length equal to 10^{-10} power or one ten billionth of a meter.

In other words, they are tiny guys.

They move in mysterious, rhythmic ways within the cell. They are outliers moving along the edge of cellular membranes. They are like ancient shaman living at the edge of the tribe acting as links and channels for larger consciousness seeking entry. They dissolve and reappear, yet remain active in the cell membrane.

Is it possible that the microtubules are part of the wave/particle process moving constantly within us seeking to reach out to the eco-fields all around? Are the microtubules dancing rhythmically with the wave/particle continuum?

As we see them microscopically, are we perceiving a form of the quantum field motion in our own bodies? Are we all potential shaman in a dancing movement between energetic domains?

And, as such, are we neural cells firing within a larger eco-brain lost to us because we live with the illusion that we only have an ego-brain?

Through the years my research has taken me further and further into the science of quantum fields and bio-resonators as a way to understand what was happening on an experiential level with my shamanic training.

An evolutionary propulsion sent me in the direction of introducing these shamanic experiences with plants to my inner scientist. The growth of these two sides of myself provided a creative tension that would be reflected in the forming of a community—the Earthtribe—prophesied by Bear Heart and other shaman within the council in the shadow of the *Huajatolla*.

The future seemed to be throwing out filaments of light to reel us toward itself in the birthing of a community of fellow Bridge Walkers.

16   TRIBAL BIRTHING

With fear and trembling, I invited a few people who had shown interest to come on a Sunday evening to my office to consider participating in an *inipi*, a sweat lodge ceremony.

After extensive conversations with Bear Heart, we decided that several months of preparation would be needed to make sure there was proper respect and also to provide safety for participants who were largely new to such primordial ceremonies.

Sometimes, Bear Heart facilitated other forms of sweat lodge experiences for beginning people that did not require such extensive preparation, but, in this case, we aspired to build an ongoing community and needed to lay the groundwork with considerable awareness.

Assisting in birthing an ongoing, Earth-based community consisting of a variety of wisdom traditions was new to Bear Heart, as well as for me. We were feeling our way, dreaming into the task, following our visions as best we could. We knew we were up to something big, but little did we realize how big.

Our gathering place for interested persons was a psychotherapeutic group room at my office on Marshall Street in Houston. Sitting on pillows and worn, yellow shag carpeting popular at the time, we covered an energetic theme from one of the cardinal directions each Sunday evening.

At the time, I only knew a few songs, so we concentrated on them. We punctuated our chanting with drumming and the blowing of an ancient conch shell that had been passed down in my family of origin through the generations for healing.

The people attracted to this core energy field of possibility consisted of friends, Center for Creative Resources staff, clients, health professionals, and local psychotherapists. Various religions and wisdom traditions were represented including Judaism, Christianity, Buddhism, and a contingent who claimed no religious affiliation.

A few sojourners had varying percentages of Native American blood, but most were simply American hybrids, mongrels as it were. We were learning that love is thicker than blood, or it seemed that way to us.

Bear Heart was criticized by some of his fellow indigenous elders for sharing the sacred ceremonies and other ways with *wascinas* or even mixed bloods, but he had been called by Spirit to disseminate the wisdom as part of a prophesy that all the races would come together at a crucial time in Earth's evolution.

He emphasized that while the Euro-American culture had inflicted terrible crimes on "Indians," the time was nigh for the races and cultures to converge and become part of the natural web once again. We couldn't quite express it, but returning human consciousness to the web was part of "the something big" we were up to.

There had been a time, he taught, for the careful guarding of traditions, but now was a moment to drill deeper through the various cultures to the bedrock or essence of Spirit's manifestation in Nature.

If the USA would simply acknowledge in some official way the genocide perpetuated on the indigenous people of the Western Hemisphere, it would go a long way to healing the wounds. But, short of that miracle, we were to proceed in our local gatherings as embodiments of a new possibility of love.

In this way, we could prepare for very dark times that were to come as Earth moved through a passageway from what his friends, the Hopi, called the 4th World to the 5th World.

Paul and Annette Sofka participated in these communal gatherings at my office and graciously offered us a landscape setting for the lodge near Manvel, Texas. Situated south of Houston in what then was a rural area but now is a populated suburb, the web of eco-fields there consisted of a sacred grove that contained yaupon, hardwoods, and a small bayou-like stream, aptly called Mustang Bayou.

In the distance was a working oil field and neighbors who would, after a few years, complain about our drumming, singing, and chanting and send us to more secluded land. But for the time being, it seemed a heavenly home.

The day approached when our seed tribe would gather for the first time. At the last minute, Bear Heart let me know he had invited two women from North Carolina to be his assistants, and they graciously agreed to travel at their own expense to be part of this birthing. At first, we were grateful for their participation even though we knew nothing about them.

Little did I know the tension they would create.

Having already been trained in the building of the physical sweat lodge with Bear Heart's guidance, I was now prepared to take several of the would-be participants to nearby creeks in search of white willows, the preferred saplings for many tribes.

This trek to connect with and cut willows or other willing trees would become an essential practice in our learning how to interact with the plant world without dominating. We soaked the willows for some-time in anticipation of the big day. With considerable effort we sank shovels into the middle of the lodge and lifted dirt from the hole we dug; sometimes this hole is called a *sipapau*, an opening into the womb of Mother Earth.

Then, we emptied the shovels of dirt a few steps from the front door of the lodge. As part of the ceremony, we cut pieces of the willow tree to make an altar in front of the *inipi* or sweat lodge.

We placed part of the cut wood that made a Y on two sides of the altar with a connecting limb in the fresh dirt. At Bear Heart's suggestion, we called this focal point an *Unci* or *oon-chee*, which translates loosely as *grandmother*.

To our great surprise, one of these cut limbs that we put in the *Unci* began to grow and sprout leaves over the years. Decades later, Paul Sofka came to visit us in our Hill Country retreat and reported that the tiny limb we placed in the ground that beginning day had flourished on its own and was now a tree some 20' tall.

It seems that the good energy of the lodge nourished it, and, when it came time to leave the Sofkas, it continued to grow as a testament to the goodwill of the day.

Only, it was not all pleasant or easy.

We arrived at the Sofkas near sunrise on the first day our tribe was to gather, did about twenty of us. Right away we danced into a heart-shaped circle. All went well with Bear Heart, who was in his usual jovial form, until his assistants began questioning the women present one by one to see if they were currently in the midst of their menstruation cycle. They called it the *moon way*.

Only one of our women was in the moon condition, and the assistants told her that she could not come into the lodge. I was shocked, and the women present, as well as quite a few of the men, were incensed.

It is possible that Bear Heart had mentioned such a gender distinction, but, at the time, it seemed like news to me. It certainly was to the group.

Keep in mind this was the very early 1980s, and the women present were nearly all part of a robust feminist movement, and not just
marginally so. When the two assistants escorted our cherished sister to
a "moon hut" to sit out the day, we were saddened and angry. We didn't
understand what was happening.

Several of us—men and women—left the main circle and went to
sit with her.

It was not so much that we were disrespectful as ignorant of a
tradition practiced by many but not all tribes. Later, Bear Heart would
offer his framework for making such a discernment that stretched back
to his tribal practice.

"During her moon time, a woman is going through her own natural purification process. While that deep purification is occurring, the
spirits are renewing her energies and powers. She is being both restored
and cleansed.

"This purification process is so profound that she has untold powers, so much so that her process can draw power away from the *inipi*.
Men do not have Nature's purification built into their bodies, so they
must enter the lodge on a monthly cycle if they are to do the kind of
work I am teaching. It is different for women. They can also go into the
purification lodge, but it is a support to the natural bodily functioning."

Bear Heart could see I was confused, vulnerable, and doubtful. He
paused and continued to a concluding statement.

"Far from being disrespectful of women, it is our ultimate respect
for the significance of their biological and spiritual pathway that we observe in this practice. There are many ceremonies men and women have
in our tribe that are separate from each other, but that in no way disre-
spects women. Do you understand?"

Letting him know that I respectfully heard him but didn't know
about the understanding part, I then asked him if he was interested in
my point-of-view and that of the people attending. He was. In the days

following, we had numerous conversations. I told him I needed to describe the emotional climate of our women and men that he may or may not have in his awareness.

While his tribe had these practices in their consciousness and had millennia to digest them, we were new to such ways. He would also have to respect our point-of-view if we were to have a tribe of love. Love means respecting all the traditions and finding an integral pathway.

I continued:

"This is a moment when women in our group are in no mood to be dismissed. *Time* magazine a couple of years ago awarded its 'Man of the Year' award to 'American Women'. The women in our gathering are extremely sensitive to a patriarchal society; they view our new tribe as offering a pathway to liberation, not subservience to a new set of patriarchs.

"They easily can interpret the moon lodge as another example of men degrading women, especially outside the milieu that you just gave me."

"The women present at our gathering stand in a long line of American women crying for a vision that includes an Equal Rights Amendment to the constitution. Many have fought hard to get this amendment passed.

"Keep in mind they have just been slapped in the face by the Republican Party which removed ERA support from its platform, and the country is still unwilling to guarantee women constitutional rights equal to those of men. Just before we gathered for the lodge, the ERA had been introduced to Congress once again, only to be voted down."

I could tell that Bear Heart was taking in my burst of thoughts and feelings with considerable reflection. I always had the sense that he was deeply present, especially when our cultures clashed, and we disagreed.

I continued:

"And then there is Roe vs. Wade. Let me tell you a bit about my history with this important women's rights case because it pertains to the gender questions that have risen in the confluence of our two cultures.

"Although Texas is sometimes seen as a conservative state, it is famous for its powerful women, not the least of whom is Sarah Ragle Weddington, the principal attorney in the Roe vs. Wade case. Sarah is the daughter of Doyle Ragle, a Methodist minister I knew from my days as a Methodist clergy person. The Ragle family originated in a farming community a few miles from where I grew up, and we shared a common soil in our crops and our spiritual inclinations.

"Also, Sarah and I both attended McMurry University, a small Methodist college in Abilene, Texas. Although we were not friends since I was five years older than she, our college careers did overlap. With that connection, I followed her legal career closely. She not only has been one of my heroes, but, more importantly, she is a hero of many of the women in the lodge and also of my two daughters."

I glanced at Bear Heart to see if he was still with me since I was chasing rabbits a bit to let him know about our strong response to the isolation of one of our women in the group's first sweat lodge. He continued to be with me, and I diverted a bit further to make sure he heard the depth of the tension the moon lodge had unveiled.

"Sarah appeared before the Supreme Court in 1971. Then in January of 1973 the Supreme Court of the United States handed down its decision, overturning Texas' abortion law and legalizing abortion within the first trimester of a woman's pregnancy.

"The mainstream culture of Texas is frequently represented by a male dominant legislature that consistently finds itself at variance with the United States Constitution as interpreted by our Supreme Court."

I was aware that I was in lecture modality but couldn't stop myself, "You see where I am going, Bear Heart? Your tradition is important, and, at the same time, we are treading on the ground here in Texas where you have a conservative and repressive male population and a vigorous tradition of women who won't sit down and shut up. And far be it from me to ask them to do that very thing. Especially when none of us had any context for the moon practice that was sprung on us without notice."

I was hot under the collar.

In a characteristic gesture, Bear Heart reached down and picked up a couple of pebbles and jiggled them back and forth for a few minutes, saying nothing. He was probably waiting for me to cool down, which I was doing because he was receptive to my perspective.

Then, he replied, "Well, my helpers from North Carolina were probably too enthusiastic and not tuned in to the women in the circle. Can you see that my tribe comes from an entirely different place? We see you *wascina* as really not respecting women and their biology.

"Is it possible that you don't grasp the power of moon time? I just want you to value these practices without dismissing them out-of-hand. Will you do that?"

I had to chew on that for a few minutes as we walked before I replied. It seemed our relationship hung in that moment.

"I definitely will. I don't pretend to know the depths of your practices. This is precisely why I value our friendship. You need to know also that I will take this situation to our fledgling council which is mostly women, including Judith who is a vigorous feminist.

"We must value where they are, as well. I will go with what the decision of the council is. Like the Iroquois Federation, we will follow the vote of the women themselves so they manage what is done with their bodies. Can we continue with that understanding?"

Bear Heart slapped me on the back and laughed, "I guess that's what we can expect from a group of mongrels such as yourself. Sure, let's see what Spirit unfolds."

For several weeks, our fledgling tribe of hybrids discussed the two traditions, led by Judith and Jyl Scott-Reagan, a woman who would become a principal leader in The Earthtribe. We decided for the women to convene and decide what to do when we gathered.

Bear Heart never brought it up again, nor did he ever ask women if they were menstruating. Over the next decade, we shared hundreds of sweat lodges together, and women were never again asked to go to a moon lodge.

We had found an uneasy common ground that respected both cultures. I am aware that many tribal traditionalists criticized Bear Heart vigorously for opening some of the traditions to mixed races, various traditions, and even mainstream culture.

On the other hand, sometimes the Earthtribe has been taken to task for being too heavily weighted toward women's rights and the Sacred Feminine.

Yet, we were finding our way together. Birthing a tribe from the profound interaction of different world views was sometimes painful. From the first major ceremonial gathering, it was becoming clear to me that we were engaged in a new flowering of Mother Earth, the Sacred Feminine. This birthing would have to emerge from the intertwining of ancient cultures whose practices seemed strange to us.

Ancestral Bear Heart seems to be here in the room with me. He smiles at a picture I have of him when he was a world champion fancy dancer as a teenager. Across the room, I have an oil painting of him when I was interacting with him on a regular basis.

I ask him, "Does it seem disrespectful to tell our readers about some of the tensions that crept into our relationship? How will your Muskogee/Creek tribal members react when they discover that we didn't follow the moon lodge tradition, at least to the nth degree?

I recall that sometimes you were criticized by organizations who saw you as co-operating with 'spiritual colonizing.' Are you OK with how we are evolving?"

He responds:

"From the vantage of the far edges of the Milky Way, the big test is Love. Sure, we had our disagreements, and still do. Open your eyes, Will, change and decay all around you. Chaos too. So far you haven't told them about the prophesies which are not pleasant to hear. The ones that tell us for thousands of years that this time was coming.

"So, yes. Confusion. But underneath is the Love that is much bigger than these practices you mention here. We talked about lodges of love. We talked about the yearning for communities that are deeply connected with the movements and cycles of Nature.

"We talked about healing people of fear and disjointed connections with creatures and plants. We talked about how this healing is part and parcel of the larger healing. So, with that backdrop Love takes many forms."

I am now seven decades into a cycle of life that gives perspective to our differences, and Bear Heart has the advantage of the vantage point of the eternal now and nonlocality.

But the Will and Bear Heart of this 1980's story did not move so easily through the tensions.

17   STRETCHING THE RAWHIDE

We come to a phase of our story that challenged me.

By "phase," I mean a slowly growing tension between me and Bear Heart as we pushed deeper into our various idiosyncrasies, closer to our souls. Such tension is par for the course, normal development in the energetic unfolding of any relationship, especially since we came from such different backgrounds. Gradually, we experienced points of constriction.

Our rough spots kept pointing me to a key question inherent in any long-term community. It was a question that I had avoided in other attempts at forming an intimate network.

How do you resolve tension and conflict?

All communities rise and fall on that question. Most relationships that fail do so as the relational ship crashes on the rocks of conflict and unresolved tension.

Notice, I said, "Unresolved." Tension is normal and necessary, but not too much. Balancing the tautness is key. A golf teacher once told me that you have to hold the club with the tension you use in holding a delicate bird. You hold the bird firm enough to keep it from flying away but not so tight that you hurt it.

In the Earthtribe, we speak of the coyote as a trickster who plays tricks on us to keep us loose and to jar us out of the rigid patterns of our everyday personalities.

And herein is a large trick: our Creator asks us to pick up the bird and hold it firmly while at the same time relaxing without hurting it. Vitality in life grows out of our ability to balance tension and relaxation. This paradox seems central to the fabric of the Universe itself, certainly to intimate relationships. The key is to live in vital balance.

After a long period of harmony, Bear Heart and I stumbled into a straining imbalance. Here is how it happened.

Bear Heart's wife, Edna, became gravely ill, and died. Being a therapist, I wanted him to express his grieving feelings openly. Being a shaman, he kept them close to his chest except in rare moments.

In addition, Judith's and my marriage was experiencing the stress of the growth of the Earthribe and its demands coupled with a radically different worldview presented by Bear Heart. My shamanic jaunts sometimes came at the expense of my family.

Reginah WaterSpirit became Bear Heart's medicine helper and traveled with him to our home. In time, their relationship flowered until one day they would wed, a beautiful turn of events, but also an added complexity. Integrating a new person into our relationship presented its own tensions and challenges.

Professionally, my referral sources were questioning this radical approach to healing through an integration of modern psychotherapy practices and primordial wisdom. A local family physician sent many patients to our clinic for psychotherapy. On several occasions, patients would return for their annual physical and report to him that they were doing much better.

The physician inquired how the progress happened, and, naturally, they expressed the benefits of walks in the woods, sweat lodges and vision quests. Instead of being grateful for the remarkable developments in the health of his patients as I might have hoped, my referral source felt vulnerable and became testy.

He was fearful that sending patients to me might result in malpractice suits for both of us, a fear which was entirely understandable. Reluctantly, he told me that he could no longer refer to me because of the unusual excursions into the wilds described by his patients. He was not alone; other professionals in my network took a similar position.

Calls came in from fellow faculty members at the local medical school affiliated with our clinical practice wanting to know what we were doing and whether it was professional or not. One professor from the medical school was a psychiatrist who became deeply involved in the Earthtribe. While it was very meaningful to her, her colleagues had difficulty in wrapping themselves around the medical and psychological efficacy of our nature-based practices.

They questioned her; she questioned me; I questioned Bear Heart.

These questions led to a conversation about whether The Center for Creative Resources, Inc., the organizational title of our clinical practice, could continue an affiliation with a medical school.

Additionally, we lived with the possibility of reprimand from the Texas State Licensing Agency for Psychotherapy. As a member of that licensing board in the 1970s, I knew how that drill would go. Just the thought of explaining our new therapeutic approaches to such a board sent chills down my spine.

In that regard, I testified before a senate committee on mental health in the Texas Legislature. A senator from East Texas—a bastion of cultural conservatism and still a hot bed of racism directed toward Native Americans—grilled me about the practice of psychotherapy.

He chaired a sunset review committee that decided whether psychotherapeutic licensure was to continue for an extended period of time for practitioners in our state. At the time, I was Chair Person of that aforementioned licensing board and in that role I was called on to testify before the senate committee.

My responses as chair were crucial to the continuation of licensure for hundreds of professional mental health workers in our state. So, there was, indeed, tension.

The East Texas Senator asked me, "Dr. Taegel, what is psychotherapy?"

I proceeded with what I thought was an erudite answer that lasted longer than needed. Finished and proud of myself, I looked at him with a satisfied smile, thinking I had made a good case. Needless to say, I did not mention my work with Bear Heart.

With a smirk on his face, he invited me into a high school type skirmish, "On the outskirts of my hometown in East Texas, we have a gypsy woman who tells fortunes. It sounds to me that's just about all you do."

At the time I said nothing because the senator's ignorance of the psychotherapeutic process was a minefield. Yet, I also knew there was a certain grain of truth in his comment.

As I sometimes say to my faculty colleagues, "Nobody is smart enough to be wrong all the time." The senator was not wrong in associating my work with the primal. I was just beginning to use the term the Mother Tongue, but I knew I would be tongue-tied to expose my work to such representatives of the mainline culture. Hence, an inner conflict in how to present myself floated to the surface.

Who was I? Pscyhotherapist? Shamanic worker? Professor? And how could I possibly put it all together?

As years with Bear Heart flew by, I became more and more vulnerable as I contemplated the possibility of having to be accountable to state mental health oversight about taking my students, supervisees, and clients to sweat lodges, vision quests, and other nature-based events.

Much of the time, I was aware of the risk of pushing the boundaries with therapeutic approaches growing out of the confluence of my psychological methods and ceremonial vortexes inherent in shamanic work. At other times, I wasn't in balance at all and tended to push Bear Heart away during such states of mind.

As pressure mounted from the reductive rationalism of academia on the left and the fundamentalism of East Texas legislators on the right, I became more and more testy with Bear Heart.

In some ways, I wished I had never taken this red road. Things reached a boiling point when an issue of Baptist Sunday School curriculum included a section on Satan and how the powers of darkness were descending through the epidemic of AIDS and through satanic ceremonies.

The article explicitly named sweat lodges as a heathen practice that Christians should take note of as a threat to their way of life. Letters and phone calls poured in. My secretary left a pile of notes on my desk from Earthtribers who were being confronted by neighbors and friends concerned about their attending our ceremonial events.

Meanwhile, Bear Heart himself was experiencing other forms of stress beyond even Edna's death and the subsequent new relationship with Reginah WaterSpirit. He was the target of criticism from younger warriors within the indigenous movement. Some called him a plastic shaman who was just making money from spiritual work. As an elder, he patiently confronted each of these accusations, but I knew it hurt him.

Within his own tribe, people understood their responsibility to offer support for their healers. He didn't have to instruct them about financial responsibilities.

However, such was not the case when Bear Heart interfaced with people outside a tribal setting. The mainline culture did not know that a substantial gift was expected so that the shaman could live. Bear Heart laughed and said, "I have a closet full of fancy boots given to me by well-meaning people I have doctored. They don't know fancy boots don't pay the rent."

Embedded in his comments was the fact that his family needed money to live in their little town north of Albuquerque. Giving tobacco to the shaman was a token of respect, frequently mistaken for compensation for work well done.

Further gifts were needed. I could only imagine what it was like for Bear Heart to fly across country to provide a service only to receive a pair of boots in payment, especially when his family needed food for their table.

On one occasion, I received a call from a friend of Bear Heart's in New Mexico telling me he needed some serious dental work and would I help? On another occasion he had optical problems. While I was glad to help, we both experienced the awkwardness of unclear expectations.

In his culture, we were supposed to know that one took care of the shaman. So, I would pick an amount of money and give it to Bear Heart when we he came to Texas to assist with the Earthtribe ceremonial events, but I never knew if it was too much or too little. In my culture, the healing and teaching agent was paid a very clear cut fee.

The tensions within and between us mounted. One day Bear Heart and I sat under a towering pine tree to discuss these growing strains.

"A piece of raw hide connects us," my friend and mentor said as he dangled a strand of buffalo hide. "Notice how hard it is. Take some water from your bottle and pour it over the leather."

I did, and the leather softened. Rawhide is more susceptible to water than leather, and it quickly softened and stretched as I held one end, and Bear Heart held the other.

We sat long enough for the leather to harden. He explained that traditional moccasins were made by taking rawhide from freshly skinned elk or buffalo and placed on the hunter's feet the way modern people might put on socks. The leather was then left to dry and take the shape of the hunter's foot.

As the leather hardened in the strip that connected us, we added water so we could stretch it knowing that we couldn't stretch it too much or it would break.

This learning experience went on for some time, and then Bear Heart, with a characteristic twinkle said, "The rawhide between us is stretched pretty tight right now. It would be tempting for both of us to cut it or stretch it until it broke. If you were primarily a student, I would cut you loose the way I do some who need to go off on their own in order to know how to be independent. Being independent isn't a problem for either of us, is it? Maybe, the opposite. So maybe we can discuss how to add some water.

"What would you suggest?"

I didn't have any immediate suggestions, but the two of us persisted.

We endured.

18 PLANT MEDICINE

At the outset of the first Earthtribe vision quest, Bear Heart sought to prepare the vision questers before they hiked out to their vision circles. Each of the vision questers sat with the two of us before they loaded their back packs for the journey to their site.

As our Earthtribe evolved, we added more ceremony, support, and safety to sending out vision questers. In the beginning, though, it was just Bear Heart and I giving instructions.

Bear Heart spoke to each quester, covering important essentials. "Be awake to every aspect of your vision circle. Our Creator will seek to open you up to your deeper soul and will speak in unexpected ways.

"Sure, you might hope for an eagle to fly by or a wolf to come up to you or for a vivid dream. But don't forget the unassuming power of a blade of grass. Notice how the sun dances with the blade; how the wind moves it; how it tickles the bottom of your feet. Even the smallest leaf is seeking to assist you in your pathway and open very large visions."

Through the years, Bear Heart and I talked with many questers before they bridge-walked out to their circle, and I noticed that he gave rich instructions and imparted a variety of stories to assist in setting the mental framework for the questers. But a recurrent theme became apparent in his pointing to long narrow leafs as a conveyors of powerful medicine in the awakening of a larger consciousness. Such a thematic emphasis eventually caught my attention, and I contemplated the deeper meaning as to why he spoke in this way about grass in particular and plants in general.

Captivated as I was by an European-dominated culture fascinated with lawns, I thought of grass as a nuisance to be mowed. My eco-field-of-origin is the Llano Estacado or Southern High Plains of the Panhandle of Texas. In its pre-Euro-American state, the Llano Estacado was known for grasses that, according to Coronado in 1540, came up to the belly of his horses, and sometimes higher.

Llano Estacado is Spanish for staked plain and referred to Coronado's driving lances into the ground so his soldiers could find their way through the tall grass when they made their return to Mexico.

Much of the tall grass described by Coronado gave way to the wheat fields so prolific in my childhood. Still, there were patches of wild prairie left where the native grass grew over my head during the rainy years of the 1940s, and I could easily get lost or make delightful hideaways. I knew about the healing medicine of grass first hand from these childhood experiences, intuitive though that knowledge was.

Then as an adult and as an eco-field researcher, I became interested in the evolutionary role of grasses. Keep in mind that an eco-field is a space configuration in which every aspect of the landscape is exchanging information and meaning with every other aspect that results in a potential wisdom of the larger whole. The more or less constant exchanges occur through the nonlocality of quantum fields.

Any landscape consists of eco-fields which overlap into wholes that become parts nested in a larger whole and so on *ad infinitum*. Grass grows at the base of the eco-field emerging out of rocks and soil. Put another way, waving grasses transmit the firings of an eco-field's eco-brain. Grass is to the eco-brain what cellular microtubules are to the ego-brain.

Grass is hair on Mother Earth's arms transmitting firings of information. This delightful family of plants includes approximately 10,000 species. Since grass in some form feeds most land creatures, nearly every bite we take, including protein, is grass in one form or another. Eat a piece of chicken or a bite of hamburger; it is grass once removed.

No wonder Bear Heart wanted us to take a break from everyday thinking and realize that wild forms of grass have something to say to us. Inherent in these grasses is vast potential for healing.[1]

Bear Heart and I often chewed on stems of grass while we talked and allowed its vitality to flow into our conversations. On another ceremonial occasion, I introduced him to a form of sage from the red slick rock canyons of my boyhood.

My mother, Juanita, and I made trips to the canyons near our family land to gather this particular plant known locally as *K-war-renu sage*, the Comanche word for antelope.

My Comanche brothers and sisters loved to eat antelope fattened on pungent sage. Bear Heart knew that I had a Comanche uncle by marriage who was a friend of Quanah Parker's and that Quanah's band of Comanches partnered with this particular sage in their healing ceremonies, as well as their diet.

On the subject of Quanah Parker and plant medicine, Bear Heart expounded with great flouish:

"You Earthtribe people need to know about Quanah Parker because he was a mixed breed like many of you. He was a Bridge Walker between the ancient wandering tribes and the America you know today.

"He really was the last shaman to be wild and free of Euro-American domination, and, at the same time, he was a principal leader in finding a way to practice Earth-based spirituality in the nation that replaced his. And it was the plant people who showed him the way.

"Quanah's name means 'smells good.' You know, like sage. His mother, Cynthia Parker, chose a beautiful valley around a lake near where you grew up. This valley had a wonderful fragrance of sage, bluebonnets, Indian paint brushes, and it was called by her *quanah*, and so she named her son.

"It was about 1874 when Col. MacKenzie of the U.S. army embarked on the strategy of killing all of the buffalo on the Southern Plains as a food source. They were following General Sheridan's policy of killing the Indian's basic nourishment. He was the general who also said, 'The only good Indian is a dead Indian.'

"MacKenzie and his army had been soundly defeated in a place called Blanco Canyon, also near where you grew up. General Sheridan and the powers that be in the U.S. government couldn't stand being trounced by these 'savages', so they hatched the notion of exterminating the Comanches the way they had other Indian people.

"They had a fancy name for it: *assimilation*. But that's a funny word to describe killing men, women, children, and food sources. It's about time you waked up to what the *wascina* culture has done to grab our land and wipe us out. Stay with me here; I am making a point about plants.

"MacKenzie's strategy was very successful, and he nearly accomplished his mission of exterminating the buffalo. But Spirit touched Captain Charlie Goodnight, who was under MacKenzie's command, and told him not to let such a terrible thing happen.

"So Charlie, who owned a nearby ranch and who was shocked by the callousness of his commanding officer, spirited about 50 head of buffalo off to his ranch in the dead of night. He risked court martial but couldn't bear to see the demise of such a sacred animal. If he had not acted in such a responsible and spiritual way, the sacred buffalo might have been lost to North America.[2,3]

"MacKenzie also killed thousands of Comanche horses, but still Quanah and his band would not be defeated. They slipped out of the canyons and disappeared into the waves of grasses on the Llano Estacado. At that time, the Comanche, the buffalo, and the grass were one piece of cloth that was ripped apart.

"At the end of his rope and without food, Quanah rode one of the last horses not killed by MacKenzie to the rim rock of one of those canyons you love. He slid off the horse's bareback, and drew a circle in the red dirt to prepare for a most important vision quest.

"He cried for a vision about what to do with his people who were starving. The white immigrants had been coming in waves for three hundred years, and he saw no end to their invasion.

"At first nothing happened in his vision circle but into the second day of his fast he saw a wolf come toward him, howl, and then trot off to the northeast. He interpreted this to mean that there was a new beginning, a birthing of a new way of life that would require much persistence and courage on his part.

"Then, a golden eagle glided overhead and flapped its wings in the direction of Ft. Sill to the east. He saw that there would be immense challenges if he went in that direction, but he sensed that the wings of the eagle would carry him and his people through what seemed the end of his world and way of life.

"He sang the eagle song I taught you: 'Kweenah, yo wah no, yanna, hey.' He kept singing it as the eagle led him and his people to Ft. Sill.

"You see the *wascina* never conquered Quanah and his antelope people. Great Spirit gave him the vision of a new life, and he moved with flexibility into the invasive forces coming his way even though it meant giving up everything he knew and the way of life on the Llanos he loved so much. MacKenzie thought he won. He bragged about it. Your history books continue to confirm his bragging as they always do.

"But Quanah was never defeated.

"He led his tribe into Ft. Sill with his head held high and the vision of his eagle carrying him forward. But once in the fort, Quanah felt trapped and sick at heart and was near death with a raging fever.

"Some accounts say he was gored by a longhorn, but the story passed on to me says he was sick in his soul. Maybe, the longhorn punctured his exterior to get to the interior of his deeper soul. Maybe his fever was Mother Earth burning through his rage that was really the anger of generations of us Indians.

"Whatever the case, his tribal members escaped Ft. Sill with him in tow and carried him to a Toltec healer, a curandera, on the border of Texas and Mexico about 500 miles away.

"Singing a *calls the Spirit song*, she cooked him up peyote tea that he drank for several weeks many times a day. She taught him that this unusual plant was a living being and carried a special kind of intelligence. It had been sent by our Creator to save humans from themselves.

"Peyote is not only an opening to the Creator spiritually but also a strong antibiotic. Maybe grandmother peyote helped with his wound. Plant medicine is strong. Slowly, he gained strength.

"He stayed with the curandera for an extended time. It's worth noting that it was a woman who healed this great man. Maybe, this turn of events forecast prophetically what you and I have been talking about in terms of the Grandmother returning in Her power with Grandfather Bear paving the way.

"Once back at Ft. Sill and as Chief of the Comanche peoples, Quanah provided his tribe with forceful and pragmatic leadership. He supported the construction of schools and was elected to the local school board and encouraged young people to learn the *wascina* ways. He became a judge to settle disputes. It wasn't long until this great man figured out how to navigate the white world.[4]

"As part of this bridging between the worlds, Quanah heard about Charlie Goodnight's good deed of saving the buffalo and formed a ranching partnership with Goodnight and Burk Burnett, another local rancher.

"You are going to love this: these two ranchers were among the most influential people in the Southwest, and they became students of Quanah's red path. The *wascina* thought they defeated us, but you see what's happening? We just hibernated like a big bear until you so-called advanced folks fouled your environment.

"Now you need us.

"We have kept the Earth-based ways hidden away in the caves of our souls. Now is the time for you to return. Nature is calling.

"Can't you hear?"

I wasn't sure I did. Such teaching with a tinge of anger was unlike Bear Heart, but it got my attention. And truth be known, I didn't hear and even remotely grasp his point. This was the early 1980s. It would take a decade or so before I began to see.

I wasn't alone in my ignorance and denial of climate upheaval. Earth was searching for voices to set forth these inconvenient truths. Much time would pass before I could piece together our Earthtribe visions into a prophetic mosaic that attempted to give us a path through the looming chaos.

I dragged my feet in knowing the only hope of our species would be a massive and conscious re-entry and re-joining of hands with all living creatures. It would be a long time before I saw that the plants provide medicine for our lost souls.

No wonder Bear Heart was red-in-the-face. He could see he had a slow learner. I preferred to deny the climate judgement coming down the road. In 1980, it seemed outlandish.

Then, later, we had environmental doomsday prophets who themselves did not see our only hope lies in the underlying, regenerative power of Earth Herself. The upheaval is coming from the heart of Nature, and, therefore, solutions will have to emerge from humans deeply connected to Nature.

Bear Heart continued.

"You might think Quanah gave up his tribal ways, but that is not true. He found an opening to bring economic and cultural success together with his tribal practices.

"He built a twenty-two room house for his seven wives, and he refused to cut his long hair. Some historians consider a twenty-two room house meant he sold out to excess, but keep in mind that he housed many people in need, including his twenty-five children.

"He slept in a small room when he wasn't sleeping under the stars. He painted stars on the roof of the house to link him with celestial bodies even when he was in his small room, and, to this day, that house is standing and known as Star House.

"President Teddy Roosevelt soon heard about this remarkable wisdom keeper and came to stay at Star House. They became friends, and Roosevelt was a hunting partner on a huge piece of land out where you went to college."[5]

When Bear Heart brought up the part of the story about Roosevelt, I recalled a relationship I had with the 6666 Ranch near Guthrie,

Texas, that figures into the narrative as the landscape to which Quanah took a sitting President.

In the late fall of 1960, I rolled out of bed at dawn on a cold morning to go with a team of students from McMurry College to a tiny rock church on the 6666 Ranch to help with a gathering of Methodists.

They didn't have a large enough congregation to merit an ordained minister, so the college volunteered to have a few youth lead singing and speak with a certainty as only sophomores in college can speak.

There were about 25 people present on that Sunday morning, mostly ranch hands and foreman. I can't recall his name now. I do recall that Burk Burnette's granddaughter, Anne Tandy, was in the gathering and later came to run the ranch, which consisted of over 275,000 acres.

The ranch foreman had much to say about Roosevelt and Quanah since he was a small boy when the Comanche chief brought the President to hunt on this ranch, which had been part of the vast Comanche hunting grounds. I double-checked my memory and Bear Heart's story and found a photo of the hunting party, including Roosevelt and Quanah.

The ranch foreman and Anne Tandy had us over for lunch, and they told me that Quanah gave Burnett the name *Mas-Sa-Suta*, or "Big Chief."

The two men were inseparable in many ways, and the church goers I talked to thought Mas-Sa-Suta joined Quanah in his peyote spirituality. We can pick up on that part of the story now, as Bear Heart continues to expound on the power of plant medicine.[6]

"Quanah rejected Christianity, even though his son, White Parker, first-born of his third wife, became a Methodist minister. Well, actually, Quanah himself became a Methodist. Like you, he ended up challenging its practices. He had seven or eight wives and twenty-five children, and the Methodist bishop came to him and told him he would have to get rid of his wives since he was now a Methodist.

"'OK,' Quanah told the starchy bishop, 'You go out there and tell them and all my children they will have to leave Star House.' Well, the bishop took one look at the blazing eyes of all seven women and the straight spines of the twenty-five children and left without a word. That's how smart Quanah was.

"When I say he veered away from Christianity, I actually mean he rejected the churches in his area as being too tame, too wooden. He thought they had lost touch with the fires of the Jesus they claimed to follow.

"He had a saying, 'The white man goes inside to a church house to hear and read about Jesus. We go to our peyote circles in a tipi under the stars to talk to Jesus because he sometimes makes a guest appearance from the ancestral world.'

"We actually see him in our midst. In Christianity, they think Jesus doesn't appear any more. He's in heaven. That might be for Christians, but for us simple Indians he appears all the time. The spirit of the plant and Jesus spirit, along with many spirits, come together in our midst when we sit on the bare ground and drink the tea. It is our sacrament."

"What were the peyote circles Quanah mentioned?" I asked.

I was surprised and a bit taken back by Bear Heart's account and faintly recalling Anne Tandy's telling me her father, Burk Burnett, sometimes sat in a tipi with Quanah and ingested the peyote sacrament.

Bear Heart elaborated.

"When Quanah returned from his trip to South Texas and the ceremonies with the Toltec curandera, he had found a new spiritual pathway, one opened by the medicine of the peyote plant.

"On several occasions, Quanah took the scriptures he had learned as a Methodist and went out on vision quests where he ate peyote buttons and drank peyote tea over several days.

"On the vision quest I mentioned earlier, the eagle and the wolf returned to him and gave him the vision of combining the scripture of his Methodist way with the scripture of Nature he was discovering in his quests aided by the tea.

"He returned from this vision quest knowing that he would found a new church where they would sit on the ground all night, drink the peyote tea, and be open to the spirit world, including an honored Jesus.

"He and John Wilson, a Delaware/Caddo shaman, formed a deep partnership and implemented guidance from the peyote plant to start what would become known as The Native American Church.

"Now that he could no longer roam the grasses of the high plains and bathe in the sage of the canyons, Quanah needed the assistance of the peyote plant."

As Bear Heart talked, quite lengthy for him, I grasped tenderly a medicine pouch made of deer hide that he had given me to wear around my neck. I had wondered what he put in the pouch, and so I asked him if he had placed a peyote button in the medicine bundle?

He responded, "Yes. And I gave you another peyote plant to put in the eagle bundle that surrounds your sacred pipe. The plant asked me to go with you to guide you and open you to visions and to assist in the forming of The Earthtribe. The plant told me you need all the help you can get."

"But I have never ingested the plant. How could it give me visions?" I protested.

"You absorb the medicine of the plant by having it around your neck. Its wisdom seeps in through your sweat next to your heart. It will connect your heart to the stars. You know, like the stars on Quanah's house.

"Are you part of the Native American Church?"

I was wondering exactly who this man, Bear Heart, was since I had known him for some time and now was stumbling onto a new dimension of his life that seemed hidden and, frankly, bizarre. It was a stretch for me to practice the ceremonies with the *inipi* sweat lodge and the vision quests, much less to think of the role of the plant medicine, peyote.

This was early 1980s, and Ronald Reagan was launching a war on drugs just at the time Bear Heart was telling me about peyote and the Native American Church.

I had an extensive psychotherapy practice that included many good folk in recovery from addiction, and I was quite involved in that process. I felt myself tapping the brakes of our relational car. I would need to know more before I could continue.

Peyote became another point of tension and stretched the leather strap between us until it was taunt.

19 COMANCHE WOMAN, PUHAKUT

The Native American Church has largely been an obscure subject for American historians, a hot potato for people in recovery from addiction, and a curiosity for spiritual seekers in general. It was no different for me.

As part of my research and in the service of shedding light on my memories of this part of Bear Heart's life, I talked to Molly Larkin, who co-wrote *The Wind Is My Mother*, with Bear Heart.

I told her I wasn't sure of the reader's response to Bear Heart's use of peyote in the ceremonies of the Native American Church, a subject of some controversy among cultural creatives, including members of The Earthtribe.

She laughed and said, "We had to fight several battles with our editors on Bear Heart's book, and especially they resisted our chapter about The Native American Church. They were afraid it would turn off many of our readers. We lost some battles and won some. But we included his relationship with the sacrament of peyote. Bear Heart insisted on it—it was important to him."

Her words encouraged me to delve into this dimension of plant medicine even though I had mixed feelings.

Although I had a rich relationship with visionary plants in a variety of ways such as ceremonial burning, ingesting the powerful plants was foreign to me. I wondered what prompted Bear Heart to enter the Native American Church and its practice of drinking peyote tea? Did the loss of his son send him searching for new resources?

Lost in a profound grief that came and went like a sudden storm, Bear Heart considered giving up his practice of *doctoring*, a tribal way of describing shamanic work. Two of his adopted brothers from the Otoe tribe knocked on his door to offer their compassion and suggest an opportunity to enter a ceremony that might help with his grief. They called it a *tipi ceremony*.

They told him that he didn't have to come to the ceremony because they knew it was strange to him. They were there not to recruit him but to ask his permission to offer prayers on his behalf using the peyote sacrament. He could attend for the whole experience, they explained, or he could come for the conclusion at breakfast after the all-night event.

As he related this phase of his life, Bear Heart paused and looked me in the eye, "I knew that the medicine of this plant was for me, and I told my Otoe brothers that I would come for the entire ceremony. That was my introduction to the Native American Church and its sacrament of grandmother peyote.

"In 1918, this new church was formally chartered at El Reno, Oklahoma. As a new Indian religion, it flew under the radar for nearly thirty years, and not many know about it, even today. We don't meet regularly but only when someone is in need. You see the meetings—we call them tipi gatherings because they are held in a tipi—are for specific healing. You have to be invited."

No immediate invitation was forthcoming as Bear Heart likely picked up on my caution. That was fine with me at the time because drinking the sacrament of peyote offered still another complication for my life.

It was about this same time that I met Huston Smith, a scholar who—Bill Moyers said in a PBS series—knew more about world religions and wisdom traditions than any other person on the planet. On a visit with this renown scholar, I sought information about using plants or other mind altering substances for expanding consciousness.[1] Huston offered compassion for my confusion about the subject and became a mentor to show me the way through.

To my great surprise, I learned that Smith had been instrumental in guiding Richard Alpert, who later became Baba Ram Das, in the use of LSD as means of grace. Huston told me that at the outset of his experimentation with mind altering substances, he thought LSD would be crucial in the next great awakening. In that regard, he also worked as an elder with Timothy Leary with considerable anticipation only to see Leary's use of LSD drift into the dysfunctional.

Given these developments, Huston became disillusioned with LSD because of the missing support of ongoing community and the lack of a spiritual tradition as a context. Taken out of the matrix of either scientific investigation or mature communal practice, LSD lost its potential and became harmful as a street drug.

So called "bad trips" were the result of recreational rather than the deep ceremonial experience needed for such powerful journeys. Nevertheless, Huston said plants like peyote and ayahuasca were NOT hallucinogens but rather *entheogens*. By that term, he meant that what you experience through plants in a proper ceremonial setting is *God* herself.

The plants do have a chemical impact on the brain, but the brain, under the influence of the plant, merely opens to a larger consciousness of God. The plants don't create a vision of God but rather open a channel to God. Hence, Smith used the Greek word for God, *Theos*, to form the word *entheogen*.

On one beautiful, summer afternoon, Judith and I sat on Huston Smith's back porch in Berkeley, California. I asked him about the exploration of life in the Native American Church since I knew he coined the aforementioned word *entheogen* and might be both objective and sympathetic. He surprised me with a brief history of the Native American Church.[2]

"The ceremonial use of peyote as a tribal sacrament reaches back at least 10,000 years and continues to flourish from its fountain head along the Texas border with Mexico not far from where you live. Legally speaking, in the USA it is to be used only in the Native American Church. In Mexico the Huichols, Tarahumaras, and other tribes make it a primary pathway to the Divine where it is legal.

"Huichol religion has much in common with Christianity. In both religions the Creator is aware of the vulnerability of humans and, out of profound compassion, enters the time/space continuum by limiting herself to a particular life form.

In Christianity, the Creator becomes flesh in the form of the man Jesus who dies but also offers life beyond through a resurrection, all on behalf of a larger consciousness for humans.

"In The Native American Church's ceremonial use of peyote, the Creator has great compassion for the human condition and chooses to enter the world in the form of a *plant* on behalf of not only humans, but also all creation.

"The plant is willing to give up its current form as a sacrifice for the Whole and for the consciousness of the seeker. Then, the consciousness of the plant lives again; indeed, it is resurrected in tribal consciousness."

Huston adjusted himself in the lawn chair and continued:

"Consider the humility of this story: The Creator sees fit to engage a plant to save humans, rather than vice-versa. Embedded in many Mexican tribes existed a talented group of artists/shaman/scientists called the Toltecs who arguably gave us the Nahuatl language, a Mother Tongue of Meso-America.

"The Nahuatl word peyotl or peyutl describes the pericardium or the envelope surrounding the heart. The name describes the ability of the plant to hold and reveal the heart.

"From as early as 1560, European immigrants to the New World misunderstood native spirituality, especially peyote. The Franciscan Friar Sahagan reported it to the Spanish Inquisition, which immediately declared it diabolic and made it illegal, punishable by torture and death.

"Even so, the practice continued to flourish throughout Meso-America. The form of peyote practice that reached Bear Heart through Quanah Parker's Native American Church is known as the Half Moon style of meeting, and remained freer of Christian influences than other branches.

"Today, the Native American Church of North America consists of eighty chapters, and in the continental USA, every state west of the Mississippi has at least one chapter."

Huston Smith's sage summary assisted and quieted the questioning of my inner skeptic, and I pretty much forgot about the issue until one day Bear Heart called.

It was December 20, 1982, when Bear Heart gave me the news that he had arranged for me to attend a *tipi* peyote gathering in Oklahoma. He was excited because this particular meeting included some of the most revered elders from a number of tribes.

Excited but still cautious, I asked when it would be.

"December 24," he replied.

"But that is Christmas Eve, and I have two daughters for whom that day is very important," I protested.

"I know," he said quietly.

"I'll talk it over with Judith," I told him, but I already knew that I would not go.

We had limited time with our two children because they spent part of the holidays with their biological mother. When I called to inform Bear Heart, I could tell he was disappointed, and I wondered if I had failed an important test.

Perhaps, I had.

Nonetheless, another invitation came a few months later, and I chose to attend because I felt I owed it to myself to explore the traditions of this person I had come to hold respectfully close to my heart.

Another feature was a questioning I had for myself about addictive impulses. Questions came into my vision circle: was I over indulging with alcohol? Sugar? Was I being over-responsible with family, friends, and clients who struggled with addictions? Enabling them? Did I need to be needed? Co-dependent? And, very important: how would the sacramental use of peyote fit with these questions?

Bear Heart picked me up at the airport in Oklahoma City, and we drove east on I-40 toward the gathering place a couple of stone's throw from the tiny town of Okemah, Oklahoma. Driving considerably under the speed limit and talking expansively, Bear Heart pointed to various towns that included a concentration of Potawatomi and Shawnee, among other tribes.

We drove past Okemah, and Bear Heart told me that this town of about 3,000 people was the headquarters of the Muscogee/Creek—called the Thlopthlocco Tribal Town—and the site of his birth. It also was the birthplace of the famous folk singer, Woody Guthrie, which prompted a spirited sing-along with Guthrie's, "This land is your land, this land is my land..."

We arrived in the early afternoon at the ceremonial site in time to meet many of the elders who were principal participants and leaders. I was paired with a Comanche woman, a *Puahkut*.

Puhakut is a Comanche term that describes a shamanic worker or, in this case, a medicine woman. Quite descriptive and pregnant with meaning, *puha* is this tribe's word that refers to a power that derives from the breath of Great Spirit.

The wind (*puha*) is the physically manifested breath of the Sacred Mystery. Puha is the contraction and expansion of the continents; it is the power of the flaring forth of the Universe a moment after the Big Bang.

It is the bump when one Universe bumps into another and produces a third, according to string theory in the newer physics. It is the beat of a hummingbird's wings against the sky in its trip across the Gulf.

A *Puhakut*, then, is one through whom *puha* moves freely connecting with many aspects in the eco-field. Of all the descriptions of holy persons such as shaman, healers, therapists, teachers, ministers, and sages, this term—in my view—best describes the qualities in a person who might offer assistance in time of need.

I called my spiritual mentor for the ceremony, *Breath-That-Moves*, because I couldn't pronounce her name in Comanche, and she seemed to like the description.

As I looked at her, it was as if the archetype of the Sacred Feminine was embodied in her. The boundary between her as a historical human and an archetypal representative of a parallel dimension, maybe a goddess, faded back and forth. Add my rich imagination, and you have a vivid being pulsating with an *élan vital*.

At the time, I was in my early forties, and she seemed ancient. Actually she was about the age I am as I write these words, mid-seventies. She had shoulder-length, gray hair with a single eagle feather attached to her crown chakra.

Beaded earrings covered the outside of each ear. She had a white shirt with a brown vest. Around her neck and hanging across her breasts was a beaded medicine bag with feathers and plants issuing out of the bag. A long skirt was held up by a belt of leather punctuated with silver discs. In her lap was a sacred pipe that had dots along the stem and a red catlinite bowl with carvings on its side in a language I did not know.

We talked for sometime, seeking connections between our two different worlds. When I mentioned that my uncle by marriage was Comanche and that he knew Quanah Parker, she was delighted. We discussed Quanah's relationship with the 6666 Ranch in Guthrie, Texas. We laughed a bit about some people saying 6666 meant the ranch was the headquarters of satan, but the opposite was her view.

She told me that the tiny town of Guthrie sits in the middle of the hunting grounds revered by her kinfolk for centuries and that her people spoke glowingly of its vast buffalo herds, its wild horses, and its abundance of antelope.

A narrative came to mind about the owner of 6666 Ranch, Burk Burnett, in which he talked about preparations for a famous hunt with Quanah and President Roosevelt.

"It may be the last time," Burnett lamented, "I get to hunt with Quanah, and I want to make the soul of that good Indian happy once more if I never do another kindly act on Earth."[3]

In this Native American Church gathering—strange as it was to me— this simple but elegant woman was returning Burnett's favor by acting kindly to a young man feeling his way along the bright path of consciousness.

Breath-That-Moves introduced me to folks as they arrived, and twenty-five of us ambled in no particular order toward the door of the tipi. The tipi was red on the top half and blue on the bottom with a yellow circle painted over the door.

The tall poles of the structure had been raised earlier that day, hard work for five young men dressed in ball caps and tee shirts that had pro football monikers on the front; one read, "The Kansas City Chiefs," and another, "The Dallas Cowboys." I smiled at the cowboys and Indians motif.

Children were riding horses bareback and filling the air with laughter. Dishes being cooked permeated the air from food I didn't recognize but would later turn out to be buffalo stew. They told me that we would have a tribal meal at the conclusion of the ceremony the next morning, and my mouth watered since I had begun a fast.

The sun went down about 7:00 p.m., and soon we lined up to enter the sacred space. The participants gathered at the tipi, more men than women, dressed in a variety of informal attire. I was the only person there not an active person in the Native American Church, and I was alerted to follow the Roadman's directions in order to be respectful.

Roadman is a term they used to describe the person leading us on the peyote road; and Bear Heart was, I discovered, a Roadman for the ceremony.

Stooping over, we pulled back the flap of the tipi and stepped onto the bare ground that had been swept with a broom until it revealed a cool and firm surface. The smell of dirt and burning herbs filled the structure. Looking up, I could see the night sky beginning to take shape through the flap at the apex of the tipi.

The last light of dusk shown through the bottom of the tipi as one of the leaders continued to sweep the dirt floor with a broom while another formed a half-moon altar in an activity that appeared something like someone building a sand sculpture on a beach.

As I seated myself in a cross-legged position, the half moon dirt sculpture became a living being and immediately took me into itself as a mother would a child.

Soon, I was lost entirely in a vision space and heard a voice saying, "I've got you, Billy. I've got you, Billy." The use of my childhood name brought up a burr-headed boy who was confused by the dynamics of his family and by grown-ups bickering over family land. In the background, I heard beautiful chants, repeated over and over.

Wey ya hey nah yah,
Wey ya hey nah yah.

The sound of a distinctive drumbeat took me deeper and deeper into the vision. A focal point of energy in our tipi circle was a water drum. The top of the drum appeared to be stretched over a container that looked like a cast iron kettle.

Later, Bear Heart taught me about brain-tanned deer or elk as the preferred hide for usage with such kettle drums. The top of the drum looked to be 8" or 10" in diameter. A rope was woven about the kettle to create an instrument I had never before seen or heard.

He also told me that inside the kettle were water and rocks or marbles, and, later in the night, the chords around the drum were adjusted to yield different sounds. A vibration new to my ears was part of what opened a passage into a moving vision.

After an eternity of nonlocality in vision space, Breath-That-Moves touched me on the shoulder. Startled, I looked into her eyes. She knew I was already in another world, and softly she asked if I wanted to drink the peyote tea.

Not opening my eyes, I took the ladle and drank, returning to the vision. I didn't really think much about the enchanted tea because my vision was already startlingly vivid.

I saw my great-grandmother, my grandmother, my mother, my daughters, and especially Judith. Along with other important women in my life, they melded into Breath-That-Moves, into one Grandmother, who held me, repeating, "I've got you."

Only, now the person in the vision was not a boy, but a grown man who aged and aged, wrinkling as he went, and, finally, crossing over through death into a larger life. All around was chaos, and Mother Earth shuddered and sought a new equilibrium, having been out of balance.

I saw Bear Heart and his death and his journey through the Milky Way. I saw the possibility of our little lodges of love and other star points of Earth-based tribes twinkling in the form of communities around Mother Earth's skin. I saw hints of a great shaking of Earth when many humans would not make it.

About 4:00 a.m., I felt Breath-That-Moves touch me gently on the left shoulder once again, explaining that the tea had been passed three times. I did not recall if I drank three times, but I guess I did.

The remarkable Puhakut woman sat comfortably on the ground as if her spine was made of the rich dirt floor. I marveled at her stamina and ability to remain in such a posture that reflected equanimity for twelve hours.

The focus of the ceremony had been the healing of a man back from war, his wife, and his children. The children did not drink the sacrament. But their faces softened. They seemed lighter, as did I. As the first light of day peeked in at the bottom of the tipi, the Roadman closed the circle. Slowly walking out of the tipi, we headed for a garage that doubled as a longhouse for the participants.

After standing in line to dip from large bowls of buffalo stew, hominy, and fry bread, I sat down on an old wooden chair with a hard bottom at a long table. Breath-That-Moves sat beside me. After a while, she spoke, "You entered the vision long before you drank the tea. I could see some of what you were seeing.

"Just being in the presence of our Mother Plant is enough for you. Some people are that way. The sensitive skin of your soul allows the plants to work. The plant radiates its power all around. Just being in the circle is enough. There are many plants that will help you. Touching them is enough. Smelling their smoke is enough."

We ate slowly without speaking. I didn't know if she was saying I had direct access without drinking the tea, or that I was a hard case and not eligible, or both.

Then, toward the end of our meal, she spoke again, "You see these visions often, don't you?"

"Many nights," I said simply.

"When you journey, let plants scout out front so you don't get lost."

The sorting through of this experience would not be easy. I was torn in many different directions. Over the next few months, it would become clear organically what the Earthtribe's practice with mind-altering substances would be.

20   EARTHTRIBE RECOVERY

On the trip back from Oklahoma, the questions I raised while in the tipi ceremony began to take focus. Paradoxically, partaking of the sacramental peyote tea made explicit the undue influence addictive urges had in my life.

Did I need to pursue peyote as a healing agent with regard to addiction? Should I lead our embryonic tribe in the use of the sacrament of peyote and become a member of The Native American Church? What of the use of other substances in the Earthtribe?

Instead of inviting me to become dependent on a substance—as I might have expected from mainline descriptions of peyote as a so-called gateway drug—my dance with this sacred plant helpfully raised significant questions about addictive substances, experiences, and behaviors in myself and in culture-at-large.

The next month on a full moon at the Earthtribe sweat lodge, I noticed items in our ceremonial meal that seemed out of place after my experience in Oklahoma. In our fledgling Earthtribe, we usually started the fires of the *inipi* about sunrise and ended the day with a tribal meal. Some people brought wine as their contribution to the sustenance, as was the practice in urban America at the time. In our infant stages of development, we gave little thought as to the ramifications such a cultural habit might have on our new endeavor.

After we emerged from the sweat lodge, there were many healthy dishes on a provisional table made of a sheet of plywood resting on top of well-used saw horses. Our makeshift table held a cornucopia of delights as people sought to bring nourishment for the soul as well as the body.

But when it came time to pour a glass of wine after a sweat lodge where my body had been cleared of toxins, my stomach rebelled at the thought. It just didn't fit to drink wine at that moment.

So, I declined.

This refusal occurred in spite of my social life at the time, which included a small collection of wines. Judith's and my courtship had its roots in the California wine country. My newfound resistance to alcohol was curious, even baffling since dependence on alcohol didn't seem a problem.

Yet, here I was questioning its compatibility as I exited the lodge.

These were complex spiritual questions worth pondering. Over the next few weeks, I discussed with various tribal members my sense that wine and other alcoholic beverages were out of place in Earthtribe ceremonial settings. Even though no one had ever over-indulged, there was a growing sense of leaving alcohol to other social events.

Such a discipline did not in any way become a directive for Earthtribe members to give up alcohol altogether although members in recovery had already taken that step.

One major consideration was the fact that most times participants in ceremonies such as sweat lodges entered a trans-ordinary state of consciousness, and driving to their home residences was already a challenge. Add to the mix a substance like alcohol, and you were asking for trouble.

Sometime later, a new participant wanted to smoke a cigarette after the sweat lodge. Subsequently, our elders decided that recreational smoking detracted from the deep practice of the sacred pipe and decided to take the additional discipline of not using tobacco in Earthtribe ceremonial gatherings except with the sacred pipe. Participants who smoked recreationally would have to fast from that practice while in our ceremonies.

Keep in mind that in the early 1980s habitual smoking was the norm throughout industrial cultures with 35% of the adults in the USA reporting habitual use at that time.

One of the transformative miracles in mainline culture has been the radical reduction of this habit to 15% in 2016. Oddly, we were at variance with mainstream America once again in that we were introducing a sacred use of tobacco in our pipe ceremonies at the same time that many in our midst were giving up their habit of smoking for health reasons.[1]

From time to time, our Earthtribe would be challenged by visitors who would say, "How can you tell us we can't smoke within these sacred grounds when you use tobacco in your ceremonies? Aren't you hypocritical?" There were no sound-byte answers, but such questions were pushing me toward a fresh understanding of addiction that would take years to take shape.

We found that our ceremonial use of herbs and minute quantities of tobacco in our pipe ceremonies actually assisted in shifts of consciousness. But even in the ceremonies themselves, we offered the alternative of touching the pipe to the shoulder instead of brief puffs if a person felt vulnerable about tobacco addiction.

At the same time that we engaged tobacco in ceremony, we recognized the powerful addictive tendency of tobacco when extracted from sacred ritual. And, of immense importance, we were discovering a variety of addictive urges coming into our awareness circles, ones hidden from us previously. Even those not struggling with drug or alcohol dependency were discovering other addictive urges.

"You *wascina* managed to take our most sacred use of tobacco and turn it into a hotbed of cancer," Bear Heart reminded me. "It's not the plant that is the problem. It is not even individual people. It is the way you folk think. It's your stinking thinking."

Bear Heart and I continued to discuss these developments related to our ceremonial practices and their relationship with addictions, and he progressively underlined the tendency of industrial civilizations to make an addiction of almost anything.

"Why you can kill yourself by drinking too much water," he laughed.

As usual Bear Heart offered a prophecy embedded in his laughter as he foresaw the destructive possibility in consuming water; bottled water, that is.

At the time, Perrier had only recently been introduced to the American public. Fifteen years after Bear Heart made the above statement, Coca-Cola introduced Dasani in 1999 as one of the first to invite us to drink "plastic water."

Subsequent use of plastic bottles of water would swell to 200 billion bottles annually. We now drink more water from plastic than either milk or beer. The result of our compulsive use of plastic has resulted in 11 million tons of floating plastic that covers an an area of 5 million square miles in the Pacific Ocean. And that addiction to plastic water is increasing. So, yes, we can become compulsive about anything.

And who in our midst is free of "plastic addiction?"

Over the years, I ventured into a number of vision quests for me personally. In the six months prior to the quests, I adopted the practice of fasting from alcohol. This practice was a step beyond abstaining from alcohol at sweat lodges.

Soon, I expanded that discipline to caffeine and obvious sugar. Though I was not a big coffee drinker, I did consume considerable tea and diet-free, caffeinated drinks. I was surprised at the headaches at the onset of dropping the use of caffeine, including chocolate.

As my mother, Juanita, would say from the ancestral domain, "You have stopped preaching, now, and gone to meddling when you bring up chocolate as an addictive urge."

True, but nonetheless, I found that my thinking cleared considerably. I felt better. My shamanic movement between worlds increased. My work as a clinician and scientist sharpened. I had noticed for some time that even a glass of wine would induce a slight slur in my speaking. I thought it might be my native blood, but Bear Heart snorted and said I didn't have enough blood to use that as an excuse.

In such conversations about addictions, he made clear that he would not give up coffee or the right to have a beer or chocolate. I wasn't asking that for him or anyone else, unless they felt such a practice would support moving to larger dimensions of consciousness. My use of alcohol eventually dropped away naturally and became a measuring rod for other habits and addictive urges.

Here is the way I came to decide about a habitual behavior: did such a behavior inhibit my movement between domains of consciousness for the purpose of enlarging my soul and serving Earth?

It was not the same for all members of the Earthtribe in our individual practices with mind-altering substances, but we agreed that we needed to create a sacred space for our healing emphases without ingesting peyote tea and drinking the fruit of the vine as part of our ceremonies.

After my experiences with the Native American Church, I had a sense that the sacrament of peyote might well assist with addictions; that seemed like a promising hypothesis.

So, why not pursue this potent possibility for addressing addictive behavior? Especially since modern recovery paradigms seemed to hit a wall of limitations?

The key in the healing I experienced in the peyote tipi occurred within a profound ceremonial culture that knew how to engage the plant respectfully and sacramentally. Their indigenous community was the main conduit of the healing I saw and experienced there.

Our Earthtribe, embedded as it was in the mainstream, was not mature enough at the time to move in that direction. Perhaps, in the future The Native American Church might teach Earth-based communities how to engage this beautiful plant in a healing way. Perhaps, peyote within tribal practice holds promise, paradoxically, for the healing of addiction.

That said, we kept bumping into this hard fact: its use was against the law.

At almost the same time of my sojourn with Breath-That-Moves, October of 1982, President Ronald Reagan spoke to the Justice Department and declared a "war on drugs," a policy originated by Nixon in 1971.

With Reagan that war picked up steam and actually helped create an epidemic of addiction. The number of people behind bars for nonviolent drug offenses increased from 50,000 in 1980 to 400,000 in 1997. Las Angeles Police Chief, Daryl Gates, believed "casual drug users should be taken out and shot."

By 2014, such an attitude resulted in 700,000 people arrested for casual marijuana use. To date, people of color are 3.7 times more likely to be arrested for casual drug use, so the war on drugs is actually a race war, including Native Americans.

And how effective is this war? *Pyschology Today* recently wrote: "The War on Drugs has been a failure. It cannot be won. It is time that leaders develop new thinking about the issue of illegal drugs." A failure? Yes. Another of our many wars that pull us into a morass of self-destruction.[2]

As I write, the current Trump administration gears up for another iteration of the war-on-drugs paradigm that will inevitably result in an increase of drug dependence.

Albert Einstein is often quoted as saying, "Insanity is doing the same thing over and over again and expecting different results." Recovering addicts repeat this wisdom at countless meetings because it describes addictive behavior so well. The insanity of this administration's amplification of a war on drugs is also a mirror of our addiction to a civilization that has gone awry.

Maybe, it is time to consider this hypothesis about addiction: Our addiction is to the form of civilization that we have created. Until we walk across the bridge to the new era, rampant addiction will continue.[3]

What I describe here is the organic unfolding of a cross-cultural community seeking to live in creative tension with a dying Western Civilization and the birthing of an Earth-based, sustainable civilization.

To build a safe container and remain in a creative tension with our culture, we needed to develop our practices with awareness and compassion. In a Reagan-dominated culture at war with drugs, we simply did not want to take the risks of integrating illegal drugs into our tribal practice, promising though they were.

The problem was not the plants, as Bear Heart taught, but the immature culture in which we lived and our lack of a tradition such as practiced within The Native American Church.

Or maybe we lacked courage?

For us it seemed disrespectful to ingest the powerful plants outside the context of the tribes that had a profound history, and connection, not to mention knowledge about how to proceed. We have, however, used various plants as portals by holding them tenderly in our hands. We consider plants as our senior mentors.

The above discussion provides us with a context for a brief look at an Earthtribe Recovery Model. In our clinical research, we developed an approach to recovery that integrated Bear Heart's teachings with the medicine wheel and my training as a psychodramatist. The result has been a primary tool in recovery from addictions we have used for the last twenty-five years called *Ecodrama*, which grew out of our practice of pyschodrama.

Psychodrama is a form of therapy invented by Jacob Moreno that focuses on a protagonist who enters a life-scene that makes thoughts, feelings, and behaviors hidden from awareness, explicit. Through dramatic situations, the hidden aspects of the individual are brought into a clear focus of awareness.

This approach has introduced to the mainstream such living tools as role playing, doubling, trust walks, method acting, and other skills now often employed in the workplace.

Sociodrama or family drama is a therapeutic intervention developed largely by family therapist, Virginia Satir, and ushered into the mainstream by John Bradshaw. It assumes a systemic nature of any organization, including the family. It seeks to bring into the joint awareness of the family what has been hidden, including roles assumed by the families that limit individual health.

At the root of many addictions, according to this model, are family secrets and family traumas that have been buried but manifest themselves in various addictions and other destructive behaviors.

Ecodrama transcends and includes psychodrama, sociodrama, and family drama in several crucial domains. Like psychodrama, ecodrama draws hidden sub-personalities out of the personal unconscious.

These hidden elements often stem from traumatic events that utilize addiction as a failed attempt at relieving personal and relational pain. Like sociodrama and family drama, ecodrama not only pulls forth hidden elements from the family such as family secrets into the light of family awareness, but reaches a larger dimension of Earth consciousness and therefore offers expanded possibilities of moving toward wholeness.

Here is where the rubber hits the road with ecodrama in a major stretch beyond its predecessors. Using the medicine wheel and energetic allies within the natural order, ecodrama transcends and includes the individual and a network of human relationships.

Reaching beyond the social system, ecodrama connects us with possibilities from the untamed and wild features of Nature as assets in the recovery process.

Ecodrama offers us a primary tool that recognizes the root of human suffering as feeling a separation from the core of Nature. Sustained recovery, according to this model, can only be addressed when the individual is perceived as part of an eco-field.

Put another way, ecodrama provides energetic equipment to reach beyond the personal to the collective unconscious residing in the eco-fields. Most experiential therapies open the door to such a renewal of human connection within the web of fields, but then stop short.

Why is this movement to reconnect with the core of Nature so crucial?

Since the main stage of our planet today is not human culture but massive climate change emerging from the deep recesses of Nature, human recovery from addictive urges can only reach its fullest potential through drawing on that dimension of Nature not controlled by humans.

Simply put, we humans are addicted to the profligate practices of Western Civilization in both its industrial and informational forms. Current civilization can't help us because it is the very substance we abuse.

Our civilization is our drug of choice.

To ask our dominant civilization to address the issue of addiction is like asking the tobacco industry to provide a cure for lung cancer. As

Einstein wisely observed, "No problem can be solved by the same level of consciousness that produced the problem."[4]

Current recovery models are firmly wed to mainstream consciousness and thus are not sufficient to meet this staggering challenge. Sensing the need to push beyond hackneyed recovery approaches, a major publisher in the recovery field invited several elder clinicians to be part of an addictions recovery task force that subsequently created an approach called Heart Reconnection Therapy (HRT) in an effort to push the envelope of the current paradigm.

From the vantage point of my role in the task force, a key dimension of HRT is reconnecting with what I call the *wild heart*, the hidden essence of the natural order.[5,6]

So much for these broad statements. Let's use our imaginations to drop into an ecodrama scene to experience Earthtribe recovery first hand, if only briefly.

Imagine that you come to me on the land we share with many other creatures in the Texas Hill Country near Wimberley, Texas. You drive a few miles from the little village to acreage that has accepted us as collaborators and park your car in the midst of a massive juniper forest.

We give each other a hug, an *apapacho hug*, one where our hearts physically touch each other. We begin our time together by incorporating this heart-to-heart connection in a physical way, knowing that recovery begins not in the abstract heart but in a physical encounter.

As we walk along a path covered in small rocks, our attention is focused on each step because it is easy to lose footing. The path itself becomes a living partner in our unfolding ecodrama since our walk makes clear that attention to where we put our feet is necessary, else we can find ourselves on the ground with a turned ankle.

And, not to be ignored, the walking path itself may have an intelligence seeking to assist us.

Once I had a new *seeker*—and I say *seeker* because *patient* no longer works for me—who was addicted to cocaine. Even though I had instructed her to come prepared to be outdoors and to walk on rough terrain, she wore high heels and dressed in a stunning cocktail dress.

By the time we reached a place under a grove of juniper trees to talk, she had sweated through her dress and scuffed her high heels. Later, she would state this short walk was a first step in recovery in that sweating and scuffing moved her from the edges of her personality deeper toward a yearning for an essence she could not yet name.

Her story is, in many ways, all our stories.

In your imaginary walk with me, then, picture yourself with comfortable but sturdy shoes or sandals with an alert eye that draws you into the present moment. Soon the Texas sun pushes us to move under the shade of a pavilion, a structure with a roof and no walls.

The patio-type floor of the structure consists of white limestone rocks gathered on the land and laid with skilled hands; the rocks invite us to doff our shoes.

Soon, we rub our feet gently across the granularity of the rocks in a soothing motion, and we feel the rough surface massage our feet stimulating key accupressure points. We feel the electromagnetics of Earth's grounding fields moving up through the soles of our feet leaving traces of information along the way.

We sit silently for a few relaxing moments before I invite you to share at least one of your addictive urges. Our goal is to reduce its intensity. You can choose from a menu of addictive urges like electronic devices, or chocolate, or a particular food, or work, or heroin or some other opioid, prescribed or otherwise.

You notice brightly colored streamers of cloth on the juniper columns that both support the pavilion's roof and speak of the cardinal directions of the medicine wheel of East, South, West, and North. Also, there are other colors that signify the Earth, Sky, Relations, and Ancestors.

You may not know what the colors and directions mean, but, even so, you feel held by what I tell you is a medicine or healing circle. The colored cloth is uplifting and suggests an opening.

Let's say that you settle on device addiction as a focus for the moment. You explain that you check your devices all through the day and send messages when you are tired, ones you wish you could recover because they lead to all kinds of mischief. When you consider relinquishing electronics for a couple of days, you feel anxious and somewhat unhinged.

Without knowing it, you have become dependent on electronic devices to fill your life. You are so dependent that you feel a buzzing of your phone in your purse or your pocket.

Then, you check, and the device rests over on your desk across the room. You had put it aside attempting to do without it, but your body is so dependent that it produces electrical sensations even when you don't have your phone on your person. Your body needs a detox from devices.

I invite you to pause and breathe into the count of eight, hold to the count of eight, and exhale to the count of seven. Then, I ask you to rub your heart and allow your shoulders to slide down your back as your head lifts to Sky and your spine reaches into Earth. Then, I invite you to allow your mind's eye to take you on a journey through your life maybe as far back as childhood.

Back. Back. Back. Until you connect with a tree, a special tree. One you climbed. Or on which you built a tree house. Or just admired.

You are surprised at how easy it is or maybe you struggle a bit. In thirty-five years I have had only a handful of seekers who could not locate a tree. In which case, we simply walk to a tree nearby and proceed. Almost always the tree connects and provides a link between us and the rest of the eco-field. Some researchers hold that we share 60% of our DNA with trees.[7]

I point to a tree near-by that is over 200 years old. I reach in a pouch I carry to pull out Sequoia leaves 2,000 years old. I mix it with the sticky leaves of a juniper near where we sit and put them on a rock to burn.

I invite you to breathe in the smoke but not too much. You move your hands through the smoke and lean down nearer to your hands to smell the mingling of smoke and skin.

Something primordial rises in you as if you are connecting with a you that transcends space and time and descends into the origins of your species. The smoke loosens the hold of the addictive urge, not conquers but loosens.[8]

We both breathe. Not surprisingly, I find my own addictive urges floating to the surface and entering the circle of our awareness. We all, as children of this culture, have these destructive inclinations. But this moment is for you, so I don't go into my own vulnerability.

You find yourself separating from the urge. It is as if you had Velcro on your chest around your heart, and the smoke assisted you in unsticking and pulling the urge out and away from your chest so that you can look at it. View it without judgment. Judgment, no; discernment, yes.

"Would you be willing," I ask, "to descend into that urge for only two minutes?"

You pause. Or rather a part of you that has the job of protecting and controlling the world in and around you pauses. But, what the heck? You will give it a try if for only a couple minutes. You become the urge.

"What animal are you like as your enter your inner urge?" I ask.

You look surprised and say, "A tiny turtle crossing the highway that has just been grazed by a car. As a turtle, I am lying on my back exposed to oncoming traffic."

I invite you to call on a grandmother to help you, and a bear comes forward and turns you as a turtle on your right side, moving you to the grass at the edge of the road and patting you gently on your shell. Hesitantly, you poke your head out to look around to see if you are still alive.

The two minutes are up.

Now, I invite you to come back to your usual self. We sit down. Your eyes move to a nearby tree. Shifting at my suggestion, you become part of the tree. You are tall and stately, bending with the wind.

From high in the tree you can see both of us. You can see something of what lies behind your addictive urges. You can see the little turtle by the side of the road.

Then, you take the view you have with the tree-top back into your chair. You now infuse your usual ego with this new awareness. You have an "aware-go," my invented word for a wild heart that infuses the usual ego with its untamed juices. You are now an I with the power of your addictive urges loosened.

You are not so tightly wound into its clutches.

Maybe your choice is to live one day each week without your devices. Once you say that aloud to yourself, it may seem too large of a stretch. Scale it down, I suggest, just experiment with one half day of not using the devices to see if you can do it. For support, I recommend that you ask a trusted friend to be aware of your aspiration.

On the walk back, we summarize the form of recovery we just experienced. To repeat: a *wild heart* is that state of consciousness within deeply connected with the natural order that lies beyond usual human control.

Such a connection may be just a few steps away from your air conditioned space, or it may require a journey to a park or green space. We have discovered in the Earthtribe that an eco-spiritual community grounded in practices that take you to your soul's untamed and untarnished point is a key in recovery.

Then, a door is opened to hold and be held by loved ones, as Bear Heart and I were about to discover.

21   TWO HEARTS HOLDING

Reginah WaterSpirit, Bear Heart's spouse, sent word that my esteemed friend would like to talk with me, that his strength was ebbing, and that I needed to come soon if I wanted to converse with him while he was still strong enough.

Some time had passed since the two of us had been together in-person, so I jumped at the opportunity to spend quality moments and strengthen our ties after a considerable hiatus. Plus, there had been some tension between us that sat like undigested tamales in my stomach.

Speaking of my stomach, I was recovering from a parasite that I had contracted when I was on the West Coast of Mexico in council with Huichol elders. Given that I had to stay pretty close to facilities, it wasn't the best time for me to make the twelve hour drive to Bear Heart's home in New Mexico; but I had a deep sense that I needed to reconnect.

So it was that Judith and I motored from the Texas Hill Country to a suburb north of Albuquerque where Bear Hear and Reginah lived at the time. After eighteen long months of struggling with upsets in my intestinal community with uninvited guests from the microbial world, I was weak and vulnerable, and a bit testy to boot.

Late on a summer afternoon, we exited from I-25 North outside Albuquerque and wound our way through neighborhoods to a bed and breakfast called The Chocolate Turtle, located in Corrales, New Mexico, not far from Bear Heart's house. Rolling up to the bed and breakfast which sported a bright blue front door with a fancy iron gate, I began to relax into such an inviting place in anticipation of my visit with my long-time friend.

True to bed and breakfast protocol, this quaint setting had just a few rooms, and ours was called "The Hummingbird Room." It sported fresh flowers and rich chocolate turtles on the pillows.

Chocolate seemed a good remedy for my digestive malady since nothing else seemed to help. Maybe, I thought, I would break my fast from chocolate; certainly, my mother, Juanita, would be pleased from her perch in the ancestral domain. Chocolate was her cure for everything.

The presence of hummingbird art in the room brought to mind my first vision quest with Bear Heart where a hummingbird had hovered with powerful wings that awakened me to the possibility of intimacy beyond humans. That tiny moment had swiveled the course of my life.

The owners of the B&B, Denise and Keith, assisted us in getting settled, and I prepared to reconnect with my old friend by walking out toward the famous Rio Grande River to collect myself.

Bear Heart and I had spent quiet hours by this iconic river. Rushing out of the mountains in Colorado through Northern New Mexico, the river was wide, flowing from left to right from where I stood facing east. As it flowed past me, it would wind slowly toward the Texas/Mexico border and then pour into the Gulf of Mexico.

Dotting on the river were a few stray Canadian geese, cinnamon teals, and ring-necked ducks. Off in the distance, I could hear a single scaled quail with its distinctive chirp, and soon its top-knotted head bobbed in the tall grass next to the water.

Already my mood was improving. The sound of the water lapping at the edges reminded me that we were entering a new era of Earth's story where water would be the crucial player. It always has been, but we humans have remained pretty much oblivious.

As I contemplated the river, I had an eery sense that water might wake us up with powerful storms like the big wind and rain of the tornado in my first vision quest had predicted.

The next day Judith and I drove around Corrales and Rio Rancho until we reached Bear Heart's suburban neighborhood where he and Reginah had rented a small house; it was set in a very typical subdivision with neighborhoods swallowed up by an expanding Albuquerque. Such a tame and conventional scene seemed incongruent with the sometimes wild man I knew and loved.

Smiling with tender memories punctuated with an anticipatory sigh, I recalled moments I had introduced him to friends at a sweat lodge when he wore a baseball cap turned around backwards and a faded bathing suit.

More than once I heard grumbling that he sure didn't look the part of a shaman, and many times he didn't, at least by Hollywood standards. Walking up the sidewalk, I didn't know what to expect since we hadn't seen each other in some time.

Had it really been over a quarter of a century since we first sat beneath a cottonwood tree at Ghost Ranch?

When Reginah opened the door, I could see Bear Heart in the background. He had lost weight, and his long hair was thinning in his 90th year but still tumbled down his back.

Our hair told the story of how we both had evolved over the decades. When we first met, he had a flat top haircut typical of many Indians of that era, while I oddly had tried perming my hair as part of a mid-life phase. The late 1960s saw my hair long and straight, but I had succumbed to the conservative trends of the early Reagan years with foul-smelling hair treatments. He kidded me about my perm until I finally gave it up. Now, decades later, as we looked across the room at each other, we both had gone gray and tied our hair in similar pony tails.

We hugged briefly, and he laughed a deep laugh, then under his breath whispered in my ear, *"Aho! Ennake!"*

He used the Creek/Muskogee for cherished relative. With that utterance, any leftover tension melted in the fires of our connection which seemed at the moment to span several lifetimes.

I responded the same, adding the cross-cultural greetings among tribes, *Hey-ya-nah, Ennake.*

In the back bedroom, was a German woman who had heard of him and traveled that considerable distance in order to sit in his sage presence. Over the next several hours, person after person came to the door to seek his assistance.

The procession reminded me of the first time we had met as we sat beneath the cottonwood tree at Ghost Ranch where we had treated a parade of scientists and artists.

On this day, Bear Heart didn't say much to the pilgrims because he didn't have that much strength. No feathers came out. No drumming. No chanting. No herbs. Yet, each person seemed to benefit by sitting quietly in his presence. Meanwhile, the two of us enjoyed the silence between us.

The day flew by, and we made plans to go to a 5 star restaurant where his grandson was a chef to celebrate life and our reunion. The four of us—Judith, Reginah, Bear Heart, and I—squeezed into our Honda CRV for the twenty minute drive toward fine dining.

Once there, the two women went ahead as Bear Heart and I parked the car and walked at a gait that fit our ages. He placed his hand on my forearm to steady himself. He was ninety, and I was sixty-seven. Two old bears walked and talked as if they had been together for eons.

He wanted to know about my work with the Earthtribe, which consisted of lodges of love west of Houston at Deer Dancer Ranch, and the newer one west of Austin in the village of Wimberley. There were other lodges I highlighted that were part of a loose network but not officially affiliated with the Earthtribe; especially, I mentioned one west of Boston in the Berkshires. He laughed and said we were all going west, which might be better than going "south."

Once inside the restaurant, Judith and Reginah talked animatedly as I spoke to the concierge about our reservations. I quickly realized that Bear Heart was well known and respected even in these hoity-toity circles; his grandson, the local chef, had made sure we had a good table.

I could tell Bear Heart was a bit unsteady on his feet. Out of the corner of my eye, I saw him leaning against a table that held the menus. It was an antique and not that stable; soon, the legs wobbled under his weight. As he and the table started to collapse, I reached out and grabbed him with both my arms around his back just before he hit the saltillo tile floor.

Then, I lifted him to his feet so that we were face to face.

A little embarrassed by the sudden intimacy, I started to move away until I realized he was grasping my arms and then my shoulders. About the same height, we looked into each other's eyes as now we were holding on as if to make up for our time apart.

For a lingering moment, the twelve-year-old Mark who lost his father under a juniper arbor and the twelve-year-old Billy who chopped juniper firewood while his father slept off excessive drinking held each other, as boys sometimes do.

Then, in that timeless moment, the two vision questers linked arms, the sweat lodge leaders touched shoulders, and the two trail-blazers found each other once again.

Bear Heart and Star Heart held each other and slipped into an eternal circle. I had received the name, *Kola-swa Fiki* (Star Heart), and

so we were heart brothers. The Toltecs have a word for such moments—
apapacho, a Nahuatl expression for hearts that touch.

Here were collaborating elders whose hugs embraced their many
selves, healing past disagreements, celebrating their work together, and
opening doors to ancestral encounters, ones not bound by space and
time. It occurred to me that I was the age that Bear Heart was when I
first met him at Ghost Ranch.

We smiled and then laughed as we walked arm-in-arm to the
choice table covered in white linen. Bear Heart sat across from me; Judith, on my left; Reginah, on my right. I don't recall what anyone ordered but the sage, who promptly asked for a large steak, medium rare.
Reginah, ever looking out for his health, gently objected, but Bear Heart
wasn't having it.

"I'll eat what I damn well please!" he shouted so loud that heads
turned from nearby diners. He was momentarily angry, flushed in the face.

Startled at first, I was then amused at his explicit humanity. The
great ones are always very human, but what made Bear Heart stand out
was how transparent he was with his humanity. There was no pretense
at sainthood because, in later years, his awareness embraced his shadow
side, as well as his apparent foibles.

Ever so often someone will tell me a disparaging story about Bear
Heart's objectionable behavior. Some are likely true. Most of us have a
few skeletons in our closets.

Back at the bed and breakfast, I contemplated these gross moments
of humanity in great teachers. I thought of Rolling Thunder, holy person
for the Western Shoshone Nation and inspiration for the Grateful Dead
and Bobby Dylan. Once I heard him say in an interview that he felt at
ease with fierce storms. Such a kinship allowed him to predict when
weather spirits would show up.

In a communication with the legendary rock band, the Grateful Dead, he told them that thunder and lightning would interrupt one of their concerts in San Francisco. Such storms were rare in the Bay Area, but on the appointed day actual rolling thunder and lightning did arrive on cue.

It was as if the rolling thunder in the storm knew the man, Rolling Thunder, and knew him well. The interviewer was astounded at Rolling Thunder's kinship with thunder itself and marveled at this brazen intimacy with the eco-fields that so challenged the rationality of even the deadhead followers of the band.

The next question in the conversation came quite unexpectedly, "Do you ever counsel with marriages?" Rolling Thunder looked surprised, then agitated, as fear strolled across his face and as he looked out of the corner of his eyes. Perhaps, he saw something we couldn't see, maybe an apparition or maybe moments of tension within his own marriage.

He slowly replied, "Don't do no *martial* counseling: too dangerous." I noticed he confused *martial* and *marital*, or maybe not. Lightning and thunder? No problem. Relationships? Too stormy.

Such frank owning of his limitations and vulnerabilities moved me. He didn't pretend to know what to do with the boiling intimacy of marriages.

The interviewer pressed Rolling Thunder about his relationship with his wife, and he replied gruffly to end the conversation, "She make good corn bread."

The interviewer raised his eyebrows at what some would see as a blatant disregard of the feminist perspective. It didn't seem that way to me; just another example of cultural clashes.

These earth teachers like Bear Heart and Rolling Thunder seemed to have an easy way with being real as if digging their toes in the dirt of hundreds of sweat lodges would let them do no other.

At the restaurant with Bear Heart's dinner party, our meal unfolded. I looked up from my plate to notice Bear Heart's engaging gaze. We said nothing, but powerful energy passed between us. Tears welled up in both our eyes for what seemed like several lifetimes.

I noticed a drop of water in the corner of his eyes and one rolling down my cheek. Another droplet poised on the end of Bear Heart's nose.

He straightened his shoulders, picked up the edge of the table cloth, jerked it so our plates rattled, and blew his nose on the cloth. Blew it without apology or even a nodding toward the propriety of an expensive restaurant. Blew it as if he was outside a tipi or a sweat lodge with little or no regard for the rules of current civilization.

For reasons I can't quite explain, that simple and jolting act was a gift of the wild to me. Through the years people ask me to tell them something about Bear Heart, and I sometimes relate this incident, especially if we are sitting around the intimacy of a campfire.

The telling rarely conveys what I want to say about him because the listeners often crinkle their noses at such a cockamamie act, but the tears and the table cloth speak of the unruly nature of our relationship.

The act feels like the initial impulse of a cold front blowing out of the arctic north after a long hot summer. Only this wave of consciousness in Bear Heart's nose-blow was one data point in a larger challenge of the very foundations of a culture built by Euro-Americans.

Ours was a walk on the wild side. I don't know why. It just felt that way.

That night we shared many teachings. Later in a dream and as I pored over the wisdom notes he left, his words came to me in quantum packets. Intimate words that reflect the mother tongue of intimacy within the eco-fields we shared.

"Among my people, we carve from bones of animals in such a way that they speak to us, and we speak to them. I sing to the bear, and he guides me. Can we not make room for the bear to roam free at least in some part of where we live? Is he not our grandfather?

"Europeans and Ivy Leaguers look down their noses at our art from the dream world. That looking down their nose is what is wrong with our world.

"And where are the humans who can walk with bears? And see them as grandmothers?

"All living things are our relatives: those that fly, those that crawl on the ground, those that stand upright. We have but one purpose now: to be part of all our relatives. Everything else falls under that practice. We are part of the land, and we must recall the rights of all creatures to live with each other.

"You can't really love the humans around you until you love the creatures around you.

"All decisions must be made for the good of all relatives: how you make money, how you vote, who you marry. Hold your leaders to those standards. If you don't, all hell will break loose. If you don't watch it, you might elect another Andrew Jackson or Nixon.

"The eagles soar in the wind. They have charge of all the purifying winds of the universe. This is what this life form has to offer us. We are to respect them, to love them, and to appreciate them. We can have no freedom unless we respect natural life forms.

"I want to tell you about the wolf. I hesitate to mention his name. In my tribe we don't speak directly of the wolf very often. We refer to him as grandfather or to her as grandmother. He guides us on our red path. Few people know that we cannot find the way without the grandfather and grandmother wolf. If you bring the wolf back to a landscape, everything else falls into place.

"I express to our Creator, Great Spirit, that we are here to appreciate the sacredness of all life. If we can come into harmony with the forest, the desert, the hills, and especially, our water we will be OK. If not, we are in big trouble.

"Harmony is a sense of blending, loving, tolerating. If we could so live that way, the greater circle might make things better for all.

"So what have we learned together? The cycle of life. Humans were inside the circle for a while. Not so much now. Inside the circle, we appreciate all of the forces of the Great Mother Nature even when they rock us.

"Like Grandmother Moon, we are here to reflect the great light, the beauty of creation.

"The rivers seek their own level to become part of the whole.

"We have broken the circle, but we can allow our Creator to mend it through us. May the circle be unbroken.

"While we are still here, can we not connect deeply to the web of life for those who come after us? It is our privilege to do all that we can to preserve and flourish our environment. We can understand and be what we are to be as part and parcel of the rivers, the lakes, the sky, and all creation.

"Our work is to remember who we are. We cannot do this without the bears, the wolves, the trees, the water, and the stars. We simply cannot know who we are without their help.

"That's why so many folks don't know who they really are. They run around like chickens with their heads cut off.

"We are mediators of the Creator. We are caretakers of the powers. We don't possess. We allow the rivers to flow through us. The Creator creates, heals, and empowers. We just open ourselves and realize that doubts are within us. We generate those doubts and fears. Our job is to make room for the enormous compassion of the Creator to move through.

"When you hurt with a pain that won't go away, go to a clear stream and allow the water to course over you. It will leave its footprints of healing wisdom in every part of your body. These little rivers carry good memories that can replace your bad ones.

"Our time with each other is like the seven years I spent with one teacher and seven other years I spent with another. We are still learning. I am still learning on the other side. You are still learning. Our task is to keep expanding. You question. That's good, but don't stop there.

"Every person is good and has something to offer, no matter what you may think, no matter how much evil you think they are doing. No life is totally lost. Your leaders look pretty bad. I know that. Still, shoot out arrows of love and compassion.

"Will, avoid scorn and judgement of others. When you point at other people and enjoy their suffering and ignorance, one finger points at them and three point back at you.

"Stand straight and never fear a crooked shadow. No matter what other people say or think about you, that is their right. You don't control them. Sometimes, they might even teach you something about yourself.

"When you give with a good heart, you extend your life of service on Earth another day.

"Worry is like sitting in a rocking chair. Back and forth, but doesn't take you anywhere.

"When you are afraid, ask yourself, 'Is it helping?' If not, let it go. The secret is in learning how to relinquish.

"Above all, keep practicing relinquishing bad things, sure. But also good things. Don't hold onto to either very long, but hold the good longer.

"You have double doctorates, but if you don't have wisdom to guide your knowledge, you will not go anywhere worthwhile."

22 CROSSING THE BRIDGE

No matter where you are as you read this book, you are imbedded in a landscape, a region of non-material and material influences. Some of these fields of influence, like gravity and electro-magnetics, are more apparent; others are emerging into our explicit consciousness.

An aspiration of this book has been to awaken an awareness of our being part and parcel of Earth's many splendored fields of influence, as well as human-made dimensions of the fields that are not so appealing.

We are interconnected in ways we cannot even imagine!

Our human return to the web of life is a return of an awakening consciousness, including how deeply connected we are to Nature's forces that shape us. All aspects of the eco-fields are seeking a transfer of information and, sometimes meaning, with every other aspect.

A butterfly flapping its wings in Austin impacts the weather in North Korea.

That is not just a metaphor; it is experimentally true in field physics and experientially true in ancient wisdom traditions. Our participation in this book consists of such a transfer of information and potential meaning because we have co-created a field of inquiry. Together, we possess the possibility of a deeper knowing of each other within our landscapes.

Such reflections come to me as our bear walk across a consciousness bridge nears a close. As usual, I am beset with questions.

Where is this bridge walk leading?

And...

Who are the Bridge Walkers?

To address those questions and integrate our time together, I amble to the backside of the land of which I am a part, the place where ancestral Bear Heart first connected with me.

This land has selected Judith and me to pay its taxes and give it an occasional haircut. In return the landscape nourishes us, awakens us, makes us better, and calls us its own.

In our twenty-five years here, we have become Johnny-come-lately features of the eco-scape. A 250-year-old oak graciously reaches out to us as does the great horned owl who lives in its branches and reminds me of the limited role I play in what Texas law calls "ownership."

The bridge between the location of my house and the sacred area where our Earthtribe gathers monthly is linked with a twisting path outlined in white rocks that leads from our ordinary life to trans-ordinary wakefulness.

The rocks are covered with a white ash left over from their presence in a glowing red fire where they gave up their sedentary ways and changed form in order to assist us in our sweat lodges. Now, they are semi-retired as markers of the path; they are our partners in awakening consciousness.

In their own way, they may be more animated than we humans are. Einstein got it right when he said, "Rocks are very slow moving light."[1]

As I walk north and west on the path, I scuff my shoes on juniper chips spread out to show me the way and keep me from sinking into mud. Each step releases an olfactory experience, made even more pungent by an overnight rain.

I take a deep breath and listen. The sound of the crunch as I walk and the wonderful smell of local cedar invites me into a shifted state of consciousness to address questions as to where the bridge between worlds is leading.

Soon, a large fire circle comes into view. A line of rocks almost waist high leads from the fire circle to a hut we call a sweat lodge. I keep walking beyond that pile of rocks deeper into the woods where we have constructed a second sweat lodge.

Like the Heinz-variety humans in the Earthtribe, this lodge is a hybrid structure made of juniper, bamboo, crape myrtle, and yaupon. Stepping through the ribs of the structure, I put down a blanket to take a siesta. On my back, I am mesmerized by the waving of the limbs of the trees as they signal to each other and graciously include me in their confab.

Soon, I am in a hypnogogic state between waking and sleeping. It seems Bear Heart is with me once again, but I don't see him, only feel his presence. As I squirm with rocks protruding into my back, a stiff wind blows out of the north and west. Weather spirits abound, and night falls.

Like a Navajo sand painting, the colors of visions from many quests and many people form a faint cartography to assist in leading us across the bridge. It is as if I, like Tezcatlipoca in Teotihuacán's pyramids, look through a smoky mirror.

I wish for more; but smoke clouds my view; and I have only murky shapes to share with you as we move across the bridge into a new civilization.

My focus drifts so that past, present, and future intermingle to birth glimpses of a future that is pulling us within itself. The snap shots of this book merge memories and visions until they become one. As I look through the thatch of the sweat lodge and the waving arms of the juniper trees, the clouds reach down to me.

It seems as if they are the ancient Hopi, speaking to show us the way, saying, "Come to the bridge!"

The year was 1947, two years following the dropping of the atomic bomb on Hiroshima. A council of Hopi elders gathered to ponder the bombing, an act they considered to be heinous. They knew their prophesies had predicted such a horror for thousands of years and called the event *a gourd of ashes*. Even so, the destructive, pyrocumulus, and mushroom-shaped cloud of debris and smoke shocked them.

Had humankind come to this? This bomb to destroy everything?

They had guarded their wisdom carefully through the years since they suspected any allowing of dominant civilization to know their truths would result simply in another form of colonialism. Their experience told them white people pilfered whatever they could get their sticky hands on, including their spiritual insights.

Yet, with the tests in White Sands, New Mexico, and subsequent dropping of a five ton atomic bomb, a nuclear age had dawned just as their prophesies had predicted.

The elders concluded something had to be done. Circumstances forced them out of the closet to share the wisdom they possessed. Or, at least, some of the influential elders felt such an urge. Others dug their heels in the ground, put on the brakes, and insisted their truths were only for their people.

Mainline white folk were, they argued, a lost cause.

After an extended council, the elders finally agreed to send emissaries throughout the Western Hemisphere to listen to other tribal visions in order to settle the question of sharing or not. The aim of these envoys was to seek a collaborative map that might open the way to a new world.

One of these gatherers-of-visions was an esteemed elder known as White Feather, the well-spring of this story.

In the Spring of 1958, White Feather had been on the road for eleven years and was now nearing his ninetieth birthday. He was so old that his beloved sons had already stepped through the great door of death, yet he persisted with his travels.

So it was that he was hitch-hiking across New Mexico on his way to his home in the Four Corners when he saw a Ford coupe with faded black paint coming toward him.

Something stirred within.

Could this be an opening to transmit the wisdom he had been gathering to people who could carry on when his Earthwalk ended? He raised that question for himself because his sons were not available; his tribe was trapped in a squabble between factions; his time, running out.

Also on his mind was the prophesy shared by many of the tribes he had visited that a new breed of white folk, a pack of mongrels, would be crucial in giving birth to the new world.

The *Pahana*, they were sometimes called.

This prediction of *Pahana* was an aspect of their intertribal wisdom resisted by many traditionalists. Something about the old auto coming toward him was attractive, but he wasn't sure if this was his opening.

Meanwhile on the lonely road, David Young, a Presbyterian minister, saw the wizened man with a blanket thrown over his shoulder sticking out his wrinkled thumb. Against his common sense, David tapped his squeaky brakes and came to a stop some twenty yards past the hitchhiker.

Painstakingly, an aging figure hobbled along the shoulder of the two lane highway, took a seat in David's car, shook off the dust, and said nothing. David shifted into drive and pulled out onto the road.

White Feather pressed his lips lightly together in a meditative silence as David prattled on about the weather, the news, and his congregation.

Miles passed as the wise shaman pondered if this scrawny driver was the one to receive the prophecies.

Finally, White Feather spoke, "I am Hopi. I am an old man. I have wisdom to pass on, and I am guided to give it to you."

Puzzled, David listened. He had no idea that White Feather had chosen in that moment to open the doors of ancient wisdom to Earth's larger tribe.

Time and distance rolled by as the elder talked. When he finished, he asked David to stop the car and let him out. The old man disappeared into the sunset.

The two men never saw each other again, yet the ripple of influence started with this unlikely duo would carry immense possibility and point toward a span leading to a new day.

David drove down the road a mile or two and slammed on the brakes. "What just happened?" he queried himself.

Then, he wrote as fast as he could in a notebook he had kept in the back seat for sermon notes. He filled it up. Back on the road, he now asked himself, "Who can I tell about these strange markings?" He was both ecstatic and frightened.

He could not tell his parishioners; they would think him a heretic. He couldn't tell his ecclesiastical superiors; that would ruin any chance he had for promotion. He knew of no academics who would be interested because of their affair with an odd form of objectivity that reduced everything to the material.

Pondering, he finally settled on passing this ineffable wisdom to his youth group that Sunday evening. This strategy seemed as outlandish to him as Spirit moving through a manger in Bethlehem or a Bodhi tree in Gaya.

The wisdom was being passed from one unlikely vessel to an even more improbable carrier, more like a virus selecting an unsuspecting host than a revelation.

To prepare for that meeting, Young transferred his notes to a stencil which he then put in a mimeograph machine. As he turned the handle of the machine, he got purple ink all over his hands, even on his tan trousers. Soon, he had about fifty copies, many of which had the tell-tale stains on them.

That Sunday night, a warm early June evening, he passed out the duplicated notes, and, to his great surprise, the youth were totally enthralled.

Later, I would learn this unlikely youth program occurred on the same weekend that I had been questing with a tornado on Rattlesnake Island not far from where White Feather hitchhiked.

In a few months, I would began a life-long process of connecting the dots imbedded in the prophecies, dots that comprise this book.

The summer passed in that same 1958, and I loaded my three year old salmon pink and charcoal gray Chevy with all my worldly possessions and sped off to college. By that time, I had repressed the Rattlesnake/tornado vision and settled on traditional Christianity as a momentary guide for a path beset with smoke and mirrors.

McMurry College, a Methodist institution in Abilene, Texas, fit the bill for my early education. The college had been founded in 1923, by Jim Hunt who was born and grew up on the Kaw Indian Agency in Oklahoma. He had been a friend of my grandfather, Lee Stephens, and they shared their connection to what they called Indian spirituality, though they also were Methodists. Jim was more faithful than Lee to Methodist religion.

As part of his heritage, Hunt had instituted in the college he founded a practice of constructing an authentic Indian village in the fall of each year. Students and some faculty would build traditional tipis from the ground up, using materials suggested by Hunt's childhood on the reservation.

In a state of ignorance of such primitive building, I meandered into this ceremonial construction without much thought, mostly out of curiosity.

Seeping beneath my ignorance and resistance, the ancient architecture awakened a core resonance in me. We stayed up nights sitting around a campfire conversing as only college freshmen can talk once freed of the constraints of parents.

During one of those campfire discussions, two students from New Mexico broke out the mimeographed documents they had received from their pastor, David Young. The tell-tale purple ink was still smeared on the sheets as they passed them around. My hand trembled as I focused an old flashlight on the tattered pages that both allured and repelled me.

That night, a seed was planted deep inside, close to my essence. It would take a decade or so before the seed broke through the ground and sprouted into a conscious quest, but the presence of White Feather was palpable, a foreshadowing of the bear of a man who would one day enter my life. Or maybe they were one archetype showing up in different garbs from the imaginal realm.

The information from White Feather's ride with David Young was an attractor force tugging at me from the future. I was a long way from knowing what the prophesies meant, but I felt the draft of a sacred wind.

In my philosophy classes at McMurry, I learned that Aristotle, grandparent of modern science, spoke of such moments. The mature oak is present in the acorn, he said, and draws the acorn toward its mature self. Aristotle called this process *entelechy*, a vital life force that guides the development of an organism toward its fulfillment.

For years, I thought the guidance from the future was simply about my personal unfolding, but gradually I discovered that the story was about the transition from one civilization to another.

Even now, I can smell the fire from that 1958 night. I can feel the touch of deer hide on the tipis. I can hear my classmates disseminating information that would marinate until my halting walks with bears would burst into full stride.

The contents of that wisdom shared by White Feather with David Young provided me with a skeleton map to cross the bridge. In addition to Hopi wisdom, I have listened to hundreds of visions from Earthtribers and others that co-mingle to provide a shadowy map that can tell us who the Bridge Walkers are and where the bridge might be leading.

Both Bear Heart and White Feather poked large holes in the mainstream understanding of the human narrative, even history itself. Keep in mind that White Feather's passing of the wisdom to David Young occurred five years before Frank Waters would write *The Book of Hopi*, a masterpiece which would open additional crevices in conventional epistemology.

The wisdom from these many traditions pointed to a human story that moved in cycles. In this cyclical view, there was linear past, present, and future in ordinary conversation, but the larger vision of the human story unfolded cyclically, and provided a wise foundation for Einstein's space/time continuum.

Here is what I learned that night with a flashlight flickering on the papers.

In Hopi cosmology, there have been four major civilizations, including the one we live in now. These past civilizations point to a pre-history that reaches much farther back than current science suggests.

Their remains may be discovered underwater in areas now submerged through at least three planetary floods. Each of the first three worlds, or civilizations, cycle through a beginning, a middle, and an end in a circular fashion.

Through the various iterations, humans made enormous strides with particular reference to technology, as well as other forms of knowledge. In the manifestations of civilizations, humans lost touch with their connection with the larger sacred web, and, in a massive self-correction, Earth brought that civilization to a close, usually with prodigious climate change.

Such collaborative prophesies tell us that we are now crossing a bridge between the 4th World or Civilization to the 5th Civilization. On that night, when we were building tipis, the students from New Mexico told of prophetic signs given by White Feather that plot signals of the end of our civilization and the beginning of a new creation.

Here are the signals as I heard them.[2]

*"**This is the First Sign:** in ancient times, we were told of the coming of the white-skinned men, like Pahana, but not living like Pahana. These twisted humans will seize the land that was not theirs. They will smite their enemies with thunder and fire sticks."*

I said to myself, "This sounds like the guns of our culture." Little did I know that the Texas legislature would eventually pass laws that opened the doors for kids to carry guns to school. Such is a signal of a crumbling civilization.

*"**This is the Second Sign:** our lands will see the coming of spinning wheels filled with voices."*

Later in life, I would talk to Judith's grandmother and hear how she walked beside a covered wagon from Nebraska to Oregon in the last wave of immigrants from east to west. They passed the time walking beside the wheels with endless conversations that helped with the boredom.

"This is the Third Sign: a strange beast like a buffalo but with great horns will overrun the land in large numbers."

As I drive five miles to our small village each day, I pass by herds of longhorns that fulfill this prophesy first uttered thousands of years ago.

"This is the Fourth Sign: the land will be crossed by snakes of iron."

This reference to railroads was obvious even to a college freshman.

"This is the Fifth Sign: the land shall be crisscrossed by a giant spider web."

When we discussed this image around the fire at my undergraduate college, it was pointed out to be ubiquitous electrical lines.

"This is the Sixth Sign: the land shall be crisscrossed with rivers of stone that make pictures in the sun."

The Federal-Aid Highway Act had been passed in 1956, and it literally paved the way for 41,000 miles of interstate rivers of stone with bill boards, giant signs, and mirages.

"This is the Seventh Sign: you will hear of the sea turning black, and many living things dying because of it."

As a college freshman, I couldn't imagine the 210 million gallons of oil that gushed into the Gulf of Mexico by Deepwater Horizon, or the 336 million gallons spilled in the Gulf War of 1991, not to mention the Exxon Valdez with its oil coating of countless wildlife. The sea and its creatures, indeed, turned black at the hand of a gasping civilization.

"This is the Eighth Sign: you will see many youth, who wear their hair long like my people, and join the tribal nations, to learn our ways and wisdom."

At the time of hearing White Feather's wisdom, I had a fashionably short flattop haircut, but I didn't imagine that in just a few years I would join a generation that would fulfill this prophecy. The pictures of Judith's and my wedding sixteen years later show both our haircuts as archetypically Hopi, but unconsciously so.

"**And this is the Ninth and Last Sign:** *you will hear of a dwelling-place in the heavens, above the earth, that shall fall with a great crash. There also will appear a blue star kachina.*"

About the time I met Bear Heart, the U.S. Space Station Skylab would fall to the Earth in 1979. Many people from Australia to Oregon to Texas would speak of a blue streak across the sky.

These nine signs prepare us to hear these following two prophetic utterances that define the transition to the next era.

"*These are the Signs that great destruction is coming. The world shall rock to and fro. The white man will battle against other people in other lands.*

"*His enemy will be those who possessed the first light of wisdom. There will be many columns of smoke and fire such as White Feather has seen the white man make in the deserts of White Sands. Diseases will spread and a great dying will off will occur.*"

Do the wisdom utterances that come to us from the future refer here to the early civilizations of light like Iran or Israel? Are we seeing the first outbreaks of these diseases in ebola and AIDS? Are our bodies speaking to us of these prophecies with the epidemic outbreak of our immune systems fighting within through autism, fibromyalgia, and cancer? Massive floods in New Orleans, Miami, Pueto Rico, Bangladesh, and Houston should be enough to gain our attention, but only a few, according to these utterances, will wake up.

People, understanding the prophecies, shall be safe. Those who live in sacred places also shall be safe. After the destruction, there will be much to rebuild. And soon—very soon afterward—Pahana will return. He shall bring with him the dawn of the Fifth World.

He shall plant the seeds of his wisdom in our hearts. Even now the seeds are being planted. These seed people shall smooth the way to the emergence into the Fifth World.

As a young man, I hardly knew what to make of these prophecies. In some ways, they seemed like fanciful after-dinner conversation, but over the years they kept coming back to me.

In addition, I listened to myriad visions from questers who brought back a patchwork that fit together and offered convergent lines of evidence and data from the other side of the bridge supporting the Hopi wisdom.

Such synergistic, prophetic wisdom may well point the way. Let's move deeper into the domain of prophecy to discover if we are able to cross the bridge.

23   THE RIVER IS FLOWING

As we complete our time together, I want to tell you about my understanding of prophecy. After all, we might be talking about not only where the bridge is leading on our bear walk but the direction of humanity. No small subject.

When I was in my 20s, I co-authored a book with a Greek scholar, Claxton Munro, in which he parsed the Greek word *prophesia*. I still recall the day when we were on retreat writing the book, and he told me that he translated the word *prophecy* as an act of witnessing or seeing from a distance the panorama of the human condition from a sacred perspective.

Prophesy, he told me, is a deeply felt seeing and story-telling with a wide angle lens that reveals what most humans don't see because their eyes are clouded by our overly rational culture. Prophecy has its roots in an intensely personal experience that allows an ascent of the mountain of consciousness until reaching a pinnacle called the witnessing presence.

In notes that didn't go into the book, I wrote my own grasp of prophetic unfolding.

Prophecy is a mosaic of visions pieced together into a cosmic map.

Prophecy allows Spirit to lift us high enough to see the spiral of evolution itself.

In vision quests, we taste a little bit of death and inch into eternity. From the perspective of nonlocality and eternity, it is possible to catch glimpses of the past, present, and future rolled into one. They co-exist in one cycle.

Prophecy often does not make sense to mainstream historians because it takes place in a vantage point beyond history itself.

It is not rational; it is trans-rational, counter-common-sense, and thus intuitive.

A glimpsing occurs through a rip in the veil of history.

And then we participate as part of an attractor force pulling Earth toward herself into another manifestation.

Bear Heart and I pondered many Earthtribe vision quests and how Mother Earth was unfolding a map for a pathway through challenging times. Those discussions led us naturally to explore a Hopi hieroglyph called Prophecy Rock, located on the face of a cliff in the four corners area near Oraibi, Arizona.

He had actually seen the pictograph with his Hopi elder friends and described it to me. He noted my interest and pointed me to other indigenous wisdom holders who had distinct interpretations of the rock.

The site of the original Prophecy Rock pictograph is now off limits to all except Hopi elders, so my knowledge of this important rock painting is second-hand.

Even so, I have seen an alternative rendition by a revered elder, Thomas Banyacya. Contemplating his work, I noticed similarities with ancient pictographs I had experienced first hand at an premordial site on the Rio Grande called the Cave of the White Shaman. Both expressions of indigenous art resonated with visions I was hearing from questers. Such prophetic insights inspired a rock painting of my own, seen below.

Following are my interpretations of the conglomerate visions. Figure A represents an archetypal figure called by the Hopi, Massau'u, who is an embodied expression of the Sacred Mystery and who taught the Hopi way of life to the remnant people as they emerged through the opening, the sipapu. They walked out of the caves of the 3rd World to the current 4th World with Massau'u acting as the mid-wife.

Figure A

In my vision quest in the Cave of the White Shaman, I deeply connected this archectypal shaman with the birth process, and she is honored in my painting. More about this archetypal form when I get to Figure H.

Figure B represents our solar system, and the moon is depicted in eclipse mode between the White Shaman and the Sun. This solar eclipse speaks to the Divine Feminine of the Moon temporarily blocking out the Divine Masculine for the journey across the bridge. The time is nigh for the Sacred Feminine to be at the forefront.

Figure B

Figure C speaks of the role of the Star Nation and the gift of the star heart for the birthing process of the new era. The star, the sun, and the moon all are on a line to the shamanic heart.

Figure C

In a series of vision fasts—one of which was actually inside the Cave of the White Shaman at the confluence of the Rio Grande and

Pecos Rivers—this chant came from the future and seemed to comment on the star in the rock prophecy:

> *Stars in the night*
> *Stars in the water*
> *Stars in my heart*
> *Stars in my head*
> *Stars in my hands*
> *Stars in my feet*
> *And then, repeated over and over:*
> *I am a human being...*

Dancing across the bridge for a brief moment in this vision, a voice of the Invisible spoke the words, Star Heart (Kola-swa Fiki), and the words have followed me as I work on the rock paintings. The chant and rock art speak to an important reality: we are all made of star dust.

Figure D, represents the cave, an incubation in the womb. Note that the black tear drop in the cave represents the power of the subconscious (ground consciousness) and the direction of the west in the birthing process. It might be seen as a shamanic cave or Plato's cave.

Figure D

Figure E, note the top line as it leaves the teardrop womb and the bottom line just below the teardrop and at the edge of the shamanic hand. Upon leaving the archetypal cave, most industrialized humans in the 4th World take a separate path (top line) in an estrangement from

Earth-based humans (bottom line), who continue in a straight line toward a new era. Some interpreters see the two lines as good (bottom line) and evil (top line) or the line of the material (above) and the line of the spiritual (below).

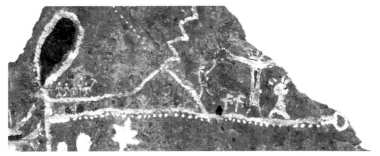

Figure E

Let's look at the upper line or path (Figure F) and see where it leads. The task of Western thinking humans was to ascend, to walk the path of scientific inquiry and critical thinking, and to develop along the way astounding technology.

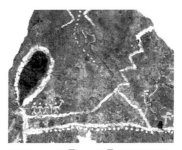

Figure F

This is the path Plato chose. He left the cave and taught that liberation lay in ascending to the heights of absolute forms. It was not an evil or bad path, but one that eventually lost its connection to primal energy and drifted into unrooted abstraction.

Plato, the Abrahamic religions, and mechanical science all developed the practice of separating from the flow to gain a bird's-eye view and thus more objectivity. Such an impulse carried the wilderness quest practice of detaching to the extreme, stretched humans away from the flow of life, and led us into our pervasive split and subsequent estrangement.

It is not seeking momentary separation that is the problem but rather losing connection with the grounded Whole.

This path (F) led humans to a state of misguided arrogance where we think of ourselves as the apex of evolution: homo sapiens, sapiens. Thomas Banyacya's and my drawing—both influenced by Prophecy Rock—show the people holding hands on this upper line.

That image might denote our current yearning for community or even the genius of the Renaissance, but look closely and notice that their heads are separated from their bodies. Could this be a prophecy of the internet where we are connected yet not really? Where our heads, our hearts, and our bodies are more and more separated and thus alienated?

And, is such separation the seat of rampant dysfunction?

In Figure G, we see an infamous part of the drawing, "the zigzag way." Notice that this crooked line leads upward to more and more separation, abstraction, and disconnection from the rock until it disappears over the edge.

Figure G

Such a path takes humans first into the terrible suffering of depression, anxiety, addictions, and then into an oblivion suffused with a mirage of individuality.

Are constant wars, even world wars far behind?

Are we pre-determined to oblivion? Do we have a choice?

As we proceed, the pictograph shows that we—participants in Western Civilization—come to a major fork in the drawing at a descending line, our bridge (Figure H) moves downward at a slant and offers the possibility of reconnecting with the mainline of the drawing.

Figure H

In contrast to many spiritual traditions and some versions of Darwinian evolution which lead upward, the bridge path descends in a return to Earth consciousness.

Through the recovered practice of vision questing, we gain the ability to move apart from the patterns of every day life and glimpse the Whole *without losing connection*.

Note the figure on the bridge with a dot of white (mongrel Pahana), inspired by The White Shaman—one image at the birth of the painting and one standing in the plant world. In a moment, I will describe the characteristics of people who choose the path of Figure I. This image is important because it represents those of us that aspire to be Bridge Walkers.

Figure I

That brings us to the figure standing in the midst of the corn plants (Figure J). This is the next embodiment of Great Spirit, a new Massau'u. When White Feather visited the Toltecs at Teotihuacán, he encountered their story of Quetzacoatl, the Toltec version of incarnated Great Spirit.

Figure J

Notice, Christians have a similar story with the return of Jesus. Also, note how similar the Hopi word, Massau, and Jewish word, Messiah, are. In my early tribal journey, I was introduced to a Comanche figure by the name of Massa-u-ta, meaning Infinite Chief Who draws all to a sacred point. I also encountered such a energy-form in the Cave of The White Shaman.

In all cases, this archetypal figure is seen as crucial to the 5th Civilization. Over the years, I have had a sense that this figure might be a return of the Divine Feminine or a web of communities that honor the Sacred Feminine by adopting Earth-based values and practices.

To me, the new figure standing in the plants unveils our archetypal Mother expressed in Earth-based community. Or maybe the plants themselves are the messiah?

Turn your attention to Figure K, the two circles (black blobs). Most interpreters, including Bear Heart, see the circles as WWI and WWII. Figure L is also a circle (black blob), and occurs as the Bridge Walkers began their return to the Earth-based path.

Figure K

Some elders see Figure L as WWIII. I am not clear on that point, though with the current dearth of global political leaders that seems a likelihood.

Figure L

In my visions, Mother Earth in L is rebalancing herself through climate change precipitated by the 4th Civilization and also by her relationship with Grandfather Sun.

Mother Earth experiences a shuddering and disequilibrium through massive disruption in climate upheaval, human wars, and over-population. We can expect massive weather events of a class never before experienced. Their purpose is to awaken us as we return to the red path.

Notice how vivid the path is with its yellow dots. The Choctaw rightly call this Earth-based pathway, the bright path.

The mosaic of visions are ruthless in their telling of these larger truths, and they are not bedtime stories. Figure H walks the bridge and lands smack dab in the middle of this shuddering. But as the walk continues, it takes the human story into a nourishing world of plants where the new civilization, steeped in plant life, flourishes.

What are the characteristics of this remnant group of mongrels, the Pahana who cross the bridge into the 5th Civilization?

Can we be included?

First, Bridge Walkers to the 5th Civilization are people who are immersed in the wisdom and conscious practice of water. The Muskogee/Creek and Hopi rotate their lives and ceremonies around the experience of water or lack of water.

That is also true of the Toltec in Teotihuacán and of the Cahokia along the Mississippi. Our bodies are 70% water. Mother Gaia is composed of 70% water. If we are to be part of the Great Return to the main pathway, we will need to learn the language of the watershed.

Such a primal education rests in the matrix of a dawning of regenerative consciousness.

In the 5th Civilization, we will treat our fellows as if everyone is downstream from someone else. This commandment supports a new water-related ethic.

We will need to become proficient in the practical application of water wisdom. As a bare minimum, we will need to know how to collect water. Bridge Walkers are water collectors, even if it is a small amount. In my visions, we will be judged not by what we believe or by dogma.

The simple judgement of Mother Earth is this: Does our consciousness include the water we need and enough to share, especially with neighbors with whom we disagree?

Finally, water herself will visit us in massive storms with the intent of awakening us from the hypnotism of consuming and "plasticating" the planet.

Second, Bridge Walkers to the 5th Civilization have a direct and conscious relationship with the sun that connects us to solar power. It was reported that the solar eclipse of 2017 drew the largest audience in human history.[1] That is a significant step in solar consciousness, but then there needs to be a translation into practice.

Suppose, as climate researchers predict, that we have an extended period when the grid collapses. Let's say for a period of two weeks in the near future. No electricity (witness Puerto Rico). What do we do? To run our devices, stoves, and refrigerators we need about 12–15 kwh per day as a minimum. Even if we have water, we need juice to pump the water through the house.

It is not a far off god who judges and decides who enters the gates of a new world. This simple question is our judge: how well connected are we to photons and electrons, offspring of our Sun? We can't eat without them.

Third, The Great Return from the abstract line that leads from oblivion to the main pathway features a remnant of people whose toes and hands dig into soil. We have much to learn from the ancients about soil.

As archeologists have recently learned, the first inhabitants of the western Amazon created a broad strip of earthworks that stretched between southeastern Bolivia into western Brazil.

The earthworks constitute a 700-mile swath of raised-bed fields roughly the size of France. "The vast fields have canals for water channels—tall settlement mounds; circular pools; permanent zigzag fish wiers; mile-long, raised causeways, ranging from simple, irregular ditches in the south to elaborate geometric arrays in the north."[2]

According to Clark Erickson, a University of Pennsylvania researcher, the region is a model of how human beings can use even the most apparently unpromising areas to create and maintain environments that match their needs.

Because the mounds, soil, and fields required enormous labor to construct and maintain, Erickson hypothesizes that these civilizations must have had hundreds of thousands of people. Carbon dates suggest they reached an apex three thousand years ago but may reach back 8,000 years.[3]

This previous civilization can point the way to soil-based humans whose consciousness smells like dirt.

Humans who become Bridge Walkers know that the word human comes from humus, the organic component of soil. Both words are deeply connected to humility, and humility is an apex quality of the new humanity.

Humility is, in this context, defined as an acute awareness that we humans are a species among species, a conglomerate of sub-atomic particles in a vast sea of eco-field consciousness. The stupendous forces of Nature in climate change call on us to put our foreheads on the ground and humbly submit to the process.

Fourth, Bridge Walkers into the 5th Civilization have a practical and conscious relationship with plants. Notice that the pictograph shows plants along the line that leads away from oblivion. As we move across the span, we join hands with the plants and with The White Shaman as participants in the 5th World.

In the tipi with Bear Heart and Breath-That-Moves, I discovered plants are the bridges that take us into new domains of consciousness. The beautiful story that the Creator chooses in this new day to reveal herself in an intertwining of plants rather than primarily through humans is startling and refreshing.

Plants in these visions become the new messiahs linking us to the Creator in a direct, felt manner. It may be that the lily of the valley and the rose of sharon are not just metaphors. Could it be true that our new messiahs are the lily, the rose, and the plant of renown?

Was a genius of Jesus that he realized his oneness with plants?

In the Earthtribe, we choose not to ingest entheogenic plants to propel us across the bridge of consciousness; but, nevertheless, our profound linkage with trees, herbs, and organic plants becomes the energetic impulse that moves us into an explicate consciousness of engaged ecology.

The judgement of Gaia's climate change and the way across the bridge to the 5th Civilization is embodied in the question: What is your direct relationship with plants?

Fifth, water, sun, soil, and plant life all speak to us in a Mother Tongue that imparts information linking us to an ever moving cycle of consciousness.

Literacy in the Mother Tongue is required of Bridge Walkers. It, not English, is the lingua franca of the new civilization. This literacy unfolds a regenerative and, thus, sustainable consciousness of engaged eco-fields.

When we land on the far side of the bridge in the New Era, knowing how to speak the language is important. Interspecies communication is crucial. We will know we belong by our ability to exchange information with all creatures.

As eco-field mongrels, we become aspects of the sacred web that move apart from usual patterns, glimpse the Whole, and return with expanded and explicit awareness. Our highest manifestation is through engaged, aware, and, thus, intimate community.

The beginning of our book now becomes the end. I return to the sweat lodge where I wake from a siesta to a felt sense of Bear, the ancestor. As I lie on the ground and stretch, I hear Judith singing a song, one I can't quite distinguish from the wind. Is she in the house singing, or am I hearing her sing from another dimension?

In any case, the words and soft music come clear:

The River is flowing,
Flowing and growing.
The River is flowing,
Down to the Sea.

Mother carry me.
Your child I will always be.
Mother carry me,
Down to the sea.

Shifting on the ground in the lodge, I ponder the song and absorb it as a melody for the walk across the arch of history to the other side.

I crawl out of the lodge and amble to the fire where ancestor Bear Heart appeared.

I join hands with my spirit guide from the waterfalls of my boyhood.

I reach out to the youth trembling beneath a tornado at Rattlesnake Island.

I smell the ink from the mimeographed paper passed from White Feather.

I listen to myriad visions of people from Earth's tribe.

I hear the sound of our bare feet as willing walkers across to a new era.

I cherish the deep, bass voice of a war veteran, Larry Winters, a wisdom student and Earthtriber, reading a recent Hopi prophesy:[3]

> *You have been telling the people that this is the Eleventh Hour, now you must go back and tell the people that this is **the Hour**. And, there are things to be considered...*

> *Where are you living?*
> *What are you doing?*
> *What are your relationships?*
> *Are you in right relation?*
> *Where is your water?*
> *Know your garden.*
> *It is time to speak your Truth.*
> *Create your community.*
> *Be good to each other.*
> *And do not look outside yourself for the leader.*
> *This could be a good time!*

> *There is a river flowing now very fast. It is so great and swift that there are those who will be afraid. They will try to hold on to the shore. They will feel they are torn apart and will suffer greatly.*

> *Know the river has its destination. The elders say we must let go of the shore, push off into the middle of the river, keep our eyes open, and our heads above water.*

> *And I say, see who is in there with you and celebrate.*

At this time in history, we are to take nothing personally, Least of all ourselves. For the moment that we do, our spiritual growth and journey comes to a halt.

The time for the lone wolf is over.

Gather yourselves! Banish the word struggle from your attitude and your vocabulary. All that we do now must be done in a sacred manner and in celebration.

We are the ones we've been waiting for, cherished relatives.

Hey-ya-nah, Ennake!

RESOURCES

Prologue

1. everythingforever.com/einstein.htm

Chapter 1

1. Jung, C.G., ed. Sonu Shamdasani, The Red Book: Liber Novus. Norton Co., 2009, pp. 244–247.

Chapter 2

1. Williams, Bear Heart with Molly Larkin (1996). The Wind Is My Mother. New York: The Berkeley Publishing Group. Kindle Edition. p.6.

2. forum.forteantimes.com/index.php?threads/necklaces-of-ears-and-other-war-trophies.12378/

3. Jung, C.g (1963). Memories, dreams, reflections. New York: Vintage Books.

4. Mann, C. (2011). 1491.New York: Vintage Books. Kindle Edition. Loc.747.

5. Ibid., Loc. 774

6. Loc. 775

7. Jung, C.G., M. Sabini, ed. The Earth Has A Soul: C.G. Jung on Nature, Techology & Modern Life. Berkeley, Ca.: North Atlantic Books. p. 99.

8. www.religioustolerance.org/genocide5.htm

Chapter 3

1. The Healing Essence, 1995

2. archive.org/stream/MemoriesDreamsReflectionsCarlJung/ Memories,%20Dreams,%20Reflections%20-%20Carl%20 Jung_djvu.txt

3. archive.org/stream/MemoriesDreamsReflectionsCarlJung/ Memories,%20Dreams,%20Reflections%20-%20Carl%20 Jung_djvu.txt

4. archive.org/stream/MemoriesDreamsReflectionsCarlJung/ Memories,%20Dreams,%20Reflections%20-%20Carl%20 Jung_djvu.txt

Chapter 4

No references

Chapter 5

1. www.new-madrid.mo.us/index.aspx?nid=132

2. see Jean and Joyotpaul Chaudburi, A SACRED PATH, Los Angeles: UCLA Press, 2001, p. 54 for more information

Chapter 6

No references

Chapter 7

1. ghostranch.org

2. ghostranch.org

3. www.chron.com/life/travel/article/Georgia-O-Keeffe-found-a-muse-in-Palo-Duro-Canyon-5142571.php

Chapter 8

No references

Chapter 9

1. www.educationworld.com/a_curr/curr011.shtml

2. www.columbia.edu/itc/history/winter/w3206/edit/tseliotlittlegidding.html

3. www.cetacealab.org/humpback-whale-song

4. www.ilovewhales.com

Chapter 10

1. http://www.self-i-dentity-through-hooponopono.com/article1.htm

Chapter 11

1. www.medicalnewstoday.com/articles/295914.php

2. www.telegraph.co.uk/news/science/science-news/11683736/Five-day-fasting-diet-slows-down-ageing-and-may-add-years-to-life.html

3. www.collective-evolution.com/2015/12/11/neuroscientist-shows-what-fasting-does-to-your-brain-why-big-pharma-wont-study-it/

4. www.collective-evolution.com/2015/12/11/neuroscientist-shows-what-fasting-does-to-your-brain-why-big-pharma-wont-study-it/

5. www.healthline.com/health/food-nutrition/how-to-prevent-an-electrolyte-imbalance#Overview1

6. www.ncbi.nlm.nih.gov/pubmed/15829535?dopt=Abstract

7. www.consciousnessandbiofeedback.org/wp-content/uploads/2013/04/Voluntary-Control-of-Internal-States-Psychological-and-Physiological.pdf

Chapter 12

1. www.health.harvard.edu/staying-healthy/what-you-eat-can-fuel-or-cool-inflammation-a-key-driver-of-heart-disease-diabetes-and-other-chronic-conditions

2. www.rogercallahan.com/callahan.php)(http://www.emofree.com

3. Hal & Sidra Stone, Partnering:How To Love Each Other Without Losing Yourself

4. www.earthing.com/what-is-earthing/

5. www.5rhythms.com/gabrielle-roths-5rhythms/what-are-the-5rhythms/

Chapter 13

1. Travels with Charley: In Search of America.Viking: New York. Page 182.

Chapter 14

1. www.carl-jung.net/synchronicity.html

2. einstein.stanford.edu/content/relativity/q411.html

3. www.universetoday.com/48619/a-universe-of-10-dimensions/

Chapter 15

1. www.sheldrake.org/files/pdfs/papers/morphic1_paper.pdf

2. www.quantumconsciousness.org

Chapter 16

no references

Chapter 17

no references

Chapter 18

The following references are websites that I used to double-check Bear Heart's stories.

1. www.britannica.com/topic/list-of-plants-in-the-family-Poaceae-2036227

   www.plantphysiol.org/content/125/3/1198

2. www.smithsonianmag.com/history/where-the-buffalo-no-longer-roamed-3067904/?no-ist

3. familytravel.everything-everywhere.com/2013/05/in-search-of-the-last-herd-of-buffalo-at-caprock-canyons-state-park/

4. www.famoustexans.com/quanahparker.htm

5. www.voanews.com/a/comanche-chief-quanah-parker-century-old-house-falling-apart/2496109.html

6. www.pinterest.com/pin/119345458848715220/jameswfarmer. wordpress.com/tag/samuel-burk-burnett/

Chapter 19

1. billmoyers.com/series/the-wisdom-of-faith-with-huston-smith-1996/

2. Background reading: One Nation Under God, Copyright (c) 1996 by Huston Smith, used by the Council on Spiritual Practices with permission. All rights reserved.

3. texasplainstrail.com/public/upload/texasplainstrail_com/files/ Humphries_Quanah%20Parker%20and%20King%20 County.pdf

Chapter 20

1. www.psychologytoday.com/blog/wired-success/201407/why-we-need-end-the-war-drugs

2. www.cdc.gov/tobacco/data_statistics/tables/trends/cig_smoking/

3. www.drugpolicy.org/new-solutions-drug-policy/brief-history-drug-war
www.politico.com/story/2010/10/reagan-declares-war-on-drugs-october-14-1982-043552
www.drugpolicy.org/sites/default/files/DPA%20Fact%20 Sheet_Drug%20War%20Mass%20Incarceration%20and%20 Race_(Feb.%202016).pdf

4. www.brainyquote.com/quotes/quotes/a/alberteins130982.html

5. Taegel, W. and Borysenko, J. "Essential Questions About the Roots of Addiction and the Seeds of Recovery, Wisdom Recovery , Part   II. Counselor: The magazine for Addiction, and Behavioral Health Professionals,June 2015, Vol 16, No. 3.

6. Taegel, Will. Wild Heart:Nature's Hope In Earth's Crisis. Wimberley, Texas: 2nd Tier Publishing, 2010.

7. www.genome.gov/dnaday/q.cfm?aid=785&year=2010

8. www.google.com/search?client=safari&rls=en&q=how+old+sequoia &ie=UTF-8&oe=UTF-8#safe=active&q=sequoia+tree+facts

Chapter 22

1. books.google.com/books?id=9nRGwQnvGx0C&pg=PA15&lp-g=PA15&dq=Einstein:+rocks+are+slow+moving+light&-source=bl&ots=Xfg9TQcKMr&sig=9g6-RC-q65eV_4O-6q nIHN-9M3o&hl=en&sa=X&ved=0ahUKEwiGwqfwl57U-AhVH54MKHfIPAcIQ6AEIKDAA#v=onepage&q=Ein-stein%3A%20rocks%20are%20slow%20moving%20light&f=-false

2. My memory—influenced by my hearing of hundreds of visions from various quests of these prophecies is somewhat different from other sources. Here are references to other sources:

www.ancient-origins.net/myths-legends-americas/hopi-prophecy-and-end-fourth-world-part-2-002281/page/0/1

Scholars differ on the authenticity of these written statements taken from oral tradition. I do not have notes from the 1958 campfire stories and rely on my relationship with indigenous elders to correlate subjective visions and recollections. I am aware that some researchers even question the historicity of White Feather. I did not meet him directly. However, given the basic betrayal of truth in Euro-American accounts of the history of the Western Hemisphere, I choose to trust the validity of my own visions, coupled with oral traditions from various indigenous sources.

Chapter 23

1. www.telegraph.co.uk/news/2017/08/21/solar-eclipse-2017-watch-live-us-goes-dark-latest-news-images/

2. www.amazon.com/dp/B000JMKVE4/ref=dp-kindle-redirect?_encoding=UTF8&btkr=1 location 6094.

3. Mann, C.(2011). 1491.New York: Vintage Books. Kindle Edition. Loc. 747.

4. These Hopi prophecies were brought to my attention from a gathering in June of 1993 before Bear Heart died. Other influences can be seen from other tribes are integrated into this closing statement. To explore further, here is a rescource: www.matrixmasters.com/takecharge/hopi-prophecy.html